CORPORATE WELFARE POLICY
AND THE WELFARE STATE

SOCIAL INSTITUTIONS AND SOCIAL CHANGE

An Aldine de Gruyter Series of Texts and Monographs

EDITED BY

James D. Wright

CORPORATE WELFARE POLICY AND THE WELFARE STATE

Bank Deregulation and the Savings and Loan Bailout

Davita Silfen Glasberg and Dan Skidmore

ALDINE DE GRUYTER
New York

About the Authors

Davita Silfen Glasberg is Associate Professor of Sociology at the University of Connecticut-Storrs. She has published widely on issues of bank hegemony, the state in finance capitalism, and political economy. She is currently working on an examination of the Community Reinvestment Act to further explore some of the theoretical frameworks developed here.

Dan Skidmore is a doctoral candidate in Sociology at the University of Connecticut-Storrs. He has published several articles on issues of political economy, including the breakup of the former Soviet Union. He is currently working on a comparative analysis of airline deregulation and bank deregulation as legislative examples of a larger state project.

ALDINE DE GRUYTER
A division of Walter de Gruyter, Inc.
200 Saw Mill River Road
Hawthorne, New York 10532

This publication is printed on acid free paper ∞

Library of Congress Cataloging-in-Publication Data
Glasberg, Davita Silfen.
    Corporate welfare policy and the welfare state : bank deregulation and the savings and loan bailout / by Davita Silfen Glasberg and Dan Skidmore.
        p.   cm.—(Social institutions and social change)
    Includes bibliographical references and index.
    ISBN 0-202-30561-9 (alk. paper).—ISBN 0-202-30562-7 (pbk. :
alk. paper)
    1. Savings and loan associations—Deregulation—United States.
    2. Savings and loan associations—Government policy—United States.
    3. Banks and banking—Government policy—United States.   4. Savings and Loan Bailout, 1989– I. Skidmore, Dan.   II. Title.
    III. Series.
    HG2151.G58   1997   96-33416
    332.3'2'0973—dc20   CIP

Manufactured in the United States of America

10 9 8 7 6 5 4 3 2 1

Contents

Acknowledgments

We have greatly enjoyed the intellectual challenge this project represents. However, like most projects, many assisted in getting it off the ground and challenging us further at many stages in its development. The National Science Foundation provided partial support for the research on bank deregulation and the savings and loan bailout legislative processes (Grant #SES-9123753). The University of Connecticut Research Foundation provided initial support for the development of the research later supported by the National Science Foundation, as well as support for the research on political action committee donations. We thank these agencies for their funding support, without which it would have taken many more years to complete the research.

We would like to thank Dan Clawson, Kevin Delaney, Myra Marx Ferree, Mark Maynard, Julia McQuillan, Robert Mills, Beth Mintz, Mark Mizruchi, Kenneth J. Neubeck, Christy Sacks, Michael Schwartz, Ronald L. Taylor, Wayne Villemez, David Weakliem, and Mary Zey, as well as several anonymous reviewers, for their help, consultation, encouragement, and critical comments on various aspects of all or part of this book. Their generosity of time and insight, despite their own busy agendas, was greatly appreciated and of incalculable value. We also wish to thank Arlene Goodwin and Inge Peletier for their administrative assistance, and Aldine's executive editor Richard Koffler, managing editor Arlene Perazzini, and copyeditor Mike Sola for all their help in shepherding the manuscript to print.

We wish to thank our families for their love, support, and encouragement: to Cliff Glasberg, for all the late-night debates about political economy, corporate welfare, the bailout, deregulation in general and bank deregulation in particular, and power; to Gillian Silfen Glasberg and Morgan Silfen Glasberg, for all their patience and forbearance during phone calls that interrupted crucial games and conversations; to Irene, Roy, Joanne, John, Barbara, Renie, and Mary—the Skidmore committee who raised Dan—without whose support Dan would still be learning how to read and color. It is to them that we dedicate this book.

And finally, we wish to thank each other. What a long, strange trip it's been!

CHAPTER

1

Introduction:
Corporate Welfare and the Welfare State

$200 billion . . . and counting.

That's what it is costing United States taxpayers to bail out the savings and loan (S&L) industry from its crisis of the 1980s (Bradsher 1994; see also Bater 1994). Estimates are that the S&L bailout will total more than $500 billion over the next forty years (with some experts insisting that the cost may total more than $1 trillion over the next thirty years) (Hays and Hornik 1990:50). And as Congress battles over budget cutting in the 1990s, feuding over which social welfare programs will suffer less funding or even elimination, the bailout program will remain untouched and unthreatened. As we debate the desirability and affordability of continuing to be a welfare state, corporate welfare is indeed alive and well.

Interest in the nature and development of the welfare state continues to grow, particularly since the Reagan administration's apparent attempts to reduce it. In particular, many studies have been done on the development of social welfare programs, such as those of the New Deal (see, for example, Levine 1988; Berkowitz and McQuaid 1980; Brandes 1976; Clawson 1981; Quadagno 1984, 1994; Skocpol and Ikenberry 1983; Witte 1972).

Research on U.S. welfare policy has continued to focus on the welfare policies of the 1930s, though some recent analyses have examined government policy that has attacked, and in some cases dismantled, depression era social welfare programs (see Weir, Orloff, and Skocpol 1988; Quadagno 1989; Ackerman 1982; Block, Cloward, Ehrenreich, and Piven 1987; Harrington 1984; Joe and Rogers 1985; Phillips 1990; Piven and Cloward 1982; Sidel 1986, 1990; Bane and Ellwood 1994). The 1990s have been marked by a renewed vigor in debates concerning reforming and reducing the United States welfare state. The stunning victories of conservative Republicans in the 1994 elections have been seen by many observers as a rebuke of liberal attempts to increase federal entitlements,

1

often cited by their opponents as characteristic of a bloated welfare state. The agenda of the Republican "Contract with America" is a return to what many social critics have decried as the severe slashes in social welfare expenditures begun under the Reagan and Bush administrations. These critics have lamented that such cuts are evidence of a "mean season" to dismantle the welfare state (Piven and Cloward 1982; Block et al. 1987).

Do cuts in social welfare expenditures really indicate a dismantling of the welfare state? The question of whether or not we have been witnessing an attack against the welfare state hinges on how we conceptualize the welfare state.

Researchers have generally implied that the concept of the welfare state concerns *social* welfare policies and expenditures. These represent attempts by the government to redistribute wealth from the rich to the poor or to alleviate the symptoms of poverty and inequality. This narrow definition of the welfare state neglects an explicit examination of *corporate* welfare policies and expenditures that redistribute wealth to corporations and the rich. We define corporate welfare as those efforts made by the state to directly or indirectly subsidize, support, or rescue corporations, or otherwise socialize the cost and risk of investment and production of private profits and capital accumulation of corporations. These include corporate tax loopholes, reductions in capital gains taxes, subsidies to industries such as defense contractors and agriculture, tax abatements to encourage corporate development, and bailouts of ailing corporations. If we broaden the concept of welfare to include all government economic intervention designed to ameliorate the risks associated with exchange, consumption, and production in a capitalist political economy, then we can understand recent policy shifts as a dramatic expansion of *corporate* welfare policies designed to prop up ailing industries and firms.

We emphasize here that we are not making the claim that the United States has always been a welfare state with varying mixtures of social and corporate welfare. Were we to argue that the welfare state has *always* been a combination of social and corporate welfare policies, we would be making the mistake of imposing an ahistorical reconceptualization on all epochs. Such an argument would mean asserting that nineteenth-century United States was a welfare state for the wealthy and powerful: This was a period in which state policies unquestioningly benefited corporations (including the legal right to issue limited-liability shares, the implementation of tariff protections for new industries, federal land grants to the railroads, and the development of strike-breaking services to aid corporations in their fight against an increasingly militant and organized labor force), while state policies aiding the poor, the elderly, and the unemployed were noticeably absent. Rather, we are arguing that while nineteenth-century United States was clearly a period marked by state economic intervention to the benefit of corporations, we would not necessarily refer to that incarnation of U.S. political economy structure as a welfare state. That is, we argue that the *contemporary* welfare state is best understood as a structure and a historically specific process in which proponents of social and corporate welfare engage in a dialectic struggle for emphasis in state economic intervention policies.

The expanded definition of the welfare state makes one thing quite clear: the recent apparent reduction in state welfare spending was a policy shift away from social welfare to corporate welfare; the S&L bailout of the Financial Institutions Reform, Recovery, and Enforcement Act (FIRREA) was one of the most dramatic examples of this form of state economic intervention. The S&L industry failure was one of the largest and most expensive industrial crises in the United States and resulted in a federally financed bailout unprecedented in size and scope. Never before has an entire industry been rescued. What political and economic forces created so exceptional a policy?

The reconceptualization of the welfare state to include corporate welfare as well as social welfare policies and expenditures allows us to understand the contemporary welfare state as a political process involving the shifting relative emphasis of these two components over time. Furthermore, this reconceptualization invites us to explore the dynamics that influence the shift of emphasis. It also enables us to examine whether certain dynamics identified in the literature as producing social welfare policies and expenditures (such as corporate dominance, structural constraints, pluralistic politics, class struggle, and bank hegemony) are also at work in producing corporate welfare. Corporate and financial interests and actors are likely to be more explicitly and directly involved in the production of corporate welfare policies than they are in the production of social welfare policies. To explore these issues, it is useful to focus on a particular policy issue. Here the focus will be on the 1982 Garn–St. Germain Act, which deregulated banks, and the 1989 FIRREA, which bailed out the S&L industry.

The legislation that mandated the federal government to support the rescue of the S&L industry by taking over insolvent thrift institutions and selling their assets is referred to in the popular and business literature as a *bailout*, which is conceptualized here as a form of corporate welfare. The U.S. government has bailed out over four hundred corporations, with Lockheed and Chrysler Corporation as the more well-known of these (U.S. Congress: House 1979; Bearden 1982; Glasberg 1987a, 1989). The S&L case differs from these previous cases in that it is by far the largest in dollar value of all previous bailouts. Moreover, this is the first time an entire industry has been bailed out, as opposed to a single firm. In addition, it occurred after the federal government reiterated its commitment to a laissez-faire approach to the economy in the crises confronting industries such as family farms and steel. How is this industry different? Is it the fact that its members *are* banks? We look at state-corporate relations relative to capital accumulation in order to assess this.

The state directly supports nonfinancial (i.e., productive) capital accumulation interests through favorable capital gains taxes, tax abatements for relocating firms, depreciation allowances, and tax exemptions for Department of Defense industries. Moreover, the state can institute price supports and subsidies (as it has, for example, for farms), purchase commodities (as it does, for example, from military contractors), and generate trade and tariff policies that reduce or eliminate foreign competition. The state can also indirectly support nonfinancial capital accumulation interests through social welfare programs such as Aid to Families with Dependent Children (AFDC) and the Women, Infants and Children (WIC) food support program. These programs ensure that even the poor will be able to purchase some commodities. The WIC program in particular provides its recipients with coupons for specific brand name products, thereby funneling state support for specific food producers through the food support program for poor women and their children. Together, these direct and indirect mechanisms help the state support producers' capital accumulation needs. Only on occasion does the state rescue or bail out an individual firm that is in danger of going bankrupt, usually because the firm is an integral aspect of the economy as a producer or employer (as, for example, Chrysler and Lockheed).

This role of the state in securing producers' capital accumulation interests contrasts with its role in bailing out finance capital accumulation interests. In the latter case, the state is forced to assume the industry's risk, rather than provide the support necessary to continue producing a critical commodity or functioning as a major employer. Banks employ fewer workers than manufacturers and do not produce a critical commodity. They do, however, provide a crucial service in that they collectively control the single most important resource that all other industries as well as the state must access to conduct their activities. Furthermore, banks' activities are organized in common lending consortia, unlike nonfinancial firms, which tend to be more competitive.

This brief discussion of the difference between financial institutions and nonfinancial institutions raises several questions relative to an analysis of the S&L bailout:

1. What role did the organized structure of the banking community play in the bailout of the S&L industry?
2. Were the processes and relationships in this case similar to those in the other bailout cases?

3. What were the dynamics between the banking community, the nonfinancial business community, Congress, labor unions, consumer groups, and community organizations in both bank deregulation and the S&L bailout?

Earlier work on debt crises in Mexico (Glasberg 1987b) and Cleveland (Glasberg 1988) found that the organized structure of the banking community empowered banks, as the collective controllers of finance capital flows, to define the parameters of the crisis and to constrain the options available to state administrators in responding to crises. This same organized structure of the banking community similarly functioned as a powerful resource in the bailouts of both Mexico and Chrysler (Glasberg 1987a, 1987b). It enhanced that community's relative power in its struggle with labor and the state (both in the United States and abroad) and ultimately outweighed the other participants' resources and objections. The banking community became a critical factor in the shaping of bailout legislation for governments and corporations, influencing the conditions of the bailout as well as the total expenditures devoted to the legislation. Did these same processes and relationships operate to produce policies that specifically socialize the costs and risks of business of financial institutions themselves? What factors distinguish this process in the passage of the FIRREA from the bailouts examined earlier? What factors distinguish these processes of corporate welfare policy development and implementation from social welfare policy? We can examine these questions using theories of the state.

THEORIES OF THE STATE

Two trends dominate the recent literature on theories of the state. One trend pertains to the object of inquiry, the other to the theoretical approach itself. First, throughout the 1980s and into the 1990s, case studies of the creation and administration of social welfare policy, particularly the New Deal, have dominated policy formation research. Analysts have repeatedly examined this case to support a particular theoretical predilection—primarily *business dominance, state-centered,* or *structural Marxist*—and to disconfirm competing theories (Allen 1991; Amenta and Parikh 1991; Brents 1992; Domhoff 1987, 1990, 1991a, 1991b; Finegold 1981; Griffin, Devine, and Wallace 1983; Levine 1988; Quadagno 1984; Skocpol 1985; Skocpol and Amenta 1986). Second, state theory has taken an "accommodationist" turn. Rather than reject some positions in favor of others, current research agendas seek to identify the conditions under which the policy formation mechanisms specified by the three "grand" state theories complement and augment each other (Gilbert and Howe 1991; Hooks 1993; Jenkins and Brents 1989; Prechel 1990; Quadagno 1992). We argue that despite statements to the contrary and solid research showing the importance of this approach, the theoretical foundation of the accommodationist position remains largely unsystematized (see Hooks 1993). In our elaboration of the accommodationist position, we apply Jessop's *contingency* theory of the state to the creation and implementation of the FIRREA—the U.S. federal government's 1989 response to the crisis-ridden S&L industry (Jessop 1990).

The structural contingency approach to the deregulation and bailout of the banking industry developed below recognizes active political contests between and within class groupings (such as the internally contentious class of finance capitalists that frequently transcends differences between members in a more unified position in conflict with consumer, labor, and community groups) and the role of nonneutral state structures in shaping state policy. From this perspective, the FIRREA was produced by the interaction of historically contingent "state" and "societal" forces, as emphasized by the accommodationist position, within the nonneutral structures of the state.

UNDERSTANDINGS OF INTRACLASS UNITY AND POLICY FORMATION

With the possible exception of the recent accommodationist turn, research in political sociology's three dominant theoretical positions has traditionally had a competitive tone. Authors in each perspective have argued the other two describe processes and mechanisms that are somehow less fundamental than those identified by the author's perspective (see Domhoff 1990; Esping-Anderson, Friedland, and Wright 1976; Evans, Rueschemeyer, and Skocpol 1985; Akard 1992).

Three Grand Theories

Where other state theories posit the state as more or less autonomous from direct political coercion, business dominance research points to mechanisms through which business leaders and business-controlled organizations dominate the policy formation process. Business leaders and their direct representatives hold strategically important state leadership positions or dominate crucial informational, advisory, and decision-making bodies (Domhoff 1978, 1990; Burris 1992; Dye 1990; Useem 1984; Mills 1956; Zeitlin, Ewen, and Ratcliff 1974; Zeitlin and Ratcliff

1975). Mills and Dye, for example, identify corporate leaders who have become presidents, vice presidents, or important members of White House cabinets (Dye 1990; Mills 1956). Alternately, Domhoff and Akard argue that corporate control of policymaking and implementation bodies such as the Council on Foreign Relations, the Council on Economic Development, and regulatory agencies makes the direct involvement of corporate leaders in policymaking unnecessary (Domhoff 1990; Akard 1992). Others identify the coordinated campaign contributions of corporations, wealthy families, and wealthy individuals as potential influences on decision-making (Allen and Broyles 1989; Clawson, Neustadtl, and Scott 1992; Mizruchi 1989; Neustadtl and Clawson 1988).

Some researchers have analyzed the influence of the corporate sector in the formulation of social welfare programs. Middlemas (1983) and Cloward and Piven (1983) have discussed the role of corporatism as a prevailing value influencing social welfare policies and expenditures. Sheak (1990) more specifically argued that corporate mobilizations in the 1970s and 1980s had directly affected state policies such that the material conditions of the working class were eroded: unions' power was undermined and wages and benefits declined at the same time that critical social welfare programs suffered serious cutbacks. None of these analyses specifically address the question of corporate welfare and the processes by which that develops, nor do they define the process by which this influence occurs: is this influence the result of conscious corporate influence, or of structural constraints of capital accumulation imperatives that leave the state no other choice?

Several analysts have recognized the ability of private corporate and capital accumulation interests to influence state policies and expenditures for their own direct and indirect benefit. For example, some have examined the ability of defense contractors in the military-industrial complex to influence defense spending by convincing the Department of Defense and the State Department of the need for particular equipment or by sending representatives to meet with the secretary of defense and leaders of the three branches of the military (Cypher 1975; Roose 1975; Cobb 1976). Gough and Steinberg (1981) described how taxes divert a portion of surplus value to the state, which then uses it for social services and other social welfare expenditures. These expenditures support the reproduction of labor power, thereby subsidizing capitalist interests. Miller (1978) noted how large corporations, banks, and a financially squeezed middle class, which carries an increasing proportion of the national tax burden, have attacked the notion of the welfare state in terms of social welfare expenditures.

While military spending is perceived to benefit everyone in the development of a strong defense, social welfare expenditures are perceived as benefiting only its recipients, some of whom are not always seen as deserving. Together these groups have called for a decrease in social welfare expenditures and an increase in state support for the private sector. Such support might include a decrease in capital gains taxes, relaxation of antitrust laws, and deregulation of industries. Miller identified this approach as "recapitalization of capitalism" (p. 5).

Although not vulgarly conspiratorial, the business dominance position implies that political leaders from business operate on the basis of a clear, fairly unified conception of both the business community's interests and the policies needed to address those concerns. Given sufficient threats and mechanisms that grant access to the policy formation process, business leaders consciously organize the political and economic resources of the business community around successful passage of pro-business policy (Useem 1984; Akard 1992; Prechel 1990).

In some sense the antithesis of business dominance theory, research from a state-centered perspective focuses on mechanisms that allow the state to operate independent of outside forces (Amenta and Parikh 1991; Amenta and Skocpol 1988; Hooks 1990; Skocpol 1980, 1988). In reaction to business dominance and structural theories (below), state-centered theorists argue that the state is the site of bureaucratic political power; it is neither necessarily capitalist in nature nor subject to capitalist demands. As an institution, the state has interests separate from the demands of external groups or economic pressures, making it possible for it to create policy to which all interest groups object. State policy is shaped by policy precedents, political and party needs, and state managers' interest in expanding their administrative domain and autonomy. Skocpol specifically argued that "governmental institutions, electoral rules, political parties, and prior public policies" (1992:527) influenced the contours of the American social welfare state (as well as that of other countries). She rejected the role of structural imperatives or class conflicts emphasized in other perspectives. In sum, in the state-centered view, the state is impervious to mechanisms of intraclass unity identified by business dominance theory and unaffected by the capitalist nature of state structures assumed by Marxist structuralists.

Structuralist theorists disagree with the business dominance understanding of the policy formation process in the capitalist state. Capitalist-state structuralists argue that state policies are forged by the structure of the state itself and its position within the larger capitalist economy (Jessop 1990; Mandel 1975; O'Connor 1973, 1981; Vallochi 1989; Wright 1978). State managers are constrained by the imperatives of the capitalist political economy to create and implement policies that reproduce capital accumulation processes or thwart capital accumulation crises. Were the state to somehow operate outside these structural parameters, it would court economic and political legitimacy crises state managers can ill afford (Habermas 1973; Offe 1974; O'Connor 1973, 1987). Moreover, because the state is the structural unification of contradictory class relationships, it remains free from direct control by class-based organizations. Procapitalist state economic intervention is not, therefore, produced by the participation of business organizations in policy formation. Rather, policy is a product of the contradictory relations of power embedded within state structures themselves; it is an expression of the state's underlying procapitalist structural bias (Poulantzas 1976, 1978). The state regulates and absorbs the functions of the economy because of the increasing contradictions and crises of capitalism.

On the other hand, the state needs the major private corporations for jobs for the working class. Economic crises create legitimacy crises for the existing political leadership (see Offe 1972a, 1972b, 1974; O'Connor 1973; Habermas 1973). State social welfare expenditures may reduce or detour class struggle by mitigating some of the negative effects of these crises for the working class (Piven and Cloward 1978). State regulation of the economy may also delay the onset of fiscal and economic crises (O'Connor 1973). Some structuralists argue that state managers exploit labor-business conflicts to increase their range of discretion and power (Block 1977). Other researchers, particularly those analyzing New Deal legislation and the creation of the welfare state, suggest that sweeping transformations in state policies result only when capital accumulation crises do not respond to more conventional remedies (Benda 1979; Block 1981; Bowles and Gintis 1982; O'Connor 1973, 1981, 1987; Wright 1978). This implies that corporate welfare is stimulated by capital accumulation crises that remain unresolved through more standard approaches.

This is distinctive from a business dominance perspective, which argues that there is a conscious, deliberate, and often unified effort by corporate interests to dominate the legislative process. A structuralist analysis suggests a less conscious, less unified determination to affect policy; rather, such an analysis looks for the effect of relationships on the legislative process. These relationships are rooted in the structure of capitalist society, such that corporate interests are positioned to be more compelling to the state than other interests. The state has little choice but to serve corporate interests, since to ignore them could pose profound negative consequences for the economy and society (such as bankruptcies, massive unemployment, recession, or depression).

Class-dialectic theorists principally view the state as mediator of class antagonisms. The state produces policies that benefit labor while simultaneously supporting and legitimating the broader political economy; state policy is the mediation of labor-business conflicts. Social welfare policies, particularly those of the New Deal, are linked to dynamic struggles between business and labor played out in the state. The policies that emerged out of these struggles organized labor into institutional forms (i.e., trade unions) amenable to capitalist interests (see, for example, Whitt 1979, 1982; Zeitlin et al. 1974; Zeitlin and Ratcliff 1975; Quadagno 1989; Quadagno and Meyer 1989). Policy derives from state interference and mediation into labor-business conflicts (Galbraith 1985; Schmitter 1974). According to these theorists, the state has far greater autonomy in its major role than business dominance theorists or even structuralists would allow. The state can produce policies to benefit the poor and working class while simultaneously still supporting broader interests of the capitalist class. Thus, unemployment insurance, food stamps, and Aid to Families with Dependent Children are social welfare programs developed to aid the poor. However, they "incorporate working class demands into legislation on capitalist terms" (Quadagno 1984:646; see also Maney 1989). These programs also benefit capital accumulation interests by maintaining minimum levels of consumption in the general economy.

Levine (1988) and Witte (1972) linked social welfare policies (particularly those of the New Deal) to dynamic struggles between capital accumulation and working-class interests, which are played out in the state. The policies that emerged out of these struggles organized labor into trade unions, which were consistent with capitalist interests. What sets these analyses apart from a purely structural one is the argument that the resultant New Deal legislation was not constrained by structural imperatives, but rather was derived from a dialectical process of conflicts both between and within classes. This suggests that corporate welfare results from the state's autonomous mediation of class antagonisms.

More recently, some researchers have shown how race and gender struggles are woven through class struggles to affect policies of the welfare state (see, for example, Gordon 1994; Quadagno 1994). They argue that the intersections of race, gender, and class affected the politics generating the welfare programs of the Progressive Era and the later War on Poverty, which in turn affected the preexisting race and gender relations. While these analyses offer a much-needed nuance to class-dialectic analyses, they remain focused on the production of the social welfare state, and do not necessarily highlight much about corporate welfare or the relation between social and corporate welfare as components of the welfare state.

Yet other researchers have implied the relationship between corporate and social welfare as components of the welfare state. For example, Devine (1983) found that while revenue policies of post–WWII United States have favored capital accumulation interests, expenditures have favored labor. The net result of these two divergent emphases has been a preservation of market-driven inequalities rather than a redistribution of wealth. While this analysis implies a tension between social and corporate welfare it is largely focused on outcomes of that tension rather than on the process by which the policies and expenditures occur.

Finally, bank hegemony theory, an offshoot of structuralism, recognizes that capitalists are not necessarily unified in their assessment of capital accumulation interests. Despite these divisions, bank hegemony theorists argue that banks' collective control over finance capital empowers them to impose structural restrictions on the range of policy alternatives open to the state; state decisions tend to serve the interests of the banking community in general and the large commercial banks in particular (Glasberg 1989; Mintz and Schwartz 1985). In brief, bank hegemony theory describes the processes through which the power of finance capital translates finance capital's particular interests into state policy.

The Accommodationist Turn

Taken together, these seemingly competing theories and typologies of the welfare state suggest interesting frameworks for understanding corporate welfare as a component of the welfare state. However, they are limited because they have stalled in a debate predicated on the presumption of theoretically mutual exclusivity. As our discussion suggests, there is, in fact, some overlap in these various perspectives, which one can synthesize into a more complex analysis, a synthesis for which many theorists have recently pressed (see, for example, Gilbert and Howe 1991; Hooks 1993; Jenkins and Brents 1989; Prechel 1990; Quadagno 1992; McCammon 1994). Though none of the theorists below refer to themselves as accommodationist and some defend positions nearly as categorical as the those just reviewed, the following research does represent a shift in state theory. Regardless of his or her theoretical home turf, ideally, the accommodationist drops the assumptions that have faced the most consistent critiques and have made his or her position particularly contentious. Yet, the following theorists retain each theory's unique insights and loosely combine these insights with "rival" theories to gain a more rounded understanding of the policy formation process. Accommodationist research agendas are oriented around two ideas. First, class-based political mobilization is contingent, requiring both a perceived threat to that class's or class segment's interests and the organizational resources with which to advocate a political position. Second, state agencies and policies interact with class-based political organizations in a dynamic process that modifies both the state and the political organizations. The specific relation between state agencies and class-based political organizations is historically contingent.

The first theme of the accommodationist position is an indirect response to critiques of the structural-Marxist and business dominance theories. Critics have argued that the structural-Marxist position, though claiming historicity, actually denies the importance of political processes and political organizations through its "overdetermined" approach to policy formation (Domhoff 1990). Alternatively, "instrumentalist" conceptions of the business dominance approach have been criticized for their inattention to both structural constraints on policymaking and the requirement that the state have some autonomy from total capitalist domination. According to these critics, policy is shaped less by the direct participation of business elite in government, and more by structural pressures on the state to maintain business confidence and support continued capital accumulation; the state must be able to incorporate the demands of labor into state policy on capitalist grounds, without the interference of more narrowly focused large capitalists (Block 1977; Quadagno 1984). Business dominance theorists have particularly chafed at the critique that the business dominance position posits the uncontested power of business irrespective of the political or economic climate.

In response, one goal of the new accommodationism has been to specify the conditions under which business exhibits intraclass unity and the variable importance of this unity under shifting political-economic conditions. Prechel's (1990) analysis of state import-export policies found, in opposition to the position that business dominates the state through mechanisms of intraclass coordination, that the capitalist class need not be unified to limit the state's autonomy. State structures themselves can become the means through which one class segment exercises control over the state. Building on Prechel's idea that business dominance is contingent, Akard argued that one must specify the "historical conditions under which intraclass cohesion and business influence on the policy process are *more or less* likely" (1992:598). He identified state policy that threatens business and business's organizational capacities as two factors determining the extent of business unity. In sum, he argued that neither the political mobilization nor the political success of business could be assumed a priori. Business does not automatically get its demands met; it is forced to contend with other political coalitions in the policy formation process. Moreover, once the political threat that unifies business fades, that political unity dissolves. It is important to emphasize again that neither Prechel's nor Akard's research is intentionally accommodationist. Rather, they exemplify this theoretical turn to the extent to which they challenge the assumptions of their theoretical milieu for the sake of keeping that position current with their theoretical "competitors."

Prechel's work also influenced Brents's (1992) research. She found that class unity is affected by the impact of economic and historical conditions on a class segment's particular interests, the organizational capacities of capital and labor at a given time, and state structures and agendas. For example, during World War I, the organizational capacities of American capital depended in part upon the state's war agenda. Temporary state agencies created intra- and interclass truces among both capital and labor. Following the war, these agencies became points of division as small, competitive-sector business split with big business over welfare and labor policies. Big business feared the welfare policies the state might produce without its intervention. New Deal policies, then, were a product of big businesses' desire to socialize the costs of welfare capitalism (and labor peace) and the enfranchisement of business into the policy formation process. Brents argued that although all three grand state theories are weak, elements of each may be incorporated into an explanation of the political positions, tactics, and successes of a variety of business coalitions in the creation of "capitalist welfare" policy.

As in research similar to Prechel's, studies of Political Action Committee (PAC) contributions seek to specify the conditions under which capitalists exhibit coordinated political activity. Researchers have argued that the coordinated political activity of business depends on a number of organizational factors, particularly interlocking directorates among corporations, interfamilial connections, and ideology. Other research indicates that the political unity of business varies according to the differential material relations of capitalist class segments to finance capital—relations affected by the historically specific conditions under which capital accumulation occurs (Allen 1991; Allen and Broyles 1989; Mizruchi 1989; Mizruchi and Koenig 1986; Neustadtl and Clawson 1988; Glasberg 1989). In sum, the first part of the accommodationist turn posits that business political unity depends both on leading capitalists' perception that businesswide interests are threatened and the organizational resources of both capital and labor.

The second part of the accommodationist position holds that the relation between the state and class-based political organizations is indefinite. Historical vagaries, state agendas, and the particular strength or weakness of different class segments affect the "state-society relation" (an accommodationist shorthand for the relative influence of state or societal factors on policy formation) and modify the state and society-based political organizations themselves. Those who argue for this dynamic conception of the state-society relation present both a response to the state-centered position and a continuation of critiques of state-centered theories (Jenkins and Brents 1989; Gilbert and Howe 1991; Quadagno 1992).

Jessop (1990) argued against analyses that attempt to "simply combine" state- and society-centered approaches to the state; the assumptions underlying such an endeavor reify an artificial dichotomy between the state and society, implying that each is a self-contained, self-determined entity. He held that such an analysis precludes examination of points of state-society intersection. Much of the accommodationist research of the state-society relation seems sensitive to this critique, and argues that our understanding of the policy formation process is incomplete unless we explore the historically specific mechanisms that are *both* of the state and of society.

Protest movements, state agendas, and business political organizations are points where the state and society intersect, and these phenomena are the backbone of the following research agendas. In their "political struggle" understanding of the formation of the Social Security Act, Jenkins and Brents argued that both structural-Marxist and state-centered approaches to theory underestimate the power of social protest and oversimplify competition among capitalists (Brents 1992; Jenkins and Brents 1989). They showed that the rise of a New Deal democratic coalition, and a split between corporate liberals and a more conservative capitalist coalition, reduced the states' resistance to mass protest; mass protests created a sense of impending crisis among politicians, forcing them to develop social welfare programs. The corporate liberal coalition held that *if* the state was to administer a social welfare program, that program should be developed by business. Through the strategic control of the policy formation process and direct investment in the electoral process, the corporate liberal position prevailed. Thus, in their revised understanding of the policy formation process, Jenkins and Brents point to the interaction of social protest, intracapitalist divisions, the dominant segment of the capitalist class, and the policy inclinations of the state. Their analysis of the formation of the U.S. welfare state underscores the reciprocal influences of state agendas and class-based political organizations.

Gilbert and Howe (1991) argued explicitly that the time to discard the distinction between state and society had come. Their research focused on the relationship between the class (societal) and institutional (state) backgrounds of state agencies, and the expression of this relationship in New Deal agricultural policy. They argued that the dominant-class bias of the state, a product of historical processes, favors some class segments over others. For example, although in the aggregate different divisions of state agencies represented a range of political positions— from ultraconservative, antilabor agribusiness through liberal, proshare-cropper social reformers—particular divisions were beholden to certain class interests. Thus, the large farmers' control of the county-level administration of federal policy meant only the most lenient production controls were implemented. Because they were instituted prior to New Deal reforms, these capitalist-dominated state institutions had the bureaucratic inertia to resist reformist pressures; newer agencies were more malleable. Moreover, whereas the dominant farm groups were unified around policies undercutting both labor's strength and the state's capacity to regulate production, the interests of labor, sharecroppers, and smaller farmers diverged by geography and their approaches to farming. In sum, Gilbert and Howe document the intersection and mutual determination of state and societal forces.

Recent research by Quadagno (1992) revolves around the reciprocal state-society relation found in Gilbert and Howe's work and Prechel's argument that societal and historical forces restrict the state's autonomy. Using her "state transformation theory" Quadagno examined the effects of mass turmoil on state policies, and the subsequent effect of state policies and structures on social protest. She documented how civil rights–related violence led the state to adopt a policy prohibiting discrimination by federal contractors. This decision made it possible for civil rights groups to protest at construction sites. Thus, in the dialectic interaction between the state and society, mass turmoil brought the state to action, and the autonomous actions of the state in turn shaped the tactics of social protest. Moreover, the influence of societal forces varied within the state itself. The Department of Labor was reluctant to oppose its political allies in the crafts unions, and thus gave little support to the Equal Employment Opportunity Commission. Alternatively, the more independent Justice Department was willing to intervene where the Department of Labor could not. In sum, Quadagno argued that the civil rights movement created actual structural changes within the state. These changes were expressed through affirmative action programs and through federal appointments and newly created bureaucracies in the early 1970s.

Finally, in his case for a state theory version of Dobbin's (1992) institutional theory, Hooks makes the definitive accommodationist statement on the three grand theories of the state: "The strong variant of each theory makes a priori commitments that only the converted would endorse" (1993:37). After critiquing strong and weak variants of business dominance, structural-Marxist, and state-centered theories, Hooks developed "middle-range" state-centered hypotheses. These hypotheses both identified processes distinct to each theory and linked these processes to the federal program or agency ("institution") in which that particular process was most evident. He found, as predicted by business dominance theory, that the business elite actively participated in the creation and administration of federal industrial policy during and following World War II. In support of his version of structural-Marxist theory, he argued that though capitalists initially objected to the policies of the federal Defense Plant Corporation, the state defied these objections to create policy that ultimately contributed to the "concentration and centralization of capital" (p. 47). Direct industrial investment by the military supported the state-centered position; state managers directed investment in and retained control over the expanding war industry. In sum, Hooks's accommodationism directly combines all three grand theories by specifying the institutional context in which each is likely to apply.

The recent outpouring of accommodationist-type theory indicates that during the last five years the U.S. state theory debate has come to a turning point. The research presented above demonstrates that theorists were unwilling to rehash old debates, ignore old criticisms, and blindly defend divisive assumptions. In short, accommodationist theory has four central themes:

1. The processes of state policy formation and implementation are characterized by sporadic fragmentation and antagonisms within class groupings, rather than spontaneous, "transhistorical" intra-class unity.
2. Class unity and political organization is affected by the presence of a perceived threat from the state and a class's organizational resources.
3. State and societal policy determinants modify one another in a reciprocal manner.
4. One must specify the historical conditions under which both class unity and the passage of policy favorable to a particular class may occur.

CONTINGENCY AND POLICY FORMATION

Bringing Structural Class Relations Back In

This research, however, does not "add up" to a new theory of the state and policy formation. Although on the surface the accommodationist position may release state theorists from the stagnant debates of the past, it has also eliminated the possibility for making general statements, beyond specific research conclusions, about the society-state relation and this relation's effect on policy formation. The new accommodationism is ad hoc, not in the sense that theories are randomly applied wherever they seem to fit, but in the sense that they no longer contribute to a theoretical system around which the disparate facts produced by state theory research can be organized. They have not specified the contours of such a synthesis.

Others have offered potentially fruitful avenues to fulfill this need. For example, Esping-Andersen offered one possible synthesis, arguing that monocausal theories of the state are too simplistic. Rather, three factors, each of which is identified by one or another existing theory of the state, interact to produce welfare states: "the nature of class mobilization (especially of the working class); class-political coalition structures; and the historical legacy of regime institutionalization" (1990:29). These factors interact to produce not one, single welfare state type, but three possible types of welfare state regimes. The liberal welfare state most closely describes the United States, Canada, and Australia, where policies to redistribute wealth are designed to accrue benefits to low-income clientele, thereby subverting market forces. Corporatist welfare states, such as France, Germany, and Italy, are commonly influenced by the church and emphasize policies that preserve class and status differentials and reinforce traditional family structures. Finally, social-democratic welfare states such as those in Scandinavia promote equality not just of minimal living standards but of standards of middle-class comfort. Entitlements to benefits are not "means tested" as in liberal welfare states, nor are they designed to reproduce class and status differences as in corporatist welfare states. The aim of social-democratic welfare states is emancipation and full participation of all members, regardless of class or status.

Esping-Andersen's analysis remains largely focused on social welfare policies. Moreover, his definition of the welfare state remains predicated on the view that it is a structure of "institutions predominantly preoccupied with the production and distribution of social well-being" (1990:1). Despite this limitation, however, the variables he identifies as differentiating the regimes, namely, the relationship between state, market, and family, offer useful hints for broadening even further the concept of welfare state to include corporate welfare. And his argument of the interactive effect of class mobilization, political coalitions, and historical precedents of regimes implies interesting guidelines for examining corporate as well as social welfare aspects of the state.

Below we explore how a structural understanding of the policy formation process—one that incorporates the findings of the preceding perspectives about the relations among the state and within and between classes—may make a generalizable accommodationist theory possible. We examine the proposition that policymaking occurs within a capitalist political-economic structure in which a limited range of policy options are entertained as practical. Policy options that challenge the underlying logic of the capitalist political economy, built around the publicly subsidized creation of private profit, are precluded by a variety of structural mechanisms; they are preempted from the policy option debate (Lukes 1974; Offe 1974; Wright 1978). From this perspective, class struggle—the political activity or structural power of labor, consumer, and other public, noncapitalist interests within and outside the capitalist state in opposition to similar activities and structures of capitalist interests—shapes decision-making and consequent state policies, as state structures shape class struggle.

Of great use here to organize the variables identified by Esping-Andersen is Jessop's (1990) concept of state projects to frame an analysis of both social and corporate welfare processes. We argue, with Jessop, that organizing the accommodationist position around the concepts of the balance of class forces and state projects helps us systematize the contingency found in the accommodationist research. However, despite his attention to the intricacies and implications of different approaches to the state, Jessop's theory lacks the concrete indicators of different social processes that would make his position easily testable. The following set of propositions examines Jessop's theory and the four themes of accommodationism, and points to crucial parts of the analysis of the creation and implementation of the FIRREA and the FIRREA-Affordable Housing Program (AHP).

A Structural Understanding of Contingency

Contingency is the central theme running through the accommodationist research. As the literature indicates, the unity and effectiveness of class-based political organizations, the dominance of the business elite, the reciprocally modifying interaction of state and society are all contingent on a variety of historical, economic, and political forces. To avoid reverting to the debates that stalled state theory, the new synthesis must incorporate contingency. Alternatively, to create a generalizable theory of the state and policy formation, we need to develop and test a set of assumptions that "systematize contingency."

The structuralist position below retains the emphasis on class highlighted by the new accommodationism, but avoids the reductionism inherent in some structural-Marxism (i.e., it was *necessary*, or inevitable, that the state adopt policies that supported continued capitalist accumulation). Rather, we begin with the assumption that the state project and apparatuses described below need not have produced a de facto and de jure procapitalist FIRREA. The state may not function to reproduce accumulation regimes and relations of production. Stated another way, the state is a *capitalist* state *to the extent* that it creates the conditions to reproduce capitalist relations of production (Jessop 1990:354). Given that the FIRREA is a procapitalist corporate-welfare policy, the research below examines the state structures, political processes, class activities, and historical contingencies that created it, shaped its implementation, and excluded other policy options. The following accommodationist propositions are built on Jessop's argument that generalizable statements about the state and policy formation begin with a general understanding of the relation between state and society (we need not assume this relation is either transhistorical or immutable). A contingency-sensitive understanding of the state-society relation can be specified through exploring (1) deregulation and the FIRREA as a state project, (2) the balance of administrative and class forces both within and outside the state, and (3) the structural selectivity of the policy formation and implementation processes.

First, by *state projects*, Jessop indicated that an analysis of state policy begins with an understanding of the state's role in society; in the case of corporate welfare, the state's economic role is of particular interest. Loosely applied, a state project is a set of state policies and/or agencies unified around a particular form of economic intervention, however transitory that unity may be. The external orientation of state projects does not mean that the state or state policy is wholly determined by outside forces. Rather, use of the concept of state project situates current and proposed state policy within the larger complex of current and historical political and economic movements, including the balance of class forces. Although neither preordained nor determined by a single actor or force, policy is not random; consistent with Esping-Andersen's notion of historical legacies of welfare state regimes, Jessop argued that more recent policies build on, are shaped by, or, in the case of dialectic movements, contradict prior policies (see also Quadagno 1992). By examining the historically established unity of state policy and agencies around corporate welfare and the AHP, we gain insight into the more general relation between state projects, and political organizations intent on preserving or modifying those projects.

Second, the state does have its own "modes of calculation and operational procedures" (Jessop 1990:366) yet the nature of these procedures remains contingent upon the *balance of forces* within and outside the state. The state's administrative powers are context dependent. The contexts within which state power operates create an ensemble of "playing fields," with no one arena necessarily competing with, in harmony with, or beholden to the same interests as any other (Gilbert and Howe 1991; Jessop 1990; Quadagno 1992).

Arguably, the central question in state theory is: How is policy created? Or, more bluntly, Who wins? From a state projects perspective, the capacity of state agents and apparatuses to mobilize social resources to their policy ends varies according to the dynamic relation between the state and political organizations. Similarly, the political strength and effectiveness of political organizations outside the state depend on factors such as an apparent need for political agitation and organizational resources. The capacities of the state cannot be divined a priori, but only through examination of the historical balance of internal and external social forces, and the actual practices that delimit the state's powers (Jessop 1990). For example, in the case of the banking industry, to the extent that some form of state economic intervention seemed inevitable to both Congress and the banking community, we should see the various segments of the finance capitalist class unified in an attempt to establish corporate welfare policy that serves their collective interests. Examination of this proposition crosses a number of theoretical boundaries: corporate political unity implies a business dominance perspective; the power of policy precedent to shape corporate demands is derived from state-centered theory; existing structures of state economic intervention is suggested by structural theory; noncorporate groups' needs articulated in terms amenable to capital is predicted by class-dialectic theory. Under what conditions might any of these factors be determinant?

Jessop's notions of state projects allows us to systematize the more ambiguous proposition that state power and state policy are neither wholly arbitrary (free from control of outside forces) nor totally determined by any one external institution. Using the notion of state projects, we can see that the formation of current policy is contingent upon unified, historical state economic policy precedents and the state apparatuses that implement these policies. We are not attempting to replace the factors identified by the other state theories with a different factor called state project; state projects are not determinant in any instance. Rather, by placing the policy formation process within the context of a set of state policies and agencies unified around a particular form of economic intervention, we argue that research will be better able to specify *the conditions under which* the factors state theories identify are important. Finally, with the notion of state projects, we associate a *mechanism* through which policy is shaped. The contingencies inherent in the policy-making processes may be systematized around the concept of *structural selectivity*. State structures "offer unequal chances to different forces within and outside the state to act for different political purposes" (1990:367). State structures and state projects select against some policy alternatives and political organizations.

Our dialectic understanding of state projects begins with the notion of the state as a complex comprised of several diverse organizations, only one of which is the legislature, and each of which is variably responsive to the pressures and constraints different state theories have hypothesized. The dialectical process of state projects then involves the ongoing struggles between finance capital and society, wherein the state mediates those struggles (see Karpik 1977; Hymer 1981; Zey and Camp 1996). The goals (interests) of the policy formation process of the state often contradict those of finance capital: the state's societal role includes defending those societal interests necessary for reproduction of the political-economic system, and its economic role reconciles those interests to the finance industry's need for capital accumulation and the maintenance of its unique role as a supplier of finance capital (as opposed to, for example, the state supplying socialized finance capital) (Offe 1984). The state project, as a set of economic policies and agencies unified around a particular form of economic intervention, is a consequence of this dialectic.

We do not posit, in the manner of pluralists, that the state is neutral in this mediation. Rather, as the notion of structural selectivity implies, the state's definitions of crisis and appropriate responses may be narrowed by a biasing or filtering process in which only some definitions become part of the process and others are ignored or never considered. The historically contingent structure and projects of the state are more responsive to particular strategies and resources than to others; few of the possible policies and organizations surrounding a given issue receive serious political consideration. Over time, selectivity perpetuates biases in the state-society relationship.

Using the concepts of state projects and balance of class forces then, we can begin to frame hypotheses of the conditions under which the elements emphasized by the various theories of the state are likely to become more or less significant in producing state policy:

1. Business interests (or segments of the business community) are likely to dominate state policymaking when the balance of class forces favors them over working-class interests, that is, when capital accumulation interests are better organized and can more readily marshall more significant resources that give them greater access to policymakers than working-class interests. Business interests are more likely to organize when faced with an imminent threat to their interests (or perceive such a threat) (for example, growing support for increasing existing restrictive regulations or imposing new restrictions), or opportunities that are conducive to such organizing are present (for example, prior policy or structural arrangements facilitating lending consortia among banks).

2. Capital accumulation interests are likely to elicit advantageous state policies when the state is faced with either fiscal or economic crises or when major industries face crises that have a strong likelihood to become catalysts for such crises. This ability to garner advantageous policies is likely to be intensified when past policies in the larger state project set a precedent and thus act as selectivity filters biasing policymakers' collective definition of the problem and the appropriate legislative solution. This ability is also likely to be intensified when working-class interests are not well organized to present alternative perspectives as viable and to

widen the selectivity filter to include such interests in framing legislation.

3. Working-class interests are likely to derive advantageous state policies or favorable provisions within state policies that are largely advantageous to capital accumulation interests when working-class interests are well organized and can marshall significant resources to bear on the struggle such that the balance of class forces becomes favorably altered. Such resources can be tangible (control of labor power, pension funds, large voting blocks in critical election years, or large PACs), or intangible (threat of recession due to significant job losses, threat of labor or community unrest). Working-class interests are more likely to organize when faced with an imminent threat (or perceived threat) (for example, growing legislative interest in antilabor legislation, growing crises in the economy that are likely to produce recession) or when opportunities conducive to such organization exist (for example, prior structures such as labor unions, or public discourse identifying issues and potential allies and encouraging coalitions around specific issues).

We can explore this systematization of the conditions under which the various elements identified in seemingly competing theories of the state become more or less salient in an examination of the 1989 legislation that bailed out the S&L industry—legislation representing one of the most expensive pieces of corporate welfare.

State structures and state projects (as shaped by the forces identified above) thus select against some policy alternatives and political organizations. The historically contingent structure and projects of the state are more responsive to particular strategies and resources than to others; few of the possible policies and organizations surrounding a given issue receive serious political consideration. Over time, selectivity perpetuates biases in the state-society relationship.

Additionally, as seen in accommodationism, state policy is not neutral. State programs may systematically favor some groups, or a particular set of political responses to social crises, over others. Thus, in our examination of the corporate welfare state project, we consider de jure and de facto state policies (both the letter of the law and its implementation) that have historically favored one class segment over others (Brents 1992; Gilbert and Howe 1991; Quadagno 1992). Keeping with our understanding of state projects and our prior research on the political power of finance capital, established relations between the state, banking industry, and affordable housing community prior to the creation of the FIRREA should be reflected in the formation and execution of the FIRREA (Glasberg 1987a, 1989; Glasberg and Skidmore 1992). As implemented, emergent state policies in some way either support or undermine existing state projects.

We examine the preceding propositions in our study of the creation and realization of the FIRREA-AHP. To study the historical balance of forces and the state project surrounding this legislation, first we will examine the development of the relation between the state and the banking community prior to the creation of this policy. What was the state's role in banking? How was the state organized to carry out this role? What were the state's responses to the early crisis in the S&L industry and the crisis following deregulation, and how did this shape the later bailout? We then describe the legislative process creating the FIRREA and AHP. What groups were represented? How were their demands met? Finally, we look at the implementation of the FIRREA-AHP. What state agencies were responsible? How was implementation affected by state structures and mandates, the balance of class forces, and the larger political/historical forces surrounding affordable housing?

The legislative hearings that created the FIRREA and oversaw its execution provide the bulk of our information. Legislative hearings are one point where state and society meet—where representatives of capital, labor, and community groups debate and are interrogated. Thus, these hearings present both intra- and interclass conflicts in the larger context of pending legislation. Was the threat of state economic intervention a source of class unity? In what ways were the class biases inherent in the state evident? Assuming these biases are not transhistorical, what series of historical contingencies explain them? Finally, after analysis of the preceding propositions, we contrast the implementation of FIRREA corporate welfare policy and the FIRREA-AHP. To what extent, and for the sake of what class interests, did state economic intervention subsidize or mitigate the risks associated with private capital accumulation? What is the relationship between corporate and social welfare processes here?

METHODOLOGY

The 1989 FIRREA mandated the federal government to support the bailout of the S&L industry through payments to depositors at failed institutions and by taking over insolvent thrift institutions and selling their assets. What factors shaped and led to the passage of passage of 2the FIRREA? How did the initial crisis in the S&L industry and the 1982 Garn–St. Germain banking deregulation act effect the FIRREA? What factors caused Congress and the executive federal government to contradict the prevailing laissez-faire philosophy and agree to the most expensive bailout in U.S. history?

Since the S&L bailout crisis and legislation deregulating banks underwent intensive congressional investigation (both before the same congressional committees), there are thousands of pages of testimony transcripts and supportive documents, contained in thirty-four volumes. The testimony transcripts function as interviews, and reflect the verbatim knowledge, expertise, and viewpoints of a wide range of critical actors and informed sources, access to whom might otherwise be difficult for a researcher to obtain. Furthermore, these government files contain documents and research reports from corporations and their executives, banks and savings and loan associations, university researchers, business analysts, accountants, labor representatives, consumer groups, community organizations, and other institutional actors and experts. Many of these documents would otherwise remain inaccessible were it not for the power of congressional committees to subpoena them. Therefore, these government documents provide an opportunity for us to access substantial and rich data to trace the relationships, resources, and dynamics critical to investigating the development of corporate welfare policy and expenditures (see Glasberg 1989:195–200).

We examined these documents using content analysis. Witnesses providing testimony to the Committee on Banking, Finance, and Urban Affairs (CBFUA) were coded according to the groups or organization they represented or with which they were identified as affiliated: the S&L industry, commercial banks, regulatory agencies (i.e., FDIC or FSLIC), labor, consumer groups, community groups, or Congress. In the case where a witness was a member of more than one group, she or he was coded by the group with which she or he was identified in the testimony or documents. Coalitions between groups were coded as well.

The testimony of witnesses before the CBFUA was examined for evidence of support for the deregulatory or bailout legislation, with attention paid to the sections of legislation with which each group agreed or disagreed (no group agreed with every single provision of both pieces of legislation). For example, as we see below, some groups sought re-regulation of the industry, federal use of seized property for affordable housing, community or worker control of S&L institutions, or modifications in the federal insurance programs. Moreover, the testimony of each group's representatives and their accompanying documents were examined for evidence of the sorts of political resources that group brought to bear on the policy formation process. For example, did the testimony of S&L representatives express their perception of their critical importance to the U.S. economy, their unique niche in the financial community, the amount of capital they control, their role as suppliers of campaign capital, or their unity as an industry? Any one of these could be considered evidence that this group might be able to influence the process. In what instances were these or other resources effective or ineffective? Thus, the bulk of the following excerpts from testimony are not intended to represent the views of a "quantitative majority" in the hearing process. Rather, we excerpted testimony to illustrate both the structure of relations between the state and the other participants in the policy formation process and the conditions under which the resources brought to the hearing process by all involved were politically effective. Finally, we placed the testimony within the context of the final legislation, and the follow-up "oversight" hearings, to see not only which groups received de jure legislation, but what pieces of this legislation the state de facto implemented.

While this methodology will be the basis of most of the chapters, the analysis of the role that bank PACs may have played in getting both bills passed requires quantitative analysis of Federal Election Commission data as well. We will address this methodological issue in that chapter.

ORGANIZATION OF THE BOOK

The remainder of the book explores the expansion of corporate welfare through an analysis of the S&L bailout. We begin in Chapter 2 with a historical examination of the development of the S&L industry in the 1930s and its rise and decline through the 1980s, leading to the 1982 bank deregulation as a state project. Chapter 3 fleshes out this broad analysis by examining the Silverado Bank and the Columbia Savings and Loan Association as case study illustrations. Chapter 4 then unravels the FIRREA as a continuation of the state project and analyzes the balance of class forces that erupted in the battle over AHP. Chapter 5 explores the role that bank PACs may have played in the passage of both bank deregulation and S&L bailout legislation. Chapter 6 considers the implementation of the bail out as a state project: what factors affected decisions concerning which banks to bailout and which to foreclose? Who benefited and who was hurt, and why? Finally, Chapter 7 returns to the question of the meaning of the welfare state and an analysis of whether or not we have been witnessing a dismantling of the welfare state. This chapter thus offers a discussion of the theoretical and policy implications of the analysis of corporate welfare and the welfare state developed here.

CHAPTER

2

Bank Deregulation

The state projects of economic intervention that produced the S&L bailout did not just emerge ad hoc in the late 1980s. The bailout was an extension of a history of state projects that together attempted to address capital accumulation crises. Indeed, the S&L industry itself was the product of such a state project. To place the S&L bailout in this broader perspective, we must back up several decades. How did the S&L industry develop in the first place, and what was its purpose? How did it get into such severe difficulties, and why did the state respond to those difficulties with bank deregulation legislation? How did bank deregulation, which was supposed to alleviate the industry's crisis, actually exacerbate the problem?

THE S&L INDUSTRY AS A STATE PROJECT

The S&L industry's very existence can be understood as an outgrowth of the larger welfare state regime's project of economic intervention: it was initially created as part of the United States' economic recovery efforts following the Great Depression of the 1930s. Large commercial banks had routinely abandoned housing lending in favor of more lucrative corporate and state lending, or had charged interest rates that made home mortgages too dear for moderate-income Americans. Congress mandated "thrift" depository institutions (S&L banks and mutual savings banks) to fill this void. The S&L branch of the banking industry was created to supply affordable mortgages to working-class families. The spirit of this market niche was to ensure that the American dream of home ownership would not slip beyond the grasp of the working class. To ensure an ongoing commitment to the home mortgage market, thrifts were prohibited by law from offering high interest rates on deposits and from investing in speculative instruments like real estate, stocks, and development projects (U.S. Congress: House 1989a). Up until the late 1970s, S&Ls prospered under regulations securing low-cost, long-term residential mortgages as their industry niche. What happened to suddenly undermine an industry that had a clearly defined market with little competition and that had performed well for almost sixty years?

The legacy of the state project set the stage for the crisis. Formal laws and regulations creating the S&L industry had structured it so that the thrifts could not compete effectively with commercial banks or roll with the punches in the economy. For example, the *Q differential*, or *regulation Q*, enacted in 1966, established interest rate ceilings for the entire banking industry and created an interest-rate differential between commercial banks and S&Ls. This differential—one-Quarter of 1 percent on thirty- and six-month small-saver certificates—allowed thrifts to compete with commercial banks by offering a slightly higher return on savings; this provided thrifts the capital they needed to fulfill their mortgage mandate. However, despite the Q differential, by the end of the 1970s deposits—and therefore mortgage money—began to dry up. According to Paul Volker, then chairman of the Federal Reserve Board, in 1976 thrifts provided almost 65 percent of all residential mortgage money. By 1979 this amount had fallen to 37 percent and the estimated annualized rate based on lending for the first half of 1980 was 16.4 percent (U.S. Congress: House 1980:49).

Contradictorily, regulation Q (a form of state economic intervention designed to preserve the integrity of the banking industry) in some sense precipitated the S&L crisis (Barth 1991). In the late 1970s, nondepository financial corporations such as Merrill Lynch and retailers like Sears began offering investment products at "market rates": rates higher than the rate-controlled depository institutions were allowed to offer. As savers became increasingly sophisticated about the effects of inflation on their savings, passbook accounts became less desirable. Small depositors, the primary source of thrifts' capital, withdrew their savings to invest in higher-rate instruments such as the money market mutual funds offered by nondepository financial institutions. According to Edwin Brooks, then president of the U.S. League of Savings Associations (or simply the U.S. League, a S&L trade group), in the first four months of 1980 S&Ls acquired net new savings of $587 million and closed mortgage loans of $18.4 billion representing a 93 percent decline in savings and a 35 percent decline in mortgages from the same period the previous year (U.S. Congress: House 1980:24, 25).

As a result of decades of mortgage lending, the asset side of S&Ls' ledgers were burdened with long-term mortgages slowly being repaid at rates as low as 6 or 7 percent. To offset these old investments, rates on new mortgages climbed as high as 16 percent. On the liability side, competition with nondepository financial institutions for deposits created losses as interest rates paid on deposits surpassed those received from loans (U.S. Congress: House 1981a:46; see also Barth 1991). The shortage of deposits, combined with high mortgage interest rates, meant that money for housing was effectively unavailable. Indicative of the historical relation between the state and the banking industry, federal legislators were concerned that the destruction of the thrifts meant "destroying the last vestige of a specialized mortgage finance supplier" (U.S. Congress: House 1981a:2). Moreover, because housing is associated with a number of industries (such as building materials, major appliances, and textiles) the absence of mortgage monies aggravated the larger downturn in the U.S. economy.

Regulatory Reactions: Forces for Structural Change

In the late 1970s and early 1980s, deregulation, as a particular form of unified state economic policies, was a state project overtly oriented around rationalization of the U.S. economy through competition. [1] This may be seen most clearly in the deregulation of the airline, natural gas, communication, and over-the-road trucking industries. Congress, the administration, and the regulators themselves proffered deregulation as the solution to the S&L crisis. In the early 1980s, industry trade groups argued that the thrift industry's role as a provider of affordable mortgages, in accordance with its congressional mandate, produced the thrift's decline—not poor management. A majority of legislators concurred, arguing that the policies constituting the congressional mandate of the 1930s were anachronisms given the economic troubles of the 1970s; the crisis required a shift in the structure of the relation between the state and the banking industry. This deregulatory shift would relax interest rate limits and remove restrictions on the intermingling of commercial banking, home banking, real estate, and securities investing. The legislature's endorsement of this analysis of the crisis—which exonerates banking management from the S&L crisis—flies in the face of later charges by consumer, labor, and community groups that those who created and benefited from the crisis should be the ones to clean it up.

In 1980, Congress established the Depository Institutions Deregulation Committee (DIDC). The DIDC's charge was to free thrifts from rate regulations that diminished their competitiveness with nondepository financial organizations. The committee was dominated by industry representatives with a variety of interests in rate regulation: the chairmen of the Federal Reserve Board, Federal Home Loan Bank Board (FHLBB), Federal Deposit Insurance Corporation (FDIC), National Credit Union Association (NCUA), the secretary of the Treasury, and the comptroller of the currency. Of these, the comptroller of the currency was the only nonvoting member, and the National Credit Union Association, although voting, was the only member not bound to the interest rates created by the committee.

According to the U.S. League, following a drop in the Treasury-bill rate, which activated the Q differential, the American Bankers Association (ABA, a commercial bank trade group) pressured the DIDC into closed-door meetings and the DIDC's decision to abrogate regulation Q (U.S. Congress: House 1980:29–30). The superseding of regulation Q created a regulatory environment in which the already weakened thrifts had to compete with commercial banks (hereafter referred to simply as banks) for deposits by matching interest rates. Inflated short-term deposit interest rates meant thrifts were paying more for deposits than they were receiving, on average, for loans. They were borrowing short-term and lending long-term. The U.S. League argued that because it forced thrifts to pay higher rates for deposits, the DIDC cure was worse than the illness (U.S. Congress: House 1981b:130–31, 1981c:42–43). This opinion was echoed by some representatives and other thrift associations (U.S. Congress: House 1981c:1–3, 42–155). Robert McKinney, former chairman of the FHLBB and the Federal Home Loan Mortgage Company (both of which are S&L groups), was angered that the DIDC was dominated by antihousing, probank regulators. He argued that their dominance on the DIDC influenced the decision-making process in favor of the commercial banks:

> The thrifts were given the powers which were supposed to make them more competitive with commercial banks. But in cold, political truth, they received only those powers the [ABA] felt would not interfere with the retention of the competitive advantages already enjoyed by the commercial banks. (U.S. Congress: Senate: 1981b:4)

McKinney's statement highlights the antagonisms between segments of the finance capitalists. That antagonism was evident as well in the ABA's response. The ABA testified that the thrifts were not hurt by the shift in the differential, but by competition from the nondepository financial institutions, which drained funds from both thrifts and banks (U.S. Congress: House 1981b:51–52). They argued that the thrift industry was troubled because it overspecialized in mortgages and faced regulations impeding its ability to compete with the nondepository financials. Therefore, they contended, the thrifts ought to be deregulated to the utmost to help them build their competitive muscle (U.S. Congress: House 1981c:156–184). Elimination of regulation Q, according to the ABA, placed banks and thrifts on equal footing (overlooking, of course, that banks were allowed to offer commercial services proscribed to thrifts) (U.S. Congress: Senate 1980a:86–87).

Thrifts asked for lending instruments designed to allow interest rates on long-term loans to conform to vacillations in the economy—essentially deregulation of their assets (U.S. Congress: House 1981c:134). For example, John Dalton, then chairman of the FHLBB, argued that S&Ls should be allowed to use adjustable-rate mortgages. These mortgages shift with the Treasury-bill rate to ensure that the lender and the borrower absorb the risks of economic fluctuations inherent in long-term lending (U.S. Congress: Senate 1981c:44–47). With the exception of the testimony of the National Association of Mutual Savings Banks (NAMSB), no one suggested regulating the booming nondepository financial corporations (U.S. Congress: Senate 1980a:170).

Like the DIDC abrogation of regulation Q, laws preventing interstate and interindustry financial mergers were altered or breached by the federal insurance companies (FDIC and FSLIC) prior to official passage of the 1982 act. De facto deregulation thus preceded de jure legislation. Emily Womach of the ABA argued that formal deregulation policy was needed to catch up with existing practices, implementing regulatory policies such as the interstate merger of S&Ls in California, New York, and Washington and the acquisitions by American Express and by a New Jersey oil company of deposit-taking institutions (U.S. Congress: House 1982b:483–87). In general, Robert Masterson of the NAMSB testified regarding de facto implementation of regulatory laws that the

> present regulatory policies are not an adequate response to the thrift problem. . . . [T]here will be a continuous waive [*sic*] of supervisory mergers, involving literally hundreds of thrift institutions. . . . [T]his process threatens to undermine confidence in the soundness of the entire financial system. . . . [T]he present regulatory policy posture points to the . . . consolidation of a huge number of independent community oriented thrift[s] . . . into a relatively small number of nationwide depository organizations. Thus, our Nation faces a radical revamping of the financial structure by regulatory fiat, without adequate congressional consideration of the public's interest in the outcome (U.S. Congress: House 1982a:809).

Apparently, the type of merger activity deregulation was supposed to permit was already occurring, thereby setting a de facto precedent in policy implementation if not a de jure precedent in policy formation.

The congressional hearings leading up to the creation of the 1982 act became key institutional selectivity filters that limited the discussion of viable options to three broad topical areas:

1. the right of depository institutions to sell securities (requiring repeal of sections of the Glass-Steagall Act of 1933);
2. the ability of regulators to use mergers to prevent thrift failures (repeal of the McFadden Act of 1927, prohibiting interstate

mergers in banking and the Douglas amendment restricting bank
holding companies);
3. the federal government's obligation to reestablish the net worth
    of failing thrifts.

The Glass-Steagall act of 1933 established the FDIC and the law that
denied banks the right to engage in investment banking, particularly the
right to buy large blocks of stock and resell them in smaller blocks at a
profit. Created during the depression, this regulation was designed to
protect the investor and the federal insurance company from bank failure through speculation. Thus, prior to the 1982 act, banks and thrifts
were prohibited from handling security-based investment products. According to the Reagan administration, the bankers, and the thrifts, this
prohibition was the key to the depository financial institutions' inability
to compete effectively with nondepository financial institutions offering
money market and other mutual fund investment products. The Reagan
administration, through the testimony of Secretary of the Treasury Donald Regan, suggested that banks be allowed to establish securities affili-
ates through which they could underwrite municipal revenue bonds
and sponsor and sell shares in investment companies (U.S. Congress:
Senate 1982a:2).

The ABA wanted these powers, but argued that the separate-affiliates
requirement in the administration proposal would not greatly enhance
the security of depositors' funds. Instead, they argued, it would create
inefficiencies subverting depository institutions' ability to compete with
the nondepository institutions—the impetus and purpose of investment
liberalization (U.S. Congress: Senate 1982a:421–22). The ABA also
claimed to be at a competitive disadvantage because investment firms
could buy corporations that owned commercial banks, and were therefore somewhat engaged in commercial banking, whereas commercial
banks could not own investment firms. Securities firms complained because they could not offer banking services, but, with the passage of this
bill, they would be forced to compete with banks that did not have to
meet the securities firms' regulatory or certification requirements (U.S.
Congress: Senate 1982a:137–42).

Returning to the problems associated with inadequate mortgage
funds, the ABA argued that investments in nondepository financial corporations divert money from depository institutions providing credit
regionally and concentrate it in national financial centers. According to
the ABA, money market funds grew 900 percent from $10.8 billion in
January 1979 to $118.5 billion in April 1981 and that the first four months
of 1981 alone saw a 60 percent increase in these investments. Mutual
funds, they contended, drain money from depository institutions and
make it difficult to meet local credit needs (U.S. Congress: Senate

1981a:1293–94). Unlike the antagonistic testimony the ABA and the thrifts gave after the hasty first acts of the DIDC, in these later hearings the thrifts sided with the ABA: both argued for enhanced securities powers (U.S. Congress: Senate 1981a:1335–38, 1982b:492–512).

Congress and the depository financial industry saw the extension of investment powers as one part of the long-term radical restructuring and strengthening of the industry (the other part was increased lending powers). However, the thrifts required a short-term response to compensate for the losses created by the temporary inversion of the time-yield curve (higher interest rates on short-term deposits than on long-term loans). To meet this need, legislators considered the regulators' bill and the Net-Worth Guarantee Act (capital assistance act). According to Senator Jake Garn, then chairman of the Senate committee on Banking, Housing, and Urban Affairs,

> the capital assistance and the revised regulators bill . . . are short term solutions to long-term problems. We stabilize and preserve the thrift industry by virtue of these bills. We should also insure the industry's long-term viability by expanding the investment and lending powers available to thrift institutions. (U.S. Congress: Senate 1982b:2; see also press release, U.S. Congress: House 1981b:38–39)

Because it was produced by a compromise among the sometimes divided branches of finance capital, the DIDC represented unified action by finance capitalists to keep control of the crisis's "cure." Community, consumer, and labor interests were excluded from upper-level decision-making. However, rather than being a continued source of unity for the financial community, the DIDC, dominated by the largest fraction of finance capital, magnified divisions between thrift and commercial banks. Operating in direct opposition to its mandate, the DIDC's first action, following closed-door meetings that violated the spirit behind its creation, was to eliminate interest rate regulation in an effort to avoid the competitive advantage regulation Q gave S&Ls.

As anticipated by the bank hegemony position, differences in the objective interests of these two segments of the industry remained a point of intraclass political division. Private "market" solutions favor large firms over small ones and increase industry concentration and centralization (Bluestone and Harrison 1982). Starting with the DIDC and going through the creation of the FIRREA, representatives of the commercial banks and the administration testified in favor of "emergency" measures and market solutions that privileged the larger banks at the expense of the smaller ones. The attempt to correct the capital accumulation crises in the banking industry by "leveling the playing field" in effect gives the competitive advantage to those fragments of the industry that—as a result of their size, assets, and structural position in the banking community—held an advantage prior to the legislative changes. As the capital accumulation crisis of the 1930s prompted legislation that facilitated increasing concentration of banking assets in the large commercial banks, so too did the capital accumulation crises and legislation of the 1970s and 1980s. The deregulation and bailout of the S&L industry permitted larger institutions to purchase the assets of smaller thrifts, with the federal government absorbing the liabilities, and thereby increased the concentration of finance capital.

Early in the crisis the Reagan administration, represented by officers of the Treasury Department, favored taking no direct action at all—a policy that virtually guarantees that only the financially largest firms will remain independent and solvent. Prior to passage of the 1982 Garn–St. Germain Act, the administration and most of the commercial branch of the industry favored a bill proffered by the bank regulators (i.e., FDIC). The regulators' bill consisted of market solutions, such as mergers, to solve the industry's dilemmas. Alternatively, S&Ls favored a net-worth guarantee, which committed public funds to an accounting scheme that raised all institutions to a certain level of capital.

The deregulatory state project presented an opportunity to the commercial branch of the industry. Large commercial banks used the thrift crisis and the bailout process as an occasion to increase their financial and strategic domination of the finance industry. They wanted provisions in the FIRREA to allow bank holding companies to acquire healthy S&L institutions as well as thrifts that were capital deficient (U.S. Congress: House 1989b, Part 2:19, 27). Such a provision would concentrate their control of finance capital flows. Even more dramatically, throughout both the deregulation and FIRREA hearings, the large commercial banks, organized within the ABA, sought dissolution of the S&L industry as a whole; they argued that the thrifts were overspecialized and no longer useful:

> When [the S&Ls] were born, there was a need. [Now,] the S&L industry, the credit union industry, the commercial banking industry are beginning to drift, so that they are beginning to look similar. . . . [P]ossibly the next chapter of this, if we do it correctly, could be . . . to permit the marketplace to work through mergers and acquisitions. (U.S. Congress: House 1989b, Part 2:63)

So anxious were the commercial banks to get the permission to eliminate or acquire S&Ls, that ABA president Thomas P. Rideout urged Congress to use "fast track" procedures in the FIRREA approval process (U.S. Congress: House 1989b, Part 2:19).

In addition to legislative shifts in the relation between the state and the banking industry, the deregulatory state project also involved de facto shifts in regulatory policy. Prior to formal deregulation, restrictions on the relations between thrifts, commercial banks, nondepository financials, and bank holding companies were subverted with the regulators' permission. Citicorp's purchase of Fidelity, a California S&L, is one example of a formerly prohibited activity receiving regulatory authorization. Deregulation provided de jure approval to de facto regulatory policy. However, despite calls from the commercial banks, deregulation did not lead to the dissolution of the S&L industry. As we argue below, Congress remained entwined within the historical, structural relation between the state and the S&Ls, while incorporating the market-oriented objectives of the deregulatory state project.

The hearings for the regulators' bill thus acted as selectivity mechanisms, as they tended to emphasize the views of the bill's supporters and to ignore or minimize the voices of its critics, particularly consumers and minority-owned S&L institutions. The bill's advocates considered it an inexpensive temporary solution to a long-term capital accumulation problem. Its critics opposed it because, although it enabled a significant restructuring of the finance industry with long-term effects that undermined federal interstate banking laws, jeopardized the existence of minority-owned S&Ls, and did not ensure investments in local communities at affordable rates, it was given a perfunctory hearing as a short-term, emergency measure.

Net-Worth Guarantee Act: A Compromise

Like the regulators' bill, the Net-Worth Guarantee Act was not meant to solve the long-term problems of the financial industry. Legislators developed the act to maintain the net worth of faltering thrifts at 2 percent. According to Rep. St. Germain, "The Home Mortgage Capital Stability Act [the forerunner of the Net-Worth Guarantee Act, was] designed to provide short-term relief for mortgage lending institutions facing temporary earnings losses in the current high-interest market" (U.S. Congress: House 1982b:807).

As drafted, the Net-Worth Guarantee Act was activated when the net worth of a federally or state insured depository institution, with at least 20 percent of its assets in residential mortgages, fell below 2 percent. When this occurred, the appropriate regulatory board (the FDIC for banks, the FHLBB for S&Ls, or the NCUA for credit unions) stepped in and made a determination about the cause of the difficulty and the viability of the institution. If it determined that the failure was not the result of bad management practices—such as high operating expenses, futures trading, or deliberate attempts to receive this aid—then the regulator could provide capital to the institution such that its net worth was brought up to 2 percent. To remain qualified, the institution was required to devote 60 percent of its new deposits to home mortgages during the period in which it received aid. The bill was scheduled to "sunset" (or to expire) September 30, 1984 (U.S. Congress: House 1982a:191–213).

Congress designed the net-worth guarantee to be accomplished, if done properly, without actual cash exchanges between the institutions and the regulators. Rather than borrowing from the regulator (and thereby actually increasing their liabilities), qualified institutions issued Income Capital Certificates (ICCs), which the regulators then "bought" with promissory notes. ICCs counted as assets and increased the bank's net worth. Using this scheme, the federal government had to repay the note only in the event the institution failed (the note worked as a capital guarantee because it was backed by "the full faith and credit of the United States"). St. Germain said that the cost of the program would be "zero" (U.S. Congress: House 1982b:807). Nonetheless, the total amount of the guarantees was capped at $8.5 billion.

Critics of the cash aspect of the bill, including St. Germain, feared that money allocations for this legislation would increase the federal budget deficit, thereby increasing inflation rates and exacerbating the thrifts' dilemma (U.S. Congress: House 1982a:807). According to Roger Mehle, representing the Reagan administration from the Department of the Treasury, non–cash assistance, which lowers the budget deficit and thereby lowers interest rates, helps thrifts more than the cash assistance plan because, "[t]he reduction of interest rates is the single most important step which the Congress can take to restore the thrift industry to economic health" (U.S. Congress: Senate 1982a:157).

Second, the provision of the bill requiring that an assisted institution devote 60 percent of its new deposits to new mortgages with interest rates 1 percent above the institution's average deposit interest rate was widely disputed and almost universally rejected. The 1 percent rule meant that already weakened institutions would be forced to lend money at a lower rate than they were buying it from depositors. St. Germain, who introduced this provision, seemed to be proposing, as part of hearings on housing and urban-rural recovery, that the institutions receiving assistance had to be willing to remain in the home mortgage lending field (U.S. Congress: House 1982a:807). This was applauded by consumer organizations such as the Public Interest Research Group, who called for "specific requirements that mandate a continued role for these institutions as mortgage specialists" as justification for federal capital assistance (U.S. Congress: House 1982a:931). However, consumers' interests were drowned out by other, more powerful voices. The crucial combatants were clearly not the more traditional ones of unified finance capitalists versus labor and consumers. Rather, divisions between segments within the banking community itself were more important filters in es-

tablishing the definition of the situation and the possible policy alternatives. Non–bank interests were preempted or selected out of the policymaking process. This was most clear in the arena in which non–bank
groups addressed their issues regarding bank deregulation.

For example, as the testimony of the Public Interest Research Group
indicates, representatives from non–finance industry organizations
either responded to the agenda established by the bankers' and regulators' bills, or addressed issues marginal to bank deregulation. Consumer, labor, and community interest groups presented their views on
banking and bank deregulation amidst hearings on urban and rural
development (U.S. Congress: House 1982a). These groups included, in
one panel, the Public Interest Research Group, National People's Action, and the National Commission Against Discrimination in Housing.
Representatives from the AFL-CIO, National Housing Conference, and
the National Farmer's Union attended earlier hearings (U.S. Congress:
House 1981a).

Unlike the testimony given by the finance industry representatives,
the testimony of the consumer, labor, and community interest groups
concentrated on bills marginal to bank reform. The panel on urban and
rural development addressed cuts in Housing and Urban Development
funding, and thus dealt with the Home Mortgage Capital Stability Act
marginally; a second panel heard testimony about monetary policy.
Their primary interests in regulatory reform were job protection in finance capital–dependent industries and lower mortgage rates, rather
than looking at regulatory reform as a wage earner/consumer issue;
however, the non–finance industry organizations addressed their testimony to concerns raised by the finance industry, such as federal pre-
emption of state banking laws. Thus, the central concerns of the
consumer, labor and community interest groups regarding banking
were addressed through legislation concerned primarily with the well-
being of the finance industry. But the exclusion of these groups from
bank deregulation hearings suggested that the policymaking process
would be influenced only by the industry that would ultimately be deregulated. The participation and influence of labor, consumers, and
community groups was effectively selected out of the policymaking process by marginalizing their input into indirectly related committees.

Although it was in the final draft of the 1982 act, many argued against
the across-the-board 2 percent net-worth guarantee found in the House
bill on the grounds that it provided an incentive for bad management.
The regulators, who favored the merger-centered regulators' bill, felt the
2 percent guarantee provided a safety net for failing institutions that
undercut market incentives to cut costs and avoid losses. Richard Pratt
from the FHLBB, although admitting that some form of federal intervention in the private thrift industry was necessary, argued that this inter-

vention should be "market-disciplined . . . and Darwinian in its impact" such that weak institutions fail and strong institutions prevail (U.S. Congress: House 1982a:1505). The ABA and the FHLBB agreed that, if taken too far, capital assistance would weaken the thrifts by protecting them from the market's honing influence. For example, ABA representative William Kennedy argued that "any legislation that attempts to shield the specialized thrift institutions from the realities of the marketplace will not work and will ultimately be very costly to banking and the [thrifts]" (U.S. Congress: House 1982a:2402; cf. FHLBB statement, U.S. Congress: Senate 1982a:68).

Like the regulators, the administration feared the net-worth guarantee would undercut market forces. Secretary of the Treasury Donald Regan argued that short-term measures were only minimally required; the administration's tax, budget, and monetary policies, designed to bring interest rates down, would redeem the thrifts (U.S. Congress: House 1981b:4). According to Roger Mehle of the Treasury, "[m]andating that institutions operating with losses automatically qualify for restoration of net worth to some arbitrary level absolves both the institution and the agency of a substantial portion of their responsibility for protecting the income stream of the institution" (U.S. Congress: House 1982a:1590). In the same statement, Mehle indicated that the thrifts would best be helped through private solutions such as interstate and interindustry mergers—solutions that increase industry concentration and favor larger banks over smaller. Moreover, Mehle argued that the thrifts really were not insolvent because they always had adequate funds to meet their immediate obligations, such as withdrawals, even if their actual net worth was low (U.S. Congress: House 1981a:438). The Reagan administration favored increased deregulation of both the deposit interest rates and loan interest rates of the thrifts.

Those who favored the net-worth guarantee [thrifts, state bank supervisors, Independent Bankers Association (IBA)] did so for very different reasons than those upon which they based their opposition to the regulators' bill. They argued that increased mergers were leading to excessive industry concentration, and that mergers were producing a de facto restructuring of the industry without proper congressional consideration. S. Allen Harris, of the IBA, gave vehement support to the Net-Worth Guarantee Act to retard the growth of what he called "merger mania" (U.S. Congress: House 1982a:2433). According to Harris,

> Continuation of the merger waive will effectively void a large body of State and Federal law. This committee's role could well be reduced to that of rubber stamping a fait accompli. Basic structural changes should result from careful deliberation, not secret weekend mergers. (U.S. Congress: House 1982b:2434)

A modified form of this waiver, giving state regulators the opportunity to protest interstate mergers, was included in the Senate bill, although not in the net-worth guarantee bill (U.S. Congress: House 1982b:23–29). Its presence in the Senate bill points to the interests of large commercial banks as important selection filters in the congressional policymaking process. It also contradicts a state-centered notion of state autonomy.

Deregulation and the S&L Crisis

With passage of the Garn–St. Germain Act, the industry remained troubled. Unlike the Depression-era Glass-Steagall Act which established the FDIC and limited the securities activities of depository institutions, the 1982 net-worth guarantee allowed S&Ls to become involved in speculative, high-risk investments while simultaneously positioning the state to bail out the industry.

According to a range of congressional witnesses and a Congressional National Commission on the FIRREA, the postderegulation banking industry crisis was rooted in the regulatory shifts that modified the state-industry relation (see U.S. Congress: House 1989a, 1989b, 1989c). Deregulation blurred the lines between banks and thrifts and between depository and nondepository financial institutions, lifted restrictions on loan and deposit interest rates, removed the prohibition against interest payments on demand deposits (checking accounts), and permitted depository institutions to become involved in public revenue bonds and a wider variety of consumer and commercial loans. Deregulation, ostensibly designed to relieve the late 1970s–early 1980s S&L crisis, opened the industry to formerly state-proscribed market practices. Unprecedented, high interest rates on deposits, imprudent real-estate speculation, and participation in the junk bond market—all departures from thrifts' home mortgage niche—were state sanctioned. According to the National Commission, "Government policies made the system vulnerable to corruption. . . . [F]raud was not the cause of the debacle" (National Commission on Financial Institution Reform, Recovery, and Enforcement 1993:8).

The 1982 act also increased the capacity of the federal regulators to rescue, merge, subsidize, or sell a failing thrift, and created a net-worth guarantee for S&Ls. The net-worth guarantee and, later in the crisis, supervisory "goodwill" for thrifts below legal net-worth levels, were part of a set of convoluted accounting changes that made it nearly impossible for regulators to discern the abuse of individual firms and the health of the industry in general (National Commission on Financial Institution Reform, Recovery, and Enforcement 1993:37–39, 48–49). Moreover, by empowering the federal deposit insurance companies to insure the net worth of failing depository institutions, the net-worth guarantee converted the responsibility for the solvency of the industry from a regulatory option to a legislative prescription (Glasberg and Skidmore 1992). What role did the state play when deregulation failed?

According to testimony given by a variety of witnesses before Congress, several factors were widely regarded as responsible for the S&L crisis (see U.S. Congress: House 1989a, 1989b, 1989c). The Garn–St. Germain Act of 1982 deregulating the banking industry paved the way for previously unacceptable practices in the S&L industry. For example, deregulation allowed S&L institutions to offer higher interest rates on deposits than in the past in order to compete with those offered by commercial banks so the thrifts could attract more business. This seriously reduced their cash flow, since low-interest mortgages payments trickled into the thrifts slower than high-interest payments on deposits flowed out, eroding their cash flow and making them vulnerable to insolvency.

Deregulation also enabled the thrifts to venture into riskier nontraditional investments such as real estate speculation, development projects, and junk bonds. Some thrifts shifted their emphasis in lending away from low-interest home mortgages and decidedly toward these riskier investments. When declines in oil and petroleum prices touched off a recession and a precipitous drop in real estate values, those thrifts heavily exposed in the riskier ventures found themselves running huge deficits and becoming insolvent.

Finally, deregulation of the industry meant that there were fewer field supervisors and bank examiners to oversee the thrifts' activities. This lack of supervision facilitated fraud, overextension, and lack of prudence in investments, as well as possible criminal behavior on the part of some thrift executives. Charles Keating of California's Lincoln Savings and Loan Association became a symbol of the alleged criminal activities and excesses of the industry. Half of the insolvent thrifts were indeed found to have involved elements of fraud in 1988 (Barth 1991). However, observers have estimated that fraud accounts for as little as 3 percent of the cost of the bailout (Ely 1990; cf. Barth 1991:44); others offered a more conservative estimate of 10 percent (Barth, Bartholomew, and Labich 1989). More critical as the primary cause of the crisis appeared to be the more structural difficulties engendered by deregulation of the industry: unprecedentedly high interest rates on deposits, risky, imprudent real estate speculation, and participation in the junk bond market, all of which departed from the thrifts' traditional home mortgage business.

While much of the testimony given to Congress identified bank deregulation as a critical factor leading to the thrifts' crisis, not all observers agree with this analysis. Barth (1991) argued that several practices and policies had already undermined the industry more than twenty years before the Garn–St. Germain Act of 1982 formally deregulated banks. Barth argued that formal laws and regulations structured the S&L industry too rigidly, so that the thrifts could not compete effectively with commercial banks or flexibly adjust to shifts in the economy. For example, the laws establishing S&Ls limited the interest they could offer on time deposits and savings accounts. Since commercial banks were not limited this way, they could compete successfully against the thrifts with more attractive rates. In response, thrifts began offering interest-bearing checking accounts in the early 1970s. But while the thrifts had found a way to attract more deposits with interest, they were still seriously restricted by formal laws as to how they could invest their funds. S&L institutions were confined to home mortgages at fixed low rates for homes within fifty miles of their home office. This meant that thrifts were tied to local economic boom and bust cycles, unable to balance local recessions with investments elsewhere in the country or abroad. The problem was compounded with federal tax laws that provided incentives to the industry to focus its activities in home mortgages.

Several observers asserted that the FDIC played a key role in precipitating the thrifts' crisis (Buser, Chen, and Kane 1981; Kane 1986, 1989). Federal deposit insurance guarantees the security of deposits up to $100,000 in order to prevent depositors from getting nervous during economic downturns and causing a run on the bank by withdrawing their money. However, the insurance also provides the thrifts with incentives to "go for broke" and invest in highly risky ventures on the assumption that the insurance will cover the losses. Both Kane and Barth agree that the federal deposit insurance program thus encourages high-risk, speculative investments, more S&L failures, and mostly more failures than would be the case without such insurance.

These observations correctly identify the industry's decline as having begun prior to formal deregulation in 1982. The key word here, however, is *formal*. We would argue that all the congressional alterations of existing laws, and all the administrative practices and tax laws represented an *informal* deregulation of the industry. As such, the Garn–St. Germain Act simply formalized what was in fact well under way for more than twenty years. Barth admits that deregulation accelerated what was already happening; and both Barth and Kane have acknowledged that the FDIC's lax supervision of thrifts caused by deregulation facilitated serious high-risk ventures to continue unabated until it was too late. Bank deregulation, therefore, still remains a major culprit in the crisis of the thrift industry.

The legislation that formally deregulated banks and that many identify as the source of the present difficulty did not just happen. It emerged out of the historical legacy of a large ongoing state project of intervention in finance capital processes, and specifically resulted from the state's previous struggles with a unified banking community over bailing out Chrysler. That is, the S&L crisis is a consequence of a radical shift in federal regulatory policy that the banks themselves participated in changing. Here, the state's own role as an active participant in a previous struggle (not as a neutral arbiter or bystander) and its roles in the de facto deregulation of the industry for more than twenty years set the stage for the S&L defaults and the ensuing conflict over its bailout. Moreover, the abrupt shift in federal regulation of banking occurred not as a result of a crisis in finance capital accumulation that remained unresponsive to conventional solutions, but as a result of a power struggle over bailing out a major auto producer (see Glasberg 1987a, 1989). Deregulation legislation, then, shaped the conditions that accelerated the S&L capital accumulation problems to crises and contributed to the selective filtering mechanism leading to the biggest, most far-reaching bailout in U.S. history.

NOTE

1.   We use the term *overtly* because, as we examine below, irrespective of the intent of its creators, deregulation created a less competitive market as it spurred greater corporate concentration.

3

Anatomies of Failures:
Case Studies of Savings and Loan Crises

So far we have outlined the structural factors that undermined many S&L institutions. While individual greed and fraud certainly played an important part in the crises of some thrifts, these structural factors more importantly created a systemwide crisis beyond the actions of greedy or fraudulent individuals in the thrifts. A lax regulatory environment in which there was little or no oversight of thrifts' activities encouraged highly risky speculative investments that were previously forbidden for thrifts and that left them vulnerable to abrupt market shifts in both the real estate and junk bond markets. Now we look at some specific cases.

COLUMBIA SAVINGS AND LOAN ASSOCIATION:
LEVERAGED BUYOUTS AND THE JUNK BOND JUNKIES

The contradiction of high-interest payouts on current deposits and low-interest-rate incomes from mortgage holdings enticed thrifts to take advantage of the deregulated atmosphere in banking and speculate in high-risk junk bonds. This is because junk bonds, as high-yield investments, provided higher rates of return than real estate loans and certainly more than the old low-interest home mortgages that the thrifts still held. They turned to Drexel Burnham Lambert, Inc., the house of Michael Milken, the junk bond king, to broker these investments.

Junk bonds are high-yield bonds that have been rated as below investment quality by Moody's and Standard and Poor's. Typically, they are those which Moody's rates lower than Ba and Standard and Poor's rates BBB or lower. These ratings indicate that the rating agencies do not consider these bonds to be prudent investments, and thus the name *junk* bonds. They are frequently issued by small firms that have no equity or favorable financial history, but that must access the capital markets in order to expand their business (U.S. Congress: House 1988:2–4).

Junk bonds are not new: there have always been bonds the rating agencies deemed unworthy of investment since Moody's first began rating bonds in 1909. However, while most of the time investors have heeded the warnings against investing in these poorly rated bonds, some investors have always been willing to ignore these caution lights and have proceeded to invest. It was not until the late 1970s, when Drexel Burnham Lambert began to aggressively market junk bonds, that they became a serious investment instrument for a significant number of investors (U.S. Congress: House 1988:5). While new issues of junk bonds amounted to $0.56 billion in 1977, that figure exploded in 1986–87 to $63 billion in new issues. Junk bonds accounted for a scant 3.7 percent of all outstanding corporate bonds, but by 1984 they had jumped to 21.5 percent of the bond market. Drexel Burnham Lambert was the main trader of these junk bonds, controlling almost 80 percent of the market by 1989 (Zey 1993:153–56; see also U.S. Congress: House 1988:6–7).

Junk bonds became the instrument that fueled leveraged buyouts in the overheated market of corporate mergers, particularly hostile take-overs. This is because they were a way for acquisitive corporations to access the capital markets to finance takeovers of other firms with little or no collateral or equity. Thus, even the largest corporations could finance a hostile takeover of another firm without risking their own assets. A General Accounting Office study of hostile takeovers found that junk bonds accounted for approximately 12 percent of the initial financing supporting the takeover; an additional 42 percent of the financing came from bank loans. But the study also found that junk bonds had a secondary role in these takeovers: many of the bank loans used initially were later refinanced by junk bonds, bringing the total financing role of junk bonds in hostile takeovers to 22 percent (U.S. Congress: House 1988:42–43; see also Burnett and Philippi 1990:148–49; Zey 1993:156–57).

Moreover, the General Accounting Office examination of the use of funds cited by junk bond prospectuses found that "13 percent of high-risk bonds was issued for the purpose of carrying out acquisitions. Another 15 percent was for future acquisitions, and 23 percent was to retire debt of previous mergers and acquisitions" (Zey 1993:157; see also U.S. Congress: House 1989k:6). Thus, 61 percent of junk bonds were used not for the internal expansion of small firms, but for fueling the merger mania that gripped corporate America.

That this represented a high risk of exposure to default did not appear to bother investors. The promise of high rates of return on junk bond investments was far too attractive to ignore, and many S&L institutions, desperate to close the gap between high-interest payouts and low-interest incomes, were drawn to the junk bond market. By 1989, 183 S&L institutions owned $14.4 billion in junk bonds, amounting to 1 percent of the industry's total assets. The thirty thrifts holding the most junk bonds—concentrated in California, Florida, New York, Texas, and Missouri—together held $13 billion, which represented 91 percent of the industry's total junk bond holdings (*New York Times* 1989). Columbia Savings and Loan Association of Beverly Hills, California, was one of the biggest purchasers of junk bonds, along with American Savings, Centrust, Financial Corporation of America, Lincoln Savings and Loan, and Financial Corporation of Santa Barbara. The concentration of junk bond holdings among thrift institutions was already apparent by 1985, when just ten S&L institutions, almost all of which were in California and Texas, held $4.64 billion in junk bonds, or 78 percent of the total junk bond holdings in the S&L industry (U.S. Congress: House 1988:21, 1989k:6–7; see also Zey 1993:61; Taggart 1988).

How was it possible for thrifts to become so heavily invested in junk bonds? Bank deregulation ushered in by the Garn–St. Germain Act allowed federally chartered S&L institutions to invest up to 1 percent of their assets in corporate debt, including high-yield instruments like junk bonds. In addition, they were permitted to invest another 10 percent of their assets in junk bonds, to be classified as commercial lending. This means that a total of 11 percent of federally chartered thrifts' assets could be invested in junk bonds (U.S. Congress: House 1988:23). Although only 149 of the 3,092 FSLIC-insured thrifts held junk bonds in their portfolios by 1988, these thrifts together "accounted for 23 percent of the industry's assets" (U.S. Congress: House 1988:21; see also U.S. Congress: House 1989k:6–7).

Columbia Savings and Loan appeared to be the leader of the pack, holding $2.3 billion in junk bonds by 1986. This represented a full 28 percent of its total assets (Hilder 1988; Taggart 1988). By 1989, that volatile investment grew to almost $5 billion, a walloping 35 percent of its assets (Heins 1988:153–56). The 1987 crash of the stock market provoked the first significant damage to the thrift: it lost nearly 40 percent of its earnings. That hemorrhage was exacerbated by the Federal Reserve Board's raising interest rates in 1988 (Heins 1988).

What few regulations still existed and were being enforced at this time required Columbia to write down the value of its junk bond portfolio to rapidly declining market values, causing it to suffer a significant loss: $591 million. Columbia attempted to remain solvent by searching for a buyer for its huge portfolio of junk bonds. That portfolio had a market value of $3.5 billion (Stevenson 1990a:D1). Meanwhile, the thrift continued to post significant losses: stockholder's equity plunged to a negative $121 million, putting Columbia $259 million short of the federal requirement of $138 million to remain solvent. Thus, by federal standards, Columbia was insolvent and in grave danger of being seized by federal regulators (Stevenson 1990b:D1).

Columbia was not alone in its struggle to remain solvent in the face of the collapse of the junk bond house of cards: S&L institutions sold $2.8 billion in junk bonds in the final quarter of 1989, and just five thrifts together accounted for almost two-thirds of those sales. Columbia was among those five, selling $421 million of its junk bond portfolio (Wallace 1990:D7). Ironically, these sales also contributed to the already volatile market in junk bonds, making it increasingly difficult for the thrifts to sell their remaining holdings while simultaneously eroding their value. While the federal government had already seized all the other S&L institutions that were heavily invested in junk bonds, it kept at arm's length from Columbia, hoping to give the thrift an opportunity to find a buyer for its junk bond portfolio. Columbia wanted to find a single buyer for the entire portfolio and, despite extreme skepticism by junk bond traders and analysts that such a buyer could be found, insisted that it had several serious bids (Stevenson 1990c).

By July 1990, Columbia announced that it had, indeed, found a buyer: the Canadian investment firm of Gordon America L.P. Gordon agreed to acquire the portfolio with a $2.7 billion ten-year note held by Columbia and secured by the bond portfolio. Gordon would pay $300 million in cash. This agreement meant that Columbia remained exposed as a financing partner: in the event that Gordon defaulted on the loan, Columbia would be left holding the portfolio. Why would Columbia agree to such a proposal? Because in exchange for the risk of the volatility of the junk bond market, Columbia would receive the steady income of Gordon's interest payments of 10.5 percent on its loan from Columbia, plus a $50 million financing fee from the investor. This could mean a short-term profit for Columbia of $100 million, which would propel it closer to solvency and perhaps avert a federal takeover (Lev 1990:D1).

Shortly after this tentative agreement was announced, three Hong Kong companies controlled by businessman Li Ka-shing announced plans to acquire a half-interest in the Gordon investment group's acquisition of Columbia's junk bond portfolio. While Li Ka-shing's empire had been built in real estate in Hong Kong, he wished to reduce his exposure there, where 90 percent of his assets were tied up. This is because investors in Hong Kong were nervous that China, which was scheduled to take control of Hong Kong in 1997, would not fulfill its promise to preserve Hong Kong's economic and political institutions for fifty years. Like many business people in Hong Kong, Li Ka-shing was attempting to move as much of his assets abroad as possible. He viewed investing in Columbia's junk bond portfolio as a "window into corporate America and into further investment opportunities" (*New York Times* 1990a). The deal seemed to offer a win-win situation for investors and seller alike.

However promising it might have appeared, the agreement still had to be approved by federal regulators, whose only concern was whether or not the deal was all that advantageous for Columbia. Columbia told federal regulators that it would lose about $50 million on the proposed sale of its junk bond portfolio, because of fees from the deal (*New York Times* 1990d). That loss, coupled with Columbia's risky exposure in the financing of the deal, made regulators nervous, to say the least. But the final blow came when regulators' analysis of the deal indicated that Columbia had failed to seek the best value for its junk bond portfolio. Regulators believed that the sale to Gordon was not the highest price Columbia could get for its holdings and were concerned that the thrift had not sought any all-cash offers. The regulators rejected the proposed sale to the Gordon investment group and instructed Columbia to look more broadly for other buyers, preferably those using cash (Labaton 1990a:D1). Columbia began to seek such bids. Meanwhile, the Office of Thrift Supervision warned that Columbia might be seized before such a sale could be closed, because the huge losses incurred by the portfolio had seriously eroded its capital.

While Columbia struggled to find another suitable buyer for its junk bonds, several lawsuits were filed that opened a very illuminating window onto management behaviors under the lax supervisory environment created by deregulation, as well as the relationship between the junk bond go-go years and the S&L crisis. The Office of Thrift Supervision sought to force Thomas Spiegel, the former head of the Columbia Savings and Loan Association, to repay the thrift almost $19 million he was alleged to have misappropriated for his own use. Among the repayments the office sought were almost $3 million for an unauthorized bonus in 1989; $6.44 million in aircraft and a luxury hangar for Spiegel's personal use; $1.1 million for personal use of condominiums in Wyoming, California, and Utah; $5.75 million for losses related to a below-market-rate loan with inadequate underwriting to a friend of Spiegel's; $2.37 million for unauthorized contributions to a charity Spiegel controlled; and almost $0.5 million for personal use by Spiegel, including travel for him and his wife, concert tickets, a wine-tasting course for him and his wife, and the purchase of fifty-five guns (Hershey 1990). A federal judge ordered Spiegel to post a $1 million bond and essentially froze all his assets pending the outcome of the case (*New York Times* 1990e). Just two months later, the Office of Thrift Supervision expanded its charges against Spiegel to include charges that he further squandered the thrift's capital in the construction of a new headquarters for the bank "without any attempt to limit costs" (*New York Times* 7 September 1990:D2). The construction, which cost more than $54.7 million, had a market value of only $24 million, causing a loss to the thrift of almost $30 million.

These charges against Spiegel are certainly alarming in their magnitude, and indicate severe mismanagement of the bank's funds, and perhaps fraud. Such mismanagement and misappropriations could only have occurred to the extent they did in an lax regulatory environment: the absence of regular and careful oversight invited the sort of hubris Spiegel's decisions indicated. But as large as these figures are, they pale beside the losses incurred by the thrift's investments in junk bonds. Lawsuits filed regarding the thrift's relationship with Michael Milken and Drexel Burnham Lambert were even more astounding.

Federal regulators filed a $6.8 billion lawsuit against Drexel Burnham Lambert in November 1990, which suggested that executives like Spiegel were not alone in exploiting the minimal oversight created by deregulation. The suit charged that the securities firm had "willfully plundered" more than forty S&L institutions that were now insolvent "through bribery, coercion, extortion, fraud, and other illegal means" (Labaton 1990b:D1). The suit pointed to Drexel's aggressive monopoly of the junk bond market as a factor in its creation of the illusion of a vibrant market for junk that would not exist were it not for Drexel's manipulations. That illusion masked the losses that many S&L institutions were actually mounting and delayed recognition that the junk bond market was indeed a house of cards and therefore not a prudent investment (Labaton 1990b:D6). The government suit charged that this dominance of the market resulted from bribes given to S&L executives to purchase junk bonds, raising more capital than necessary from one thrift institution to facilitate further investments in Drexel's junk bonds, and manipulating the prices of junk bonds by trading these between thrifts (Labaton 1990c:A1).

With this suit, the federal government had cited Drexel Burnham and its "co-conspirators" as "principal culprits" in the S&L crisis that would now cost taxpayers untold billions of dollars to clean up. Essentially, the suit suggested that Drexel had used the deregulatory legislation to its advantage at the expense of taxpayers, particularly those in the middle and working classes, who were supposed to be the principal beneficiaries of the thrifts' market niche. The suit contended that Drexel's incredible success in what were supposed to be high-risk bonds resulted from "its ability to tap into enormous pools of federally insured money held at scores of savings and loan associations" (Labaton 1990c:D4). Drexel deliberately marketed junk bonds by refocusing investors' attention from the bonds' high risk to their high yield. "In fact, the 'yield' was often infinitesimal or nonexistent because the securities turned out to be worthless," the suit charged (ibid.).

Columbia Savings and Loan Association filed its own $4.5 billion suit against Drexel, charging that Drexel used market manipulation and fraud, among other illegal means, to sell junk bonds to the thrift between 1982 and 1988 (Stevenson 1990c). Columbia's then-chief executive

officer Thomas Spiegel was one of Michael Milken's "first and best customers" in the purchase of junk bonds, becoming the largest thrift hold-
er of junk bonds. Columbia's suit paralleled the federal government's
suit against Drexel Burnham, arguing that Milken and Drexel "were
essentially operating a huge scam, manipulating junk bond prices and
misrepresenting the terms of deals to create profits for Mr. Milken and
his associates, often at the expense of junk bond buyers" (Stevenson
1990c:D5). For example, in 1989 Drexel sold Columbia $15.75 million in
junk bonds issued by Braniff, Inc., but failed to inform Columbia of the
extent of Braniff's financial crises. In fact, Braniff went bankrupt shortly
after Columbia purchased its junk bonds, leaving Columbia holding a
loss of nearly $16 million. In another instance, Drexel convinced Colum-
bia in 1988 to purchase $31.5 million in subordinated debt and $16 million in nonvoting stock in Tricap, an investment partnership Drexel set
up in Bermuda with a subsidiary of the insurance firm American International Group (AIG). Drexel claimed in the prospectus it showed Columbia that it would share decision-making power with AIG in Tricap,
but in actuality Drexel controlled the investment decisions. Columbia's
suit charged that this control over investment decisions meant that
Drexel had created a "captive buyer" in Tricap to purchase junk bonds
Drexel could not sell elsewhere. Indeed, the suit charges, many of the
junk bonds Tricap purchased from Drexel were tremendous losers rather than high-yielders: Tricap lost more than 28 percent of the value of its
$249 million junk bond portfolio by 1989, and Columbia's $47.5 million
investment in Tricap-issued junk bonds became completely worthless
(Stevenson 1990c:D5).

These two cases cited in Columbia's suit against Drexel Burnham
were just two examples in a series of similar investment groups Drexel
created to entice investors like Columbia to purchase junk bonds by
creating markets that did not exist for worthless bonds. The illusion of
high yield quickly gave way to the reality of high risk for Columbia, as it
did for many other similarly exposed thrift institutions.

The federal government finally seized control of Columbia in January
1991. The thrift had stalled a federal takeover for almost a year by attempting to find a buyer for its junk bond portfolio, which by now had
fallen in value from about $4.3 billion at its height to $2.1 billion, and
was continuing to post losses. Its inability to find a buyer, and the
portfolio's continued decline left the federal government no choice but
to take over the thrift (Lev 1991a:31). By September of that year, federal
regulators closed the thrift, agreeing to sell off or return $4.76 billion in
deposits (Lev 1991b). Thus ended the largest case of a junk bond–in-
duced S&L failure. And although Spiegel clearly misappropriated the
thrift's funds for his own benefit, the amount of money attributed to his
actions is relatively small compared to the losses the thrift incurred from

its junk bond market participation engineered by Michael Milken and Drexel Burnham. Columbia cited the lax oversight engendered by bank deregulation as an important factor contributing to its incredible participation in the high-risk gamble of junk bonds. In its suit, the thrift claimed that it was "ill equipped" to handle the new investment authority it was granted under the Garn–St. Germain Act, yet it felt compelled in the highly competitive banking market to make forays into these uncharted waters. Its inexperience and lack of expertise left Columbia vulnerable to the fraud and manipulation perpetrated by Milken and Drexel Burnham (Eichenwald 1990:D5).

Junk bonds had thus served to destroy at least one S&L institution. We now know the fraud and criminal behavior perpetrated by Milken and friends in leveraged buyouts and the junk bond market. The investments in junk bonds by the S&L institutions represented enormously imprudent investment decisions, encouraged by the misrepresentations and manipulations of Milken and Drexel Burnham Lambert. Thrift executives, who were naive and inexperienced in bond investing, accepted Drexel's prospectuses as truthful and quickly leaped at the opportunity to reap high yields. That quickness to ignore the high-risk aspect of junk bonds and invest in them was prompted by the damaging gap between payouts and income created for the thrifts by a long history of state projects. Considering the exposure of many thrifts in the junk bond market, we can appreciate the role these high-yield, high-risk instruments played in the industry's crisis.

SILVERADO BANK: DEREGULATION AND UNREAL ESTATE SPECULATION

Silverado Banking, Savings and Loan Association (hereafter referred to as Silverado Bank or simply Silverado) began in 1956 as Mile High Savings and Loan Association, a bank chartered by the State of Colorado. It was a typically unnoteworthy S&L, solid but unimpressive in its growth as a home mortgage lender until the mid-1980s, when it became Silverado Bank and began showing explosive growth in assets and investments. Yet, Silverado collapsed only two years after posting significant growth, and by the end of 1988 federal regulators closed the bank. How did such an impressive success story turn so quickly into a disaster?

Silverado's story includes many of the soap opera elements found in other S&L stories, elements that often distract us from more careful analysis: power, intrigue, murky business ethics, legal grey areas, and the fall of the rich and famous (all of which we will get to shortly). But these are not the essential elements in the demise of Silverado. The story of Silverado Bank highlights another important factor in the S&L crisis: wild real estate speculation by erstwhile stodgy but solvent S&L institutions, facilitated by deregulation.

In the early 1980s Silverado Bank, like many S&L institutions, sought to close the gap between older, low-interest mortgage payments coming in and high-interest payments of deposits going out by taking advantage of the more relaxed environment created by deregulation. Colorado's economy was booming, primarily due to the oil industry, and real estate development projects grew rapidly. Deregulation now allowed S&L institutions like Silverado to enter real estate speculation and commercial development projects that had previously been inaccessible to them. Silverado entered that market aggressively; indeed, by the mid-1980s Silverado had shifted its focus from a single-family home mortgage lender to a "complex financial institution specializing in commercial real estate lending" (U.S. Congress: House 1990i:249). By 1986, $1.1 billion in commercial real estate construction loans, "the riskiest types of loans an S&L could make," accounted for 85 percent of Silverado's loan portfolio (U.S. Congress: House 1990i:68). The initial profits from Silverado's activities in these investments were considerable: its total assets grew 347 percent between 1980 and 1983, when its total assets were $370 million; it continued to show phenomenal growth until 1987, when its total assets were over $2.2 billion in 1987. Its annual asset growth rates were equally outstanding: 1984 alone posted an asset growth rate of 157 percent (U.S. Congress: House 1990i:120, 248–49, 1990j:158). Such figures would be the envy of any business.

However, this incredible balloon began to quickly lose air. Although Colorado's economy continued to boom while other state economies were in recession, that charmed existence did not last. The oil industry bust caught up with Colorado in the late 1980s, and consequently, as in states like Texas and California, the real estate market imploded. Banks like Silverado that were overexposed in real estate speculation and commercial development projects found themselves getting sucked under in the vortex of delinquencies and foreclosures, which skyrocketed in 1987 and 1988. Audited financial statements for the bank showed Silverado had a $200 million insolvency (U.S. Congress: House 1990i:67; see also U.S. Congress: House 1990j). Rather than acknowledge the problem and get out of real estate as quickly as they could, Silverado's management developed a scheme for creating the image of a still-healthy and growing institution that complied with federal solvency standards. Enter the "quid pro quo" program.

Under the quid pro quo program, Silverado would arrange a deal with borrowers that the bank would provide the loans the borrowers requested plus a premium on the loan, which the borrower agreed to use to purchase stock in Silverado Financial Corporation, the holding company that owned Silverado (U.S. Congress: House 1990i, 1990j:162–63). This arrangement created the appearance of increasing Silverado's capital structure. Two major auditing firms, Ernst & Whitney, and later Coopers & Lybrand, concluded that "Silverado directly and indirectly provided the funds for its own capital infusions contrary to applicable regulations" (U.S. Congress: House 1990i:121). Coopers & Lybrand specifically noted that these transactions did not constitute an actual contribution of new capital to the bank at all (U.S. Congress: House 1990i:257).

Silverado coupled its aggressive venture into real estate development projects with a foray into a new and complex investment tool: residual interests in real estate mortgage investment conduits (REMICs). REMICs are pooled mortgages that are sold to investors. The pool contains a hierarchy of tranches, with each tranch containing its own risk level and relative yield: high-risk tranches offered high yields. Silverado invested in the "residual" tranches—those that remained when all other tranches had been sold. These residual tranches were the highest-risk tranches in the pool, offering the highest return on investment—often as high as 18 percent return when Silverado purchased them. Like junk bonds, these high-risk tranches offered an attractive potential to earn vast amounts of money to help close the gap between high-interest deposit payouts and low-interest mortgage receipts. But, like junk bonds, the risk of a huge loss was great. The risk associated with the residual tranch of REMICs is that their yield is highly sensitive to the difference between the effective interest rates on the pooled mortgages and the international interest rate established by the London Inter-Bank Offering Rate (LIBOR). A large increase in LIBOR "could wipe out most of the value of the residuals" (U.S. Congress: House 1990i:263). A steady LIBOR could produce a very nice return for Silverado.

Despite the risks associated with investing in the residual tranches, Silverado could not resist the potential high yield, and invested heavily. By the end of 1987 the bank had invested half a billion dollars in REMIC residuals. At first the investment seemed like a shrewd investment indeed: LIBOR had dropped from 8 percent in the first quarter of 1986 to almost 5 percent by the end of that year; the following year LIBOR remained fairly stable into the first quarter of 1988. But after that first quarter LIBOR began to rise sharply, from slightly more than 6 percent in late 1987 to 9.5 percent in 1989 (U.S. Congress: House 1990i:263). The results were catastrophic for Silverado: the rise in LIBOR effectively wiped out its investments.

Silverado clearly needed to take fairly drastic measures to recapitalize, or at least to reshuffle its ledgers so as to appear solvent. In addition to the creative financing of the quid pro quo program, Silverado used some highly unusual accounting procedures. While its growth in the mid-1980s was explosive, its growth in 1986 was healthy but smaller. The bank sought to protect itself from the enormous risks the earlier loans posed by forming a "pool" of these existing loans in 1986; it then sold discounted junior interests in the pool to outside investors while retaining senior interest itself. Holders of senior interest received preferential payments of interest and principal on the loans in the pool before the holders of junior interests. Much like junk bonds, the appeal to purchasers of junior interests in the pool was the potential for high yield; the risk was that in the event of default on a loan in the pool, the holders of junior interests would be the first in line to lose their investment (U.S. Congress: House 1990i:257, 1990j:164). In his testimony before Congress, Brian C. McCormally, district counsel for the Office of Thrift Supervision in Topeka, complained that the primary purpose of the loan pools was to "circumvent the appropriate recognition of loan losses and to manipulate the institution's balance sheet" (U.S. Congress: House 1990i:13). That is, with loans pooled into one large entity, losses of one loan may be balanced out by healthier loans in the pool, thereby creating the image of a healthier bank than is the case. That practice of pooling loans helped Silverado to stall off federal regulators from noticing that the bank was actually in serious trouble.

In addition to the questionable practice of pooling loans, Silverado Bank approved several loans that raised questions of conflicts of interest, particularly between board member Neil Bush and two borrowers who also happened to be his business partners (U.S. Congress: House 1990j:165–67). Bill Walters, often referred to as the Donald Trump of Denver, was one of the most powerful developers of both commercial and residential property in that city, and a substantial borrower at Silverado even before Neil Bush joined the bank's board. Walters was also a limited partner in Bush's JNB Exploration Company, with a 6.25 percent interest. That interest was based on Walters's January 1983 investment of $150,000 in JNB. Bush insisted he had no involvement in day-to-day decision-making in the firm. Walters also owned the bank that loaned JNB $1.75 million in 1983. Testimony before Congress revealed that Bush had introduced or voted to approve $106 million in loans to Walters. Rep. Frank Annunzio of Illinois noted that Walters's complex relationship with Bush produced a powerful conflict of interest, in that Walters was both a partner and a stockholder in JNB, as well as a major lender to the firm; that power over the pursestrings would surely influence Bush to be favorably disposed toward loans Walters requested of Silverado (U.S. Congress: House 1990i:106). Grumbled Annunzio, "[W]hat makes matters worse is that all of the loans are in default and the taxpayers stand to lose every cent of the money" (U.S. Congress: House 1990i:103).

A year and a half after Walters's investment in JNB, Ken Good also became a partner with Bush in JNB Exploration Company, with a 25 percent interest. He contributed $10,000 to JNB for his interest. For his part, Bush invested a mere $100 to capitalize JNB, but he insisted that his investment was more substantially in sweat: he contributed his expertise in generating the deals for JNB (U.S. Congress: House 1990i:98–103).

In 1986 the partnership between Good and Bush was restructured, with Good retaining an option to invest another $3 million in the firm. By then, Good "personally and through various entities owned and held a 33.75 percent interest in JNB, and was both a general and limited partner of JNB" (U.S. Congress: House 1990i:103). Bush maintained that Good, like Walters, was not a principal in JNB, but was simply a funding partner and not involved in decision-making at the firm. It was not until this restructuring of their partnership in 1986 that Bush finally began to feel uncomfortable with the conflicts of interest their partnership posed, and agreed to abstain from participating in decisions at Silverado involving loans to Good. Prior to this, Bush had maintained that because neither Walters nor Good participated in day-to-day decision-making at JNB, no legal conflict of interest was posed when loans for either man came before Silverado's board. Indeed, Both Walters and Good received unanimous approval by Silverado's board for loans.

Like Walters, Good had provided Bush with loans that raised questions of conflicts of interest for Bush as a board member at Silverado making decisions concerning loans for Good. In 1984, Good loaned Bush $100,000 for a commodities deal, over which Good maintained 100 percent control and full discretion for investing the money in a high-risk pool. The loan was to be repaid only if the investment succeeded. It is unclear why Good did not simply invest the money himself instead of investing it in the name of Neil Bush. But by 1990, with the investment unsuccessful, Good forgave the loan. Even Bush admitted that this arrangement sounded "a little fishy" (U.S. Congress: House 1990i:107).

Throughout the congressional hearings, Bush maintained that there were no legal conflicts of interest, that what may have appeared to be conflicts of interest were more a reflection of life in a relatively small town:

> In a small town case where there is one banker and one lender and there are like 10 directors, like in our situation, and everybody is intertwined and there is a relationship, how can you preclude loans to be made which, you know, like a doctor in the community or the bank, the guy down the street that does the construction work on homes. It just doesn't make sense. (U.S. Congress: House 1990i:117)

Bush argued that since Bill Walters was the preeminent developer in Denver, it would not make sense to preclude making loans to him: if Silverado wanted to embark on an aggressive program of making real estate development loans, it would surely have to make some to Walters. Bush repeatedly argued that no fraud had taken place.

Annunzio later angrily retorted that Bush had "established a new legal precedent" in his characterization of his relationship with Good not constituting a conflict of interest:

> Mr. Bush argued that Mr. Good was a partner of his, but that he was not a partner of Mr. Good's. Thus, we have a new legal doctrine . . . , "Partnershipus Interuptus." Translated from Latin, it means, he's my partner, but I'm not his partner. The Marx Brothers, the Three Stooges or even Yogi Berra could not come up with logic like this. (U.S. Congress: House 1990j:5)

Federal regulators seemed to reject Bush's characterization, citing his relationship with Good and Walters as a conflict of interest. But they imposed the mildest possible penalty against Bush in what amounted to a "cease and desist" order that he not engage in such activities in the future (Tolchin 1991:D2). They did not bar him from ever again participating in the S&L industry. Five other individuals, including Michael Wise, James Metz, Richard Vandapool, Robert Lewis, and Russell Murray, were barred from future participation in the banking business, a penalty they agreed to accept. Bush refused to agree to the order, threatening a long, expensive, and protracted set of lawsuits (U.S. Congress: House 1990j:5). The U.S. government backed away from the threatened struggle, and instead imposed the mildest of sanctions against the son of the president of the United States.

Observers of corporate structures and processes generally agree that the first line of defense against management excesses and abuses is an active, "alert and involved" board of directors who "collectively are charged with providing wise counsel, setting prudent policies, and ensuring the implementation of such policies" (U.S. Congress: House 1990i:11). This is particularly so when a corporation adopts an aggressive, speculative, or unusual philosophy regarding its conduct of business. The second line of defense is the independent accounting auditors, who make annual reports concerning the health and well-being of the firm. Where was Silverado's board when decisions were being made about questionable loans and about unusual programs such as the quid pro quo program? And where was the bank's independent auditor?

Silverado's board had an unusually high level of consensus: there was unanimous agreement on virtually every decision made by the board. Like many other failed S&L institutions, Silverado's directors offered little if any critical challenges to management. And contrary to senior managers' insistence that unanimous decisions result from consensus building, internal documents from the bank indicate processes of

groupthink at work. For example, Florian Barth, a director on Silverado's board, complained in a letter to Chairman of the Board Michael
Wise that the outside directors were simply rubber stamps controlled by
James Metz, director and majority stockholder, and Wise (U.S. Congress: House 1990j:109). Brian C. McCormally, district counsel from the
Office of Thrift Supervision in Topeka, testified to Congress that one
director "admitted to leaning over to officers who attended board meetings and asking, 'Is this loan OK to approve?'" (U.S. Congress: House
1990i:11–12).

Neil Bush, son of then–vice president George Bush, was actively
recruited to serve on the bank's board by board chairman Michael Wise.
In a July 15, 1985, letter to board members, Wise noted that he had been
negotiating with Bush, then only thirty years old, to join the board. It is
unclear just what qualifications young Neil Bush might have had to
serve on the bank's board, other than his role as head of JNB Explora-
tions, an oil exploration firm. Such a qualification is weak at best: one
could perhaps argue that his role at JNB made him appropriate to serve
on the board of a bank that invested in oil projects; but the fact is that the
vast majority of Silverado's lending portfolio was in real estate, not oil
exploration. More notably, Wise made a point of emphasizing the fact
that Neil was the son of the vice president of the United States. Nowhere in the letter did Wise give any details about Bush's unique qualifications or contributions that would make him an asset to the board.
That he did, however, remind the board of his political pedigree suggests that Wise was looking for someone with an image of powerful
connections who would not be likely to know much about banking and
would not launch a challenge to senior management's lending decisions
brought to the board.

Much energy in congressional hearings was devoted to the role that
Neil Bush and his connection to the White House might have played in
contributing to federal regulators' loose rein on Silverado and their slow
pace in finally closing the bank. Indeed, although "everyone was in
agreement in 1988 that the institution was dead," it remained open and
operating; and when the Colorado savings and loan commissioner attempted in October 1988 to enforce the order to Silverado to raise $62
million or face closure, the FSLIC in Washington quickly requested a
two-month delay. Notably, it was not until the day after the national
election (when Neil's father George was elected president of the United
States) that Kermit Mowbry, president of the Federal Home Loan Bank
of Topeka, formally recommended that Silverado be placed into receivership (U.S. Congress: House 1990j:3). That delay has never been
adequately explained; the timing, however, on placing the bank on
which the president's son was a board member, into receivership is
striking. It seemed that Bush was at least initially carefully selected by
Wise for his inexperience in banking and thus his anticipated naive

complicity with the board's groupthink, and his credentials as the son of the vice president, which would to attract new investors.

And where was the bank's independent auditor during all this? Ernst & Whitney acted as Silverado's independent auditor from 1977 until 1985, when Silverado fired them. The bank originally stated that it had fired the accounting firm to avoid the appearance of conflicts of interest. Congressional investigations found that Silverado's chief financial officer, Robert M. Lewis, who was hired by Silverado in 1984, was also a partner of Ernst & Whitney. This could call into question just how independent the audit of the bank could be, and this is the reason Silverado gave at the time they fired Ernst & Whitney. Later, Silverado's officers insisted they fired the accounting firm because of substantial overcharges for the audits. However, investigations revealed that Ernst & Whitney had produced a scathing critique of the bank's business practices in 1985, including its quid pro quo program and its lending pools, and gave the bank a qualified report. Silverado felt the accounting firm was too strict in its application of accounting principles to the bank's "cutting-edge" transactions and fired the firm (U.S. Congress: House 1990i:13–14).

Ironically, they hired another Big 8 accounting firm, Coopers & Lybrand, who came to many of the same conclusions Ernst & Whitney had: Silverado was engaged in practices that did not conform to generally accepted accounting procedures (GAAP) and therefore received a qualified financial statement from the auditors in 1987 (U.S. Congress: House 1990i:236–73). The apparent attempts by Silverado Bank to have the independent auditor legitimize its cooked books had failed; the auditors' qualified report became the first loud thunderclap of the destructive storm that would soon rage about Silverado.

Silverado's house of cards quickly collapsed: It could no longer shuffle assets and liabilities to cover its disastrous investments. Finally, in December 1988, federal regulators closed the insolvent Silverado Banking, Savings and Loan Association of Denver. Its desperate attempts to recapitalize and to hide its condition long enough to buy time to do so earned it the dubious nickname of Desperado Bank (Purdy 1990:A21).

The big question, of course, is, How could the bank have managed to engage in such outrageous unorthodox accounting practices and high-flying gambling in its investment strategies for so long before someone noticed? Why wasn't it stopped sooner—before it ended up costing taxpayers so much money? The answer, for Silverado's own case and for the S&L crisis in general, lay in deregulation and its implementation. Under deregulation, there were far fewer field supervisors and inspectors than when the thrifts were more tightly regulated. Mowbry acknowledged in testimony before Congress that a lack of resources at his regulatory oversight office, particularly too few examiners, was a factor in the demise of Silverado (U.S. Congress: House 1990j:22, 37). He complained that deregulation had opened all sorts of new and complex investment and banking opportunities for thrifts without giving him the labor power necessary to oversee operations; he said that repeated requests to the Office of Management and Budget to secure more examiners were turned down (U.S. Congress: House 1990j:38). Indeed, Rep. Mary Rose Oakar of Ohio noted that her congressional subcommittee on federal employee compensation found that eighty-eight thousand federal employees, including many from supervisory offices of banking institutions, had been transferred to Pentagon activities, thereby robbing the banks' oversight and regulatory offices of personnel to adequately examine banks like Silverado (U.S. Congress: House 1990j:38).

The upshot here was that Silverado was not thoroughly examined for a period of about three years, from 1983 until December 1986, when a six-month examination "presented a devastatingly clear picture of Silverado's deteriorating financial condition, apparent conflicts of interest and unsafe and unsound practices" (U.S. Congress: House 1990i:39–40). At that point, regulators placed Silverado under receivership, but it was obviously too late. Silverado's gamble of shifting its business emphasis from low-interest single-home mortgages to commercial real estate development speculation, REMIC residual investments, and sleight-of-hand accounting practices had so severely undermined the bank that it could not recover.

Like other S&L cases, Silverado clearly had its share of fraudulent, unorthodox, and excessive management decisions, questions of unethical conduct and conflicts of interest, and a board of directors that did not perform its job of critically evaluating and perhaps challenging senior management's decisions. But these factors are not nearly as important to the demise of Silverado as its business decisions facilitated by deregulation. Its investment gambles cost Silverado its existence when the real estate market collapsed and LIBOR rose sharply. Also, the lack of complete regulatory oversight for over three years allowed the gambler to continue to pour good money after bad in a desperate attempt to recover the losses. When pressed by Congress to identify what he would have done differently if given the chance to avoid the $1 billion loss Silverado would cost taxpayers, Bush admitted, "I wouldn't have allowed for that high a concentration of commercial real estate" (U.S. Congress: House 1990i:132).

DISCUSSION

The cases of Columbia Savings and Loan Association and Silverado Banking, Savings and Loan Association together illustrate how deregulation exacerbated the thrift industry's problems rather than liberated it to compete more effectively in the economy. The state project of economic intervention involving bank deregulation as a remedy to the thrift industry's capital accumulation crisis of the late 1970s and early 1980s became one of the leading factors facilitating a devastating crisis in the industry. The state was left at this point with few options beyond the most comprehensive and expensive bailout in United States history.

4

The Savings and Loan Bailout: Continuation of the State Project

REGULATORY REACTIONS: STRUCTURAL CHANGE IN HISTORICAL CONTEXT

In the previous chapter we examined bank deregulation as part of the legacy of a larger state project of economic intervention. In this section we place the bailout in the historical context of prior bailouts and the role of Congress and the S&Ls in the provision of moderate-income housing. As with the Depository Institutions Deregulation Committee (DIDC), the Garn–St. Germain Act of 1982 was a modification of the structure of the state-industry relation. Unlike the depression-era Glass-Steagall Act, which established the FDIC and limited the securities activities of depository institutions, the 1982 Net-Worth Guarantee Act allowed S&Ls to become involved in speculative, high-risk investments while simultaneously positioning the state to bail out the industry. Yet, the bailout aspects of this bill and the FIRREA, which followed, remained a point of contention within Congress and the industry. What was the relation of this industry to the state? What specific responsibilities did this relation imply?

Despite efforts to resolve the S&Ls' crisis with bank deregulation by the Garn–St. Germain Act, the industry's crisis continued to deepen. Many observers testifying before Congress as well as a Congressional National Commission on the FIRREA cited the regulatory shifts that altered the relationship between the industry and the federal government as important factors in the crisis (U.S. Congress: House 1989a,b,c; National Commission on Financial Institution Reform, Recovery, and Enforcement 1993:8). As noted in Chapter 2, deregulation made the market niches between banks and thrifts and between depository and nondepository financial institutions indistinct, eased restrictions on interest rates on both loans and deposits, and allowed thrifts to pay interest on demand deposits (checking accounts) and to invest in public revenue bonds as well as a broad array of consumer and commercial loans. Deregulation was supposed to resolve the S&L crisis, but instead it served to deepen it: high interest rates were now being paid on deposits, while low interest rates on old mortgages continued to trickle in; and thrifts began to invest heavily in real estate speculation and the junk bond market. All of these activities represented state-sanctioned practices by the thrifts rather than illegal activities perpetrated by rogue bank managers, prompting the conclusion by the National Commission on Financial Institution Reform, Recovery, and Enforcement (1993:8) that state policy was largely to blame for the debacle that was now the S&L industry crisis.

While the Garn–St. Germain Act deregulating banks was a strong culprit in the industry's severe problems, that legislation also mandated federal regulators to rescue, merge, subsidize, or sell a failing thrift, and established a net-worth guarantee for S&Ls. But the legislation produced a set of complex and confusing accounting changes that mitigated the ability of regulators to identify abuses and imprudent investments by specific thrifts and hindered their analysis of the fiscal solvency of the industry in general (National Commission on Financial Institution Reform, Recovery, and Enforcement 1993:37–39, 48–49). The Garn–St. Germain Act thus acted dialectically to address the industry's problems while in fact exacerbating that very crisis. This dialectic set the stage for the state's next move in the larger state project of economic intervention.

Though some representatives of different parts of the state and the industry saw the Garn–St. Germain Act as a bailout, most legislators portrayed this act as a continuation of the state's role in the S&L industry, and not a bailout. Industry representatives and the administration distanced deregulation from policy precedents that ameliorated the risks associated with private accumulation. Subcommittee chairman Henry Gonzalez defended the net-worth guarantee by arguing that neither this bill nor similar prior legislative acts were bailouts; he compared the net-worth guarantee to Congress's actions surrounding Chrysler:

> [T]he Government did not give anything in Chrysler's case. . . . And so it wasn't a bailout in the sense that the Government was coming in to give [Chrysler] anything; it was guaranteeing, taking that risk on the basis that the managerial know-how was there. . . . I do want to say that I do not look upon this as a bailout of the S&Ls or the savings industry. (U.S. Congress: House 1982a:928–29)

Placed in the context of the structure of the state-industry relation, the deregulation and bailout of the S&L industry were frequently understood as a *public* service, not a service to the heads of the industry. S&L representatives argued that, unlike Chrysler and New York City, the

S&L dilemma was created by a federal mandate to provide low-interest mortgages, and therefore the government was responsible for guaranteeing the industry's prosperity. Moreover, the state's commitment to banking predated the legislation of the last decades. As argued by an economist from the Brookings Institute, the state guaranteed the solvency of the banking industry during the depression, when it established the federal insurance corporations to protect the public against bank failures and the banks against runs by an overwrought public (U.S. Congress: House 1982a:2454). FDIC chairman William Seidman noted the legislators' need to prevent a legitimation crisis, and bluntly asserted that Congress had no choice but to perform the unprecedented act of bailing out the entire industry. When congressional committee members expressed concern over writing a blank check to bailout the S&Ls, he shrugged:

> The problem is that the size of the loss is whatever it is, and there are only two sources at the moment for making up that loss. One is the premiums from the industry and other charges to the industry. The rest is paid by the Government and the taxpayers because of the fact that the depositors will not get their money unless this is paid . . . whatever the loss is, and unless the Government wants to raise questions about its guarantee to depositors, which I am sure they don't . . . then they are going to have to pay the bill, whatever it is. (U.S. Congress: House 1989b, Part 1:26–27)

Policy precedents and the historical relationship between the state and the banking industry placed structural constraints against (that is, selected against) the possibility that the state would allow the industry to fail.

The public service understanding of corporate welfare has endured through the pre- and postderegulation crises. In Resolution Trust Corporation (RTC; the federal body concerned with the closing and disposition of failed S&Ls) oversight hearings from 1990 to 1993, Treasury secretaries and RTC chairmen Nicholas Brady and Lloyd Bentsen both testified that the FIRREA was not a bailout. According to Brady:

> We are not using taxpayer dollars to bail out any thrift institution, their owners, or the savings and loan industry in general. We are living up to the government's end of the agreement represented by federal deposit insurance. (U.S. Congress: Senate 1990a:27; see also U.S. Congress: House 1993c:4)

Nonetheless, both Gonzalez and Brady sprinkled their testimony with talk of a bailout. For example, Gonzalez eventually lumped the legislative solution to the S&L disaster, along with the activities surrounding Penn Central Bank, New York City, and Chrysler, in the category of a "bailout" (U.S. Congress: House 1990a:168; see also U.S. Congress: House 1991a:32).

On their own behalf, S&Ls maintained that despite data from the past decade indicating otherwise they continued to fill an important market niche—affordable home mortgages—which the large commercial banks continued to ignore. During hearings on the FIRREA, S&Ls portrayed themselves as champions of the working class, arguing that through low-cost mortgage lending they had provided the average American access to the American dream. The thrifts maintained that this unique role in banking was the main reason why Congress had no choice but to bail them out. Jack Rohrer, president of the Kentucky League of Savings Institutions, told Congress, "The bottom line question . . . is whether you cripple the savings and loans . . . so much that they cannot perform their historic housing finance function for our citizens. That would be a terrible loss to our communities" (U.S. Congress: House 1989b, Part 1:47). As expected by the accommodationist position, state policy cannot be divined a priori. The state's administrative powers are contingent upon the actual historical practices—prior bailouts and the role of Congress and the S&Ls in the provision of moderate-income housing—that define the state's role in the industry, and thereby delimit the state's powers.

In sum, as the S&L crisis turned the industry toward the state for solutions, the *structure* of the state-industry relation, in conjunction with the larger deregulatory state project, created policy that contradictorily amplified both the level of investment risk in the banking industry and the level of corporate welfare. This *structure* included the dominance of large commercial banks in administrative decision-making (i.e., the DIDC), the state's de facto corporate bailout policy, and the state's historical responsibility (realized through the bank insurance agencies) for the solvency of the S&L industry. The deregulatory state project involved a unified set of state policies across a number of industries and state apparatuses geared toward, in the case of the S&L industry, enhanced market-based risk taking and public subsidization of the risks associated with the private accumulation of capital.

THE FINANCIAL INSTITUTIONS REFORM, RECOVERY
AND ENFORCEMENT ACT (FIRREA):
CONTINUATION OF THE STATE PROJECT

Political coalitions and divisions within the banking community and between banks and Congress helped to guide the next phase of the state project: the bailout of the S&L industry. Throughout the hearings of the

FIRREA, it was clear that the various segments of the financial community agreed on one thing: the federal government had to bail out the S&L institutions. On everything else, including what a bailout means, they clearly disagreed.

The S&L institutions capitalized on Congress's fear of the threat of legitimation crises should working-class access to finance capital evaporate. The industry clearly was attempting to exploit Congress' fear of working-class perceptions that Congress might be responsible for denying them access to the American Dream.

Though the various segments of the banking community agreed the federal government needed to resolve the S&L crisis, within the community there were serious rifts over the details of such a policy. For example, a coalition of small banks (Independent Bankers Association of America) supported bailing out the S&Ls, but they worried that the bailout plan placed a disproportionate insurance burden on them relative to the large banks. They pressed Congress to "broaden the insurance assessment base . . . to include foreign deposits and other non-deposit liabilities which the largest banks use to fund most of their lending" (U.S. Congress: House 1989b:Part II, 28).

Credit unions posted better performance rates than either banks or thrifts during the same economically distressed period that had hurt these segments of the industry. This points to the structural factors underlying the S&L crisis. Credit unions' capital is derived "almost entirely from retail deposits, not large, highly rate-sensitive commercial or brokerage deposits" (U.S. Congress: House 1989b:Part II, 6). In addition, credit unions did not make any real estate development loans, and "only a small portion of their assets [are] in long-term fixed rate mortgages" (U.S. Congress: House 1989b:Part II, 6). Finally, credit unions did not make business loans to economically vulnerable industries like energy and agriculture, to underdeveloped and developing countries around the world, or to corporations borrowing funds for leveraged buyouts. These volatile and speculative investments, which credit unions avoided, were precisely those the S&L institutions and large commercial banks emphasized. Therefore, where the thrifts were hit particularly hard by crises in leveraged buyouts, real estate, farming, and developing countries, credit unions remained healthy and profitable.

The Consumer Federation of America (CFA) agreed that not all financial institutions should share the bailout cost equally. They specifically objected to lumping credit unions in under provisions calling for increased capital and asset requirements, arguing that it would "penalize primarily the small credit unions" (U.S. Congress: House 1989b:Part II, 72–74). However, despite credit unions' structural exclusion from activities that brought down other segments of the industry, the large commercial banks insisted that they be included in any increased burdens of contributions to depositors' insurance funds. Indeed, President Bush, seeking more insurance funds, proposed that credit unions pay a higher premium to the National Credit Union Share Insurance Fund than that paid by banks to the FDIC (U.S. Congress: House 1989b:Part II, 7).

S&Ls themselves, not surprisingly, complained of the burden of the costs of the rescue to the industry. As Charles John Koch, president and chief executive officer of Charter One Financial Inc., who spoke on behalf of the National Council of Savings Institutions, argued, "[C]onsidering the condition of the industry, the costs imposed on the industry by . . . this bill and the current economic environment," Congress should not "overburden" the industry by requiring increased deposit insurance contributions (U.S. Congress: House 1989b:Part II, 15–16). He argued that such increases were more than the industry could afford, and would therefore cause more insolvencies and increase the final cost to taxpayers. Instead, he wanted all financial institutions covered by the FDIC to pay the same premiums, regardless of size or solvency. And although he linked the thrifts' ability to pay to the condition of the industry and the condition of the economy, he linked these conditions neither to the behavior of the thrifts themselves nor to the state economic intervention policies and agencies comprising this state project. Both the S&Ls and the state, which protected this market niche, went blameless.

By the time Congress passed the FIRREA, the policy provided that all segments of the banking community would share the burden of increased premiums to cover insurance costs related to the bailout (U.S. Congress: House 1989b). Notably, the large commercial banks were least hurt by this provision: they were best able to absorb these costs relative to all other segments of the banking community. In contrast, the cost of the provision carried the potential to weaken the other segments of that community, thus enhancing the already advantaged position of the commercial banks relative to the other banking institutions.

In addition to these disagreements over sharing the cost burdens of the bailout, segments of the banking community argued over the use of the valued FDIC logo, a logo designed to inspire consumer confidence in the institutions that carry it. S&L institutions wanted the right to display the same FDIC logo as commercial banks to reassure customers that their deposits were protected. The large commercial banks vehemently opposed sharing the logo because they did not wish to be sullied by association with the troubled S&Ls. Once again, the large commercial banks prevailed over the weaker segments of the banking community. Again, the greater collective financial power of the large commercial banks had convinced Congress to support their concerns: S&L institutions would use the logo of the FSLIC, and the FDIC logo would be reserved for the commercial banks (U.S. Congress: House 1989b).

Finance capital accumulation interests were not monolithic. In fact, as we have seen, the dialectical struggle occurred not only between finance capital and "social interests," described below, but also between various segments of finance capital. For example, the large commercial banks saw the thrifts' crisis and the bailout process as an opportunity to increase their concentration in and control of the financial industry. They wanted provisions in the bailout legislation to allow bank holding companies to acquire healthy S&L institutions as well as solvent thrifts that were capital deficient (U.S. Congress: House 1989b:Part II, 19, 27). Such a provision would enhance large banks' domination over the financial community and further concentrate their control of finance capital flows. Indeed, as we saw with the creation of the Garn–St. Germain Act, large commercial banks again suggested that the thrifts had outlived their usefulness and were no longer needed. The thrifts strenuously disagreed, and continued to argue that, despite the commercial-bank-provided data indicating otherwise, they still filled an important market niche ignored by the large commercial banks: affordable home mortgages. Nonetheless, so anxious were the commercial banks to get the green light to take over thrifts and eliminate their competition while increasing their domination of the industry, that Thomas P. Rideout, president of the ABA urged Congress to put the FIRREA on the "fast track" to passage (U.S. Congress: House 1989b:Part II, 19). The elimination of the S&L industry suggested by the commercial banks would have destroyed the historical structural relation between the S&Ls and the state. As indicated by the repeated (and ongoing) failed attempts by the ABA to kill the depression-era Glass-Steagall Act segmenting the banking industry, this was in the interests of neither the S&Ls nor the state itself.

Yet Congress obliged the banks' request to fast track the bill: the bailout was now accepted as the latest entry to the state project. Congress now turned to the question of how to pay for it. Here, the tension between social and corporate welfare in the United States' welfare state regime shaped the decision.

Nowhere was the differentiation between social welfare interests versus corporate welfare interests more tellingly underscored than in the debate over whether to treat the S&L bailout as off-budget or on-budget. As noted earlier, many members of the Committee on Banking, Finance and Urban Affairs (CBFUA) expressed concerns about preserving the sanctity of the Gramm-Rudman Act, which requires automatic reduction of federal expenditures across the board should Congress fail to meet targets or reduce the deficit. Since the S&L bailout was to be given a blank check (with widespread agreement that the final cost of the bailout was likely to be much higher than original projections), many feared it would be a "budget buster." The options open to Congress were limited:

(a) give the bailout a special exemption from Gramm-Rudman, (b) put the bailout in the budget and take the chance that it would provoke Gramm-Rudman cuts, or (c) place the bailout off-budget.

Expenditures that are off-budget are those which will be paid no matter what happens to the rest of the federal budget. For example, the costs of the Gulf War in 1991 were off-budget. If Gramm-Rudman cuts do occur, they are made only in programs and expenditures that are on-budget; off-budget items are spared that ax and are not affected by any congressional decisions to balance the budget or reduce the deficit in an effort to avoid precipitating Gramm-Rudman provisions.

There was widespread agreement among the members of CBFUA that it was unwise to give the S&L bailout a special exemption to Gramm-Rudman; they believed it would set a precedent and touch off nasty and endless future debates when legislators attempted to provide similar protection to their favorite programs and expenditures. It would also violate the spirit and legitimacy of Gramm-Rudman (U.S. Congress: House 1989b:Part II, 124, 164). To place the bailout on-budget would almost surely activate the feared Gramm-Rudman cuts, which would hurt social welfare expenditures, which had already suffered a decade of slashes. However, to place the bailout off-budget would be more expensive: Alan Greenspan, chairman of the Federal Reserve Board, estimated it would cost about a billion dollars more off-budget, because of the need for greater insurance coverage to ensure funding of the program (U.S. Congress: House 1989b:Part II, 164; see also U.S. Congress: House 1989c:20, 155). However, after much debate, CBFUA decided to treat the bailout off-budget. No one acknowledged that to put the bailout off-budget meant that this corporate welfare program was protected and ensured, while social welfare programs would remain part of the ongoing debates about deficit reductions, balancing the federal budget, and expenditure cuts: when cuts were to be made to reach deficit reduction targets, social welfare expenditures and programs would compete against each other for survival, while corporate welfare expenditures would continue unthreatened. This would reinforce the public perception that social welfare expenditures were the cause of the huge federal deficits, not corporate welfare expenditures.

In the end, $50 billion in borrowing for the bailout was kept off the 1990 budget; $20 billion was placed on the 1989 budget, but outside the Gramm-Rudman calculations, and the remaining $30 billion was to be borrowed, off-budget, in 1990 and 1991 (Congressional Quarterly, Inc. 1990:118). The bailout itself benefited from its role in the larger state project of economic intervention in finance capital processes and from the selectivity filter established by earlier corporate bailouts. It would later disappear from the heated debates in Congress after 1994, when the Contract with America and the welfare reform debate suggested massive cuts in social welfare to balance the federal budget and reduce deficits. Those debates are poised to redistribute the relative emphases in the U.S. welfare state from social welfare to corporate welfare more pronouncedly than at any time since prior to the 1930s.

THE BALANCE OF CLASS FORCES:
THE FIRREA AND THE AFFORDABLE HOUSING PROGRAM

That the large commercial banks got the provisions they wanted in the FIRREA is consistent with a class dialectic analysis that holds that the state mediates both inter- and *intra*class contradictions. In this case each segment of the banking community is structurally differentiated according to its primary constituents: either corporate and state business, as with large commercial banks, or working-class and middle-class mortgages and deposits, as with credit unions and thrift institutions. As a consequence of these structural differences, the political interests and relative power of different segments of the finance industry vary both in communities and in the larger political economy. Because of their more central and pivotal role in the larger political economy as providers of corporate and state financing and as controllers of the largest pool of private finance capital (including management of pension and trust funds), commercial banks tend to wield more power within the banking community as well as outside that community.

One can also see evidence of this class dialectic in the relative input into the bailout legislation from various interests throughout society. As in its depression-era origins, this state project's continuation through the FIRREA attended to the interests of those outside the industry, and expressed those interests in terms amenable to the continued private accumulation of capital. Several consumer, labor, and community groups appeared before Congress to press their interests and goals in the bailout process. For example, the CFA supported restructuring the Federal Home Loan Bank Board (FHLBB, the regulatory agency responsible for the home loan bank system)) so that only three of its nine board members would be thrift owners. CFA also urged Congress to give consumers two seats on the board, arguing that consumers' stake in the thrift industry is equal to that of the thrift owners. Although as we see below, the state met some of the demands of the consumer groups (again, on capitalist terms), in this case, the structure of the FHLBB remained unchanged. Where in the political structure did the community groups fit, and what political resources did they bring to the table?

Consumer groups, community groups, and labor appeared before Congress to argue for both more consumer oversight of S&Ls and increased S&L participation in mortgage lending, and against taxpayer funding of the bailout. The CFA—besides seeking a change in the composition of the FHLBB's board—called on Congress to compel thrifts to take up their traditional role as providers of home mortgages and insisted that community reinvestment be emphasized. In that regard, CFA asked for, and received, provisions in the bailout stipulating increased disclosure of lending information to facilitate local and state consumer groups' oversight of S&Ls. They also asked that thrifts be required to eliminate questionable investments (particularly junk bonds and real estate loans) and practices such as brokered deposits (U.S. Congress: House 1989b:Part 2, 72–74). The FIRREA re-regulated the S&L industry by increasing the amount of capital an institution had to have on hand (capital standards), eliminating "supervisory goodwill" as a form of capital, banning investments in speculative real estate and junk bonds, preempting lax state regulations with stricter federal restrictions, prohibiting brokered deposits to undercapitalized thrifts, and placing the FDIC in charge of the S&L deposit insurance fund (Congressional Quarterly Inc. 1990:119–21). Many of these provisions were in the initial FIRREA proposal made by the Bush administration, and were actually toughened during debate and compromise as the thrift crisis deepened. However, conflicts emerged over whether the bill should include some provision for increasing access to affordable housing for the poor, an issue seen by these groups as significantly linked to the S&L crisis and bailout.

Mildred Brown, president of the Association of Community Organizations for Reform Now (ACORN), argued that because of the industry's lack of concern for affordable housing, particularly for minority group members, taxpayer funds should not be used in the bailout. S&Ls redlined African-American and low-income communities and, according to a survey of 3,100 U.S. thrifts, African-American and Latino loan applicants were two to three times as likely to have mortgage applications rejected as whites in the same income group (U.S. Congress: House 1989b:Part 2:573; see also U.S. Congress: House 1989d:40). She argued that the House Banking Committee would not have agreed to the bailouts of Chrysler, Lockheed, or even New York City had they exhibited the same patterns of discriminatory practices:

> We all grow up [with] the American dream of home ownership, but no matter how hard a black or Hispanic woman or man dreams today, the dreams are not likely to be fulfilled . . . because of redlining and other discriminatory lending practices of the very industry we are here today to

lend a hand to. There should be no helping hand to an industry that has offered millions of Americans nothing more than the bitter fruits of years of discrimination. (U.S. Congress: House 1989b:Part 2, 77)

According to Maud Hurd of ACORN,

These neighborhoods are crumbling because S&Ls aren't doing the job they were set up to do. While S&Ls could have been rebuilding our communities, they were out gambling other people's money. (U.S. Congress: House 1989d:52)

Brown suggested that, instead of using taxpayers' money to bail out the thrifts, those who benefited from the deregulation that precipitated the S&L crisis (referring to financial institutions, particularly S&Ls) should raise the funds to pay for the bailout. Quoting Jesse Jackson, Brown said, " '[T]hose who went to the party should pay for the party.' We were not even invited" (U.S. Congress: House 1989b:Part II, 76). Yet organizations like ACORN, in accord with the rest of the hearing's participants, recognized that a bailout of some sort was inevitable. In this context they struggled to shape legislation that would address some of their concerns. In particular, they used these hearings to make Congress aware of the national shortage of affordable, low-income housing.

As Jenkins and Brents (1989) noted, the political effectiveness and capacity for organization of social groups is contingent upon historical circumstances. In this case, as in Jenkins and Brents's examination of the creation of the welfare state, rivalries within the capitalist class made the resources of social groups more effective. In the case of the FIRREA, community groups became better organized and used the bailout to link the affordable housing question to the needs of the banking community.

Brown informed Congress that a coalition of community groups, churches, labor unions, and civic leaders had formed in response to the crisis. Calling itself the Campaign for Financial Democracy (CFD), the coalition argued that the collapse of the thrift industry and the severe shortage of affordable housing in the United States were intricately related. They therefore insisted that Congress place provisions in the bailout legislation linking rescue of the industry to investment in affordable housing. For example, CFD suggested the formation of a national Housing Opportunity Fund, to be financed by all members of the financial community (not just thrifts). Its purpose would be to provide below-market mortgage rates to first-time home buyers and to develop "permanently affordable housing" (U.S. Congress: House 1989b:Part II, 76). The coalition also suggested that the Resolution Trust Corporation (RTC, the FIRREA-created agency responsible for the cleanup) use the residential property it seized from insolvent thrifts as affordable housing for the poor and homeless:

> These houses are worth 25 cents on the dollar to the Federal Government, but they are worth a mint to the underhoused and homeless Americans, and some money from the sale of other FSLIC assets [could] go into the Housing Opportunity Fund. (U.S. Congress: House 1989b:Part II, 76)

Ultimately, an Affordable Housing Provision was included in the FIRREA. Though community and working-class organizations had been marginalized in the bailout hearings, through organization and by threatening electoral retribution they were successful in obtaining at least a de jure link between the bailout and the affordable housing crisis in the United States. Congress balanced this provision, though, with a mandate to the RTC that it receive as high a price for any piece of property as quickly as possible—a mandate that in effect excluded the poor and working class [see Skidmore and Glasberg (1996) for an analysis of the implementation of the Affordable Housing Provision of the FIRREA]. In sum, faced with the inevitability of the bailout, an organized coalition of community, consumer, labor, and civic groups succeeded in altering the balance of class forces affecting the FIRREA—the latest piece of this state project.

The viewpoints of community, consumer, labor, and civic organizations were a relatively small and marginalized portion of the total congressional testimony concerning the industry's crisis and the solution to that crisis. Only 3.5 percent of a total of 3,300 pages of such testimony in 1989 came from these organizations or speakers, compared with 34.6 percent from financial institutions' organizations and representatives (the remainder of the pages contained testimony from either government agencies, academics, consultants, industry analysts, and builders and real estate representatives, or opening statements from legislators sitting on the banking committees themselves). Moreover, 60.3 percent of the testimony of community, consumer, labor, and civic organizations was contained in hearings on housing issues or on the problems confronting the FSLIC as opposed to the hearings directly devoted to the crisis confronting the S&L industry itself and to the debates concerning solutions to that crisis. As such, the testimony and viewpoints of these groups, which directly challenged the perspectives and interests of the banks in general and the thrifts in particular, were presented in hearings not directly concerned with the crisis and its resolution. Such marginalization contributed to the further filtering or selection of congressional perspectives, biasing it toward that of the industry itself and of finance capital accumulation interests in general.

The balance of class forces in this instance of the state project had clearly favored the banks. Challenges from community and working-class organizations, which felt that the bailout should be the industry's concern rather than the public's concern, lacked the structural power of the banking industry. Community and consumer groups are not as structurally central to the political economy as is the banking industry. Over time, the unified banking policies and agencies of this state project increased the concentration of privately held finance capital. It was within this particular state project—this historical conjunction—that the FIR-REA was created. Unlike community groups, the activities of the banking industry shape both the economic climate of the nation, and the political climate that economy creates. Further, selectivity processes engendered by the structural centrality of banks and by policy precedents provided the banking community with a prominent position in the banking committee hearings from which it could provide analysis and information. In contrast, the banking committee agenda minimized the input of community and working-class organizations that challenged the banking industry's analyses.

Although these groups had support in the legislature, particularly from House Banking Committee chairman Gonzalez, in the end, the AHP was passed as a result of a compromise between AHP proponents and proponents of the Bush administration plan to keep the bailout off-budget. The Senate Banking Committee defeated a proposal from Senator Kerry requiring that the newly created RTC offer local and state housing authorities right of first refusal on real estate acquired from S&L failures. Republicans almost unanimously opposed a House committee amendment to require federal home loan banks to subsidize mortgages to low and moderate-income families and another right-of-first-refusal amendment. In the full House, a Republican amendment to eliminate the mortgage subsidy was defeated by Democrats. Alternatively, the House Financial Institutions Subcommittee and the full Banking Committee, seeing the AHP as a continuation of the state and S&L industry's historic commitment to affordable housing, approved a right-of-first-refusal proposal offered by Gonzalez. Rep. Frank Annunzio argued that Congress had no choice but to save the S&L industry: "Americans . . . cannot do without a S&L industry that is dedicated to helping people buy homes" (U.S. Congress: House 1989b:Part 2, 97). That the administration and almost all Republicans strongly opposed the housing amendment allowed it to be played as a partisan/class issue. For example, Democratic representative Barney Frank argued that Republican resistance came from that party's lack of concern for the poor (Congressional Quarterly, Inc. 1990:124, 126–28, 130).

Thus, the final conference committee bill was a compromise. The

Senate Republicans and administration, as noted above, kept $50 billion in borrowing off the 1990 budget; $20 billion was placed on the 1989 budget, but outside the Gramm-Rudman calculations, and the remaining $30 billion borrowed off-budget in 1990 and 1991. The House Democrats prevailed in receiving both the low-income mortgage subsidy program, and the right-of-first-refusal provisions for local and state non-profit housing agencies (Congressional Quarterly Inc. 1990:131). In the end, House leaders pleaded with members to accept the compromise, despite the financing plan, fearing that "low income housing might be jeopardized by continuing wrangling with the administration" (p. 133). The conference report was narrowly accepted, with a majority of Democrats voting against it.

In sum, the FIRREA appears to be a model of democratic process and compromise. On the one hand, the thrift industry became almost a political nonentity. Though it strongly opposed stricter capital standards, capital standards were repeatedly ratcheted up as legislators attempted to "out-tough" each other in their approach to the debacle. However, over the fervent objection of consumer and community groups, the thrift industry did receive $73 billion (the extra $23 billion was a Treasury fund to cover postbailout expenses) in taxpayer funds to dispose of S&Ls that had been run into the ground through reckless and unprofitable speculation. This initial sum primed the pump for what would eventually be RTC allocations of $30 billion and $25 billion in 1991, and another $18.3 billion in 1993. Two and one-half years after the FIRREA passed, Ralph Nader of Public Citizen's Congress Watch testified that under this funding scheme the RTC had become as large and expensive a debacle as the S&L crisis itself. Moreover, bailout funding seemed exempt from the pay-as-you-go provision of the Budget Enforcement Act of 1990, which specified that new spending must be accompanied by new revenue (U.S. Congress: House 1992a:97, 106).

On the other hand, given their success with the AHP, it appears that the unity and electoral power of the community groups prevailed. As predicted by the accommodationist perspective, "state" and "social" forces modified one another in a reciprocal manner. The administration, though consistently in the corner of finance capital, ultimately succumbed to the pressure of community and consumer groups and approved a fairly progressive affordable housing program. Yet, community groups have historically had legislative "victories" with little practical impact; the Community Reinvestment Act, tax breaks for low-income housing construction, and HUD (which, during the time of this legislation, was being investigated for illegal use of funds) have all been de jure successes with minimum practical impact. In this case, given the accommodationist position that the power of the state is contingent upon the balance of class forces within and outside the state, what was the effect of the administration's continued opposition to affordable housing?

DE FACTO AHP IMPLEMENTATION

The affordable housing provisions of the FIRREA indicated a strong de jure commitment by the state to the creation of housing for low- and moderate-income families. It granted local and state housing agencies, and families with incomes below 115 percent of area median income, the right of first refusal on single-family homes under $67,500; it required Federal Home Loan Banks to establish a fund to subsidize mortgages for families with incomes below 80 percent of the area median; and it allowed the RTC to subsidize loans for multifamily property buyers that agree to keep 35 percent of rents affordable to families with incomes below 80 percent of the area median. In its implementation, the most contentious points of the AHP were the RTC's obligation to identify and publicize affordable properties, and its authority to finance low-income homes at below-market rates and sell low-income properties at below-market values.

In sum, the low-income housing program of the RTC was mandated to maximize the availability and affordability of low- and moderate-income housing (Public Law 101-73, 1989). Yet despite its apparent commitment to affordable housing, the FIRREA also contained a contradictory, overarching mandate that the RTC reduce the cost of the bailout by obtaining the maximum return on the disposal of the property of failed S&Ls. For three years following the FIRREA, consumer, community, and housing agencies battled the administration and the RTC to implement the AHP mandate in the spirit in which it was created. This battle highlights both the balance of class forces within and outside the state and the dynamic, mutually transformative relation between the state and society.

Bureaucratic Veto

The RTC oversight hearings quickly revealed the power of the administration's continued resistance to affordable housing and the inability of community groups to overcome that opposition. In the hearings immediately following passage of the FIRREA, representatives of the Consumers Union and the Center for Community Change foreshadowed the obstacles they were to face. These groups pinned the success of the program on the level of commitment the administration brought to the AHP's implementation and on the creation of standards ensuring that the affordable housing mandate is not superseded by the mandate to maximize returns on disposed property (U.S. Congress: House 1989h:477–78, 486). According to Chris Lewis of ACORN:

> Although your initiative [FIRREA] represents a significant opportunity to improve the quality of life in hundreds if not thousands of communities nationwide, it is threatened by *bureaucratic veto* if program design and implementation are unnecessarily cumbersome. ACORN is concerned that the RTC either out of ignorance of low-income housing needs or deliberate design may render this hard won program ineffective. (U.S. Congress: House 1989h:498; emphasis added)

Community, consumer, state, and local housing agencies all pointed to the many ways the RTC executed the "bureaucratic veto" about which ACORN warned. At the end of January 1990, less than six months after Congress passed the FIRREA-AHP, these groups testified in protest of the RTC low-income housing strategic pilot plan. In particular, groups such as the Texas Housing Authority, ACORN, Consumer's Union, the Consumer Federation of America, and the League of Cities noted that the pilot program failed to meet the mandate that affordable housing information be made available to those who needed it, disregarded social groups' policy input, failed to disclose the interim strategic plan for public comment, lost affordable properties by selling them to ineligible families while the banks were technically in conservatorship, and ignored the widely held opinion that without price discounts and mortgage subsidies, no low-income family could afford these homes (U.S. Congress: House 1989h).

This last point was particularly contentious. The RTC refused to discount houses more than 5 percent below appraised market value. Because many of the homes were appraised during the overheated real estate market of the 1980s, this meant they were needlessly too expensive for low-income buyers, or were ineligible for the AHP all together. Representatives of ACORN argued that the interim plan "effectively vetoed an affordable housing provision by failing to allow RTC staff to use various affordable tools to discount sale price and seller finance" (U.S. Congress: House 1989h:176). "The strategic plan is blind to the simple fact that market rate housing is *unaffordable* for lower income families" (p. 1125). "They [low-income families] will never scratch. So this is all a sham, a joke" (p. 200). Less than a week later, representatives of the administration and the RTC testified in Senate hearings; no community, consumer, or state housing groups were present. Deputy Treasury Secretary John Robson testified that the strategic plan of the RTC Oversight Board "asks the RTC to provide financing of assets sales sparingly" (U.S. Congress: Senate 1990c:27, 30). To this end, he added that whatever subsidies the RTC provides for the AHP would come only after the ninety-day right-of-first-refusal period proves inadequate.

More than a year after the FIRREA, state housing agencies continued to criticize the RTC-AHP program. Tish Gonzalez of the National Council of Housing Agencies documented a number of mechanisms that prevented affordable housing from reaching low-income families. True to its testimony, the RTC intentionally minimized its discounting and financing programs; it provided no discounts until after closure of the ninety-day right-of-first-refusal window—the only advantage the program offered low-income buyers—and provided financing from the limited coffers of state housing finance agencies, rather than from RTC de jure subsidy authority. The RTC's resistance to new appraisals, and its policy of accepting the first reasonable offer, worked against low-income families, who have no means to hire an appraiser and are less likely than investors to secure private financing quickly. Moreover, in what turned out to be a key point, the RTC was not forthcoming in disclosing the sales figures upon which it was making policy (U.S. Congress: Senate 1990b:236–51; see also U.S. Congress: House 1990a:83–86). Finally, private realtors held that RTC guidelines were unrealistic. For example, in June 1991, a president and CEO of a Texas-based firm argued that it was unrealistic to expect anyone to be able to close on a property in the amount of time allocated to the AHP period. Once these properties left the AHP program they were often snapped up at a discount by investors (U.S. Congress: Senate 1991b:163).

In July 1991, nearly two years after Congress passed the FIRREA, state housing agencies continued to argue that the RTC resisted executing its affordable housing mandate. John Henneberger, the director of Texas Low Income Housing Information Service (TLIHIS) testified that contrary to RTC reports, low-income buyers could not find private financing; the RTC needed to use the powers provided in the FIRREA to provide financing to those outside state financing agency criteria; and RTC rapid sell-off techniques, such as auctions, both received fairly low prices and excluded the unsophisticated buyer—the bidding form alone was twenty-five pages long (reduced from over forty). Moreover, maximum discounts continued to go to investors buying after the expiration of the AHP right-of-first-refusal time period. Finally, RTC clearinghouses failed to distribute accurate, complete information about affordable properties to the people and agencies for whom the program was designed. Rather than adopt a decentralized, intensive, local information network built around nonprofit organizations to market AHP housing, the RTC contracted a handful of private agencies in select cities (U.S. Congress: House 1991a:58–59). The net effect of these tactics was that affordable housing never reached low-income families:

> The lack of a marketing program for low and moderate-income buyers, along with the lack of financing and absence of any non-profit outreach to low-income families are the principle reasons [that over] 1,000 [Texas]

houses had passed through the ninety day marketing period without an accepted offer. (p. 200)

Finally, indicating the dynamic state-society relation the accommoda-tionist position posits, FIRREA-AHP implementation spurred social pro-test that led to new legislation (below). By December 1990, ACORN and other community groups had protested in and outside of court to have the RTC implement the AHP policy in the spirit of the FIRREA mandate. ACORN members staged protests in RTC-held houses, which involved breaking open locks, moving low-income families into deserted proper-ties, and getting arrested. ACORN also sued the RTC to reverse the sale of an AHP property to an investor out from under a low-income buyer (U.S. Congress: House 1990a:86). Community and consumer groups sought not a change in RTC structure—RTC had all the powers it needed to bring housing to low-income families—but legislation forcing the RTC to uphold its AHP mandate. Barring explicit congressional in-structions, administrative appointees to the corporation were unwilling to use its de jure powers. As McEvoy, of the National Council of State Housing Agencies noted, "[T]oo often, RTC only takes action to remedy the problems when Congress forces it to" (U.S. Congress: Senate 1991a:42–43).

AHP Effectiveness

Despite the reports of community and consumer groups attesting to the de facto veto of the AHP provisions of the FIRREA, through three years of hearings the RTC unfailingly portrayed the AHP as a success within the letter and the spirit of the FIRREA legislation. For example, on June 14, 1990, Treasury Secretary Brady, the chairman of the RTC Oversight Board, reported that one hundred homes were sold in the AHP pilot program, and that the average income of the purchasers was 83 percent of area median income (U.S. Congress: House 1990b:93–94). Brady testified that as of April 1991, 12,203 single-family homes had been listed with clearinghouses, 7,141 homes had been placed under contract, 2,777 had closed, 13 multifamily properties had closed, and 77 of the 471 listed had offers. The average price of the single-family home was $32,000, and the average income of the low-income home buyer was $22,000, which Brady reported was less than 60 percent of the national median household income (U.S. Congress: House 1991a:115–16). How-ever, RTC information was frequently inconsistent. While Brady testi-fied, RTC executive director David Cooke reported, in separate hearings, that as of June 21, 1990, thirty-nine properties had been sold and that the average income of the buyer was 79 percent of the area median income (U.S. Congress: House 1990c:60).

However, the promises indicated by these statistics were contradicted at every level by other testimony revealing that the RTC both failed to meet its affordable housing mandate and lacked the basic information upon which to create better policy. Ernestine Whiting of the Illinois ACORN testified that, according to its own figures, the average AHP buyer in Chicago had an income 83 percent of the area median—roughly $45,000; obviously, this was well above the low-income family category created by Congress (U.S. Congress: House 1990a:524). Currency Comptroller Charles Bowsher released a report indicating that, two years after its creation, the RTC continued to lack the basic controls to allow it to track its billions of assets. Quoting this report, House banking committee chairman Gonzalez argued that the AHP remained "an unmitigated disaster" with few of the working poor receiving low-income housing, and much of the property going to speculators (U.S. Congress: House 1991a:2). As of March 1992, Bart Harvey, of the nonprofit Enterprise Foundation, testified that the RTC still did not know what properties it did and did not have (U.S. Congress: Senate 1992b:40).

A few groups documented the extent of the crisis. Henneberger of the TLIHIS testified that not only was the RTC reticent to release figures, but, apparently the RTC did not record, evaluate, or investigate its performance for its own purposes. As a result of this inaccurate or contradictory data, research by the TLIHIS indicated that "the figures which RTC provides in reports on sales under the Affordable Housing Disposition Program significantly overstate the actual number of sales under the program" (U.S. Congress: House 1991a:197–98). For example, in the March 1991 "Affordable Housing Sales Report" the RTC reported cumulative sales of 1,931 single family units. Yet, the separate RTC information obtained by the TLIHIS, listed only 1,660 houses sold and many of those sales reported were for the same address.

Regarding average income, 449 of the buyers had a total adjusted gross income of $0.00. Because the "Number Of Days the Property Was Listed" column was left blank or exceeded ninety days for these properties, the TLIHIS assumed $0.00 meant the property was sold to buyers outside the affordable housing guidelines. Whatever average-income testimony the RTC provided was skewed by listing more than one-quarter of the buyers as incomeless. The RTC refused to provide supplementary information on buyer's income, but because those at 115 percent of area median income were as eligible for low-income properties as those at 50 percent, Henneberger argued that low-income housing tended to rise to the higher income. Finally, RTC staff reported that listings in the sales report were for single-family homes for which the RTC had accepted an offer—they were not actually sales.

In sum, Henneberger testified that the RTC had continued to resist the AHP, though in the reports it submitted to those legislators most concerned with the program, its figures looked good. "It appears to us that all the properties, whether purchased by an investor or a qualified low-income buyer, whether within or after the 90-day window, have been counted as affordable housing disposition units to Congress and the Public" (U.S. Congress: House 1991a:200).

Many homes that would otherwise be in the program were sold to people outside the low-income requirements. As of June 1991, 3,300 houses and 174 apartment complexes had passed through the ninety-day window unsold. Another 3,998 eligible houses were sold outside the program because the institution holding the deed was technically in conservatorship, not receivership. The RTC offered discounts and subsidies on all properties except those in the AHP, meaning not only did these homes go to investors, but these investors received discounts not available to families eligible to bid in the ninety-day window (*New York Times* 1991c).

Additionally, as reported by the TLIHIS, a high percentage of Texas AHP sales were for cash, though it is not apparent how low-income families obtained this cash (U.S. Congress: House 1991a:199). According to a Texas real estate agent, the 20 percent of Texas homes sold for cash moved through a legal loophole in which an investor gives the cash to a low-income friend or relative, that buyer moves out, and the house is refinanced and converted into rental property, freeing the initial investment for the next low-income turn around (*New York Times* 1991a). Finally, the General Accounting Office reported in 1992 that the RTC had yet to create a policy to verify that prospective buyers meet low-income eligibility guidelines (U.S. Congress: Senate 1992b:58).

To dispose of property that was becoming costly to maintain, RTC officials decided to move 80 percent of its low-cost assets by June 30. As noted above, high-speed sales disadvantage low-income families who cannot quickly inspect houses, receive appraisals, and secure financing. Although low-income families could also buy discounted property after the big sales push, a lot of this property was worthless: the choice properties went in auctions. Only four hundred of the one thousand properties the RTC offered to convey (give away) to nonprofits were taken. Finally, of the $142-million mortgage bond issue, the RTC subsidized only 384 loans. This left the agency with over $122-mil in unused funds, although the RTC phone hotline was receiving up to eight hundred calls a day (*New York Times* 1991c).

John McEvoy, the executive director of the National Council of State Housing Agencies, reported other methods the RTC used to appear successful. Not only did the RTC refuse to make public the actual prices at which houses were sold or the income of their buyers, as Henneberger testified, the data the RTC did release were self-serving and misleading, particularly with regard to the income levels served (U.S. Congress: Senate 1991a:42). According to McEvoy, the RTC calculated cumulative data on the 70–90 percent of sales that it considered "statistically significant" (U.S. Congress: Senate 1991a:141). The few raw data they released—in this case for Pennsylvania—revealed that the RTC had dramatically overstated sales to families with incomes below 80 percent of the area median. Fifty-six percent of the closed Pennsylvania sales were to buyers with unknown incomes (U.S. Congress: Senate 1991a:142). Repeating the theme that the agency was involved in a de facto veto requiring congressional action, McEvoy concluded,

> [T]he RTC can cure every problem I have so far described through administrative action. It's a matter of will, not a matter of law. But FIRREA amendments are necessary where RTC proves unable or unwilling to make needed changes. (U.S. Congress: Senate 1991a:42–43)

Congressional Response

As in the battles between the administration and Congress during the passage of the FIRREA, the AHP had congressional supporters. House banking committee housing advocates Gonzalez and Frank recognized the administration's attempt to nullify the program. For example, committee chairman Gonzalez noted the de facto veto, arguing that the administration was attempting to defeat this measure "by creative drafting of regulations and guidelines" (U.S. Congress: House 1990a:228–29). Similarly, Frank held that the refusal of the RTC to provide discounts and financing meant that affordable housing was going only to those at the upper range of eligibility, at or just below 115 percent of area median income, not the poor. According to Frank: "I think the majority of this board is failing to comply with the true spirit of this legislation, and it will wind up depriving us of an opportunity to do some low income housing" (U.S. Congress: House 1990a:58). In separate hearings on RTC property disposition policy he argued:

> [V]ery little discourages me as much as hearing the RTC talk about low-income housing. I have never seen a government program administered less sympathetically. It is as if we had appointed the "Marlboro Man" as surgeon general or Gandhi at the Pentagon. (U.S. Congress: House 1990c:17)

Finally, in hearings before the task force on the RTC he said, "[A] very large number of organizations who try to deal with you complain, and I share that complaint, that there does not seem to be a great deal of interest in moving this program along" (p. 29). In sum, Rep. Joseph Kennedy argued that the AHP has "been treated like the runt of the RTC litter [and] has turned the affordable housing program into a symbol of governmental neglect" (U.S. Congress: House 1990a:418–19).

Part of the state response to RTC negligence was the addition of affordable housing amendments to the $30 billion and $25 billion 1991 congressional RTC allocations. These new provisions allowed the RTC to sell property from conservatorship, extended the 90-day window to 180 days, allowed for greater discounting on single-family properties, and required buyers to certify their intent to occupy the property for at least a year. Nonetheless, in 1993, McEvoy and others continued to testify that despite legislative changes thousands of properties were lost, and that the majority of the buyers were not those for whom the AHP was intended (U.S. Congress: House 1993b:115). In the same hearings, Harvey of the Enterprise Foundation, testified to the AHP's wasted potential and, possibly foreshadowing further disappointment, noted the continued importance of bureaucratic support:

> Since 1989, the RTC has taken great strides to establish and improve its Affordable Housing Program. . . . However, in number terms, very little of the potential of this program has been realized by non-profits and governmental agencies. [The new program] can only be successful if the RTC and relevant federal agencies will devise a cohesive strategy to link efforts in property disposition with financing in ways in which nonprofits can participate. (p. 155)

By contrast, Gonzalez argued in April 1993:

> My impression is that this has been a successful program . . . even though the initial efforts of some of us to attach the affordable housing and disposition provisos . . . were met by headstrong opposition from the then administration, and . . . some of the RTC officials. (p. 1)

In sum, examination of the de facto AHP reveals a variety of techniques used by the administration to subvert the apparent political victory of the community and consumer groups. Although well supported by the most powerful members of key banking and urban affairs committees within the state, ultimately the structural power of the administration to make policies and appointments meant AHP legislation had little practical impact outside the state. Finally, as anticipated by the accommodationist position, the interaction of the state and community and consumer groups in the creation and implementation of the AHP points to the mutually transformative powers of the state-society relation.

5

Bank PACs and the Legislative Process: To Market, to Market, to Buy What?

Congressional willingness to deregulate and then rescue the banking industry raises the question of the mechanisms through which the banking industry, and corporations in general shape legislation. Research into questions of this nature has investigated the extent to which corporations, families, and individuals coordinate PAC donations, with the implication that coordinated donations create favorable legislative outcomes (Allen and Broyles 1989; Clawson, Neustadtl, and Scott 1992; Mizruchi 1989; Neustadtl and Clawson 1988). Unfortunately, because this research has focused primarily on *patterns* of PAC giving, such as whether or not PACs are "ideological" or "pragmatic" (see below) in their giving, the relationship between contributions and specific policy *outcomes* has gone largely unexamined. Few have explored the degree to which PACs target their donations to those legislators most responsible for government policy affecting their industry.

We wish to know what role bank PACs played in the passage of the Garn–St. Germain Act of 1982 deregulating banks. For those who study the role of banks in the policy process, bank deregulation presents an interesting case. When Congress deregulated the banking industry, it was not acting to protect loans gone sour, as, for example, the bailouts of Chrysler and Mexico. In other words, deregulation lacked the lender-borrower relationship commonly associated with bank hegemony processes (see, e.g., Glasberg 1989; Mintz and Schwartz 1985; Glasberg and Skidmore 1996). Mechanisms of corporate power other than bank hegemony may have filled that gap. PAC contributions to legislators' election campaigns could be an important channel through which the banking industry coordinates and articulates its interests. Oddly, although the deregulation and bailout of the banking industry have been the subject of much research, the role of bank PACs in these policies has received less explicit attention—though data from the Federal Election Commission (1984, 1986, 1995) indicate bank PACs were active prior to passage of both the bank deregulation and bailout legislation. To what extent do PAC contributions shape policy? Were bank PAC donations targeted at key legislators? Do PAC donations create influence in the form of access to Banking Committee members, or access to Congress in general? Or was some other set of mechanisms involved?

PACS AND POLICY FORMATION

What role do corporate PACs play in the policy formation process, particularly in the development of policy concerning a single industry? Some studies have found that PAC contributions are positively related to favorable legislative votes on issues of importance to the contributors (see, e.g., Wertheimer 1980; Alexander 1984; Kau and Rubin 1982; Wilhite and Theilmann 1987; Frendreis and Waterman 1985; Gleiber, King, and Mahood 1987; Ginsberg and Green 1986). Most of the sociological literature surrounding PACs examines the relation between intercorporate organization and corporate political behavior (see, e.g., Mizruchi 1989; Mizruchi and Koenig 1986; Clawson, Neustadtl, and Bearden 1986; Allen 1991; Allen and Broyles 1989). PAC donations are used as a quantitative indicator of the level of political activity and political organization of corporations and other special interest groups. Though these studies do not examine the direct link between PACs' campaign contributions and legislative outcomes, they do point to areas for exploration.

For example, Mintz and Schwartz (1985) demonstrated that indirect interlocks between corporations, particularly those organized through large central banks, are associated with higher levels of coordinated political activity than direct interlocks. Similarly, Clawson et al. (1986) used corporate PAC donations as an indicator of unified corporate political activity. They compared the level of pragmatic corporate PAC donations (donations given to incumbent candidates irrespective of their party) to the level of ideological donations (donations given to conservative challengers for incumbents' seats). They found that, at the aggregate level, corporate political activity is disunified: some companies are primarily pragmatic PAC donors while others are ideological. However, when they broke down the data by individual campaigns, they found that organized corporate political behavior (again, defined as organized PAC giving) is specific to the individual campaigns to which the corporations are donating. The disunity apparent at the aggregate level—some companies seemed pragmatic, others ideological—resulted from one group of corporate PACs donating to the pragmatic candidate in one race, and a different corporate group donating to the ideological challenger in a different race. Furthermore, Neustadtl and Clawson (1988) argued that shared conservatism was the most significant predictor of coordinated corporate PAC donations. When Clawson and Neustadtl (1989) examined the relationship between corporate interlocks and political contributions more directly, they found that the central, most interlocked firms—the firms that, from research such as Useem's (1984) study of the "inner circle," one would expect to be strategic corporate leaders—have more moderate levels of coordinated, ideologically conservative PAC donations then less interlocked firms.

In studies looking at other types of intercorporate organization and political behavior, Allen (1991) and Allen and Broyles (1989) found that campaign donations may be organized through corporate-family ties. Family ties may be a resource making possible organized and explicitly probusiness political activity. In sum, though these and the preceding studies do not directly explore the link between PACs' campaign contributions and legislative outcomes, they suggest that banks may not only organize the general business community's political activity, but may also be able to mobilize this resource to influence specific bank-related legislation. Since research indicates that banks are the most central figures in patterns of interlocking corporate directorates (see Mintz and Schwartz 1985), we should find that the PAC donations of corporations associated with the banking industry are more coordinated with respect to bank-related legislation than those of less interlocked, nonfinancial firms.

Analysts have interpreted the impact or meaning of PAC donations in a number of ways. Some researchers argue that PACs do not buy legislative outcomes (Chappell 1982). For example, several studies found evidence suggesting that PACs simply increase contributors' access to legislators (Langbein 1986; Grenzke 1989; Gopian 1984; Sabato 1984). Other studies suggest that PAC contributions buy neither legislative votes nor access, but function instead like "protection money," particularly when the receiving candidate is a powerful legislator with little likelihood of facing a serious election challenge. PAC contributions to candidates in close electoral races, while riskier, are more likely to be of decisive importance to the candidate and thus perhaps to elicit access or favorable legislation (Keim and Zardkoohi 1988).

Interpreting the affects of PAC donations raises the question of the meaning of access. While some studies define access as literally gaining an audience with a legislator (measured, for example, by the amount of time PAC representatives spend with legislators—see Langbein 1986), Neustadtl (1990) gave it a more encompassing definition. Access involves the attempt to influence legislative outcomes, to influence the phrasing or the interpretation of a particular bill during markup sessions prior to congressional votes, or both. The distinction between outcomes and phrasing is important. Access that shapes the wording or meaning of a proposed bill prior to a vote does not necessarily determine whether or not a bill passes; access targeting a particular congressional vote may not necessarily craft the contours of the bill itself. According to the testimony of industry representatives, banks attempted to influence both the wording and the votes for or against passage of deregulation. What remains unclear is the degree to which the banking community used PAC donations to shape this legislation.

The theoretical import of the preceding studies lies in the unstated *assumption* that PAC donations play an integral role in the policy formation process: one examines PAC contribution patterns based on the assumption that this money somehow translates into policy. Without this assumption, the research is meaningless. Yet, campaign *donations* are a step removed from the creation of specific *legislation*. Because this literature conflates PAC donations with political effectiveness, it *implies* a *business dominance* understanding of the policy process: a unified, interlocked corporate class exercises political power through PAC donations that neutralize the political input of other sources. Though implied, this inclusion is not tested.

Business dominance theory suggests that capital accumulation interests dominate the state's policymaking process. Theorists using this perspective have argued that business leaders and their direct representatives hold strategically important state leadership positions, thereby "capturing" the state (Miliband 1969; Useem 1984; Zeitlin and Ratcliff 1975; Zeitlin, Ewen, and Ratcliff 1974). Mills (1956) and Dye (1990, 1995) identify corporate leaders who have become presidents, vice presidents, or important members of White House cabinets. More recently, researchers have argued that capital accumulation or corporate interests influence the policymaking process by dominating crucial informational, advisory, and decision-making bodies (Burris 1992). For example, Domhoff (1990) and Akard (1992) argue that corporate control of policymaking and implementation bodies (such as the Council on Foreign Relations, the Council on Economic Development) and regulatory agencies makes the direct involvement of corporate leaders in policymaking unnecessary.

Without testing the assumption that PAC donations translate into political power, PAC research fails to directly challenge the pluralist position—the coordinated political activity of interest groups competing in the legislative process is compatible with pluralism. Indeed, pluralism's central point is that over time, and across issues, no one unified group repeatedly has its political demands met at the expense of others (see Lipset 1981; Polsby 1980). To challenge the pluralist position, it is necessary to show not only that corporations are unified politically, but that through the use of resources specific to the corporate sector (i.e., the political coordination produced by networks of interlocked directorates and the large economic reserves from which to make PAC donations) a unified corporate class tailors legislation to its specifications at the expense of the interests of other groups. That is, the political arena is not neutral, but contains a *systematic* procapitalist bias. This requires we not only look at patterns of PAC contributions, but also examine the impact of PAC contributions on the legislative process as seen in the creation of specific legislation.

In their most recent study of the relationship between campaign money and policy formation, Clawson et al. (1992) downplayed PACs' significance in the policy formation process. They found that the relationship between direct PAC contributions and large, visible pieces of legislation is negligible. Contrary to the implications of research such as Mintz and Schwartz's (1985), their research suggests that banks would be *unlikely* to use PACs to influence the most visible, critical pieces of corporate welfare legislation—particularly those which directly affect banks. According to Clawson et al., the point of corporate campaign financing is to establish access—corporations want their position heard and understood—not a legislative quid pro quo. They argue that most corporate political activity is not focused around large visible votes and pieces of legislation, but around corporate- or industry-specific loopholes in larger pieces of legislation (Clawson et al. 1992).

While offering divergent interpretations of the significance of PACs, the literature suggests important questions for our research. Do bank PAC contributions correlate with the probank outcomes of this legislation? Did bank contributions target members of the House and Senate Banking Committees? That is, did they contribute more to these legislators than to legislators on other committees? Did their contributions increase significantly before passage of these bills, and then decline after passage? Did their patterns of contributions differ from those of nonfinancial PACs, including nonfinancial corporate PACs, labor PACs, and PACs representing community and consumer interests? In the passage of bank deregulation and S&L bailout legislation, were bank PACs a resource creating banking access in either (or both) of the senses of access identified by Neustadtl (1990)? Finally, and possibly most importantly, can we specify the *conditions under which* certain potential political resources, such as PAC donations, hold political sway (Skidmore and Glasberg 1996)?

FINANCIAL PACS AND CONGRESSIONAL BANKING COMMITTEES

According to Makinson (1992), financial institutions and individuals employed by financial institutions were among the dominant contributors to congressional campaigns in 1990. Individuals employed by financial institutions were, as a group, the leading campaign contributors that year, giving a total of $16.5 million. Finance PACs were second only to labor in total campaign contributions to congressional candidates; whereas labor PACs contributed $35.5 million, finance PACs contributed $25.5 million. These PACs stand out as major contributors—the nearest total amounts in contributions came from agricultural and ideological PACs, each of which contributed "'only' $15 million" (p. 22). The finance, insurance, and real estate industries were major individual contributors and, combined, constituted the leading sector in both individual and PAC contributions. As a group, this sector contributed $43.2 million in campaign contributions, "more than twice as many campaign dollars as any other industry" (p. 43). And, importantly, most of the money (62 percent) from the financial industry came from PACs, with the remainder from individuals (p. 64).

Where was all this financial muscle going? In general, Makinson found a pattern in which "the member's profile of contributors tends to parallel his or her committee assignments" (p. 36). Thus, members of the House and Senate Banking, Finance, and Urban Affairs committees were targeted by financial institutions, receiving "substantial contributions" from commercial banks, S&L institutions, insurance companies, and investment firms. Financial institutions contributed almost $110 million to members of the House Banking, Finance, and Urban Affairs Committee, far more than they contributed to any other committee (with the exception of the pivotal House Ways and Means Committee) (p. 38).

Notably, Phil Gramm (R-Texas), John Kerry (D-Massachusetts), and Larry Pressler (R-South Dakota) were among the top Senate recipients of financial industry largess. All were members of the Senate Banking Committee. Five of the top ten recipients of financial industry campaign contributions sat on the House Banking Committee (p. 65). In particular, the three leading House recipients of commercial banks' contributions sat on the House Banking Committee (Stephen L. Neal, D-North Carolina; Doug Barnard, Jr., D-Georgia; and Peter Hoagland, D-Nebraska). Phil Gramm and Bill Bradley (D-New Jersey) were the leading Senate recipients of commercial banks' contributions. Notably, Bradley sat on the Senate Finance Committee, which oversees tax law changes (p. 66).

Contributions from the S&L industry declined by 50 percent between the 1988 and 1990 elections, primarily because of the devastation suffered by that industry. However, the U.S. League of Savings Associations, the industry's chief lobbying group, alone contributed almost $390,000 to congressional campaigns in 1990; together, the top five S&L industry contributors gave almost $620,000 to congressional candidates. The leading House recipient of S&L industry contributions (Carroll Hubbard, Jr., D-Kentucky) sat on the House Banking Committee. Phil Gramm was the leading Senate recipient of these contributions (p. 66).

Makinson found that more than half of the members of the Senate Banking Committee (eleven out of twenty-one) received at least one-third of their large campaign contributions from committee-related PACs, with seven of these members receiving more than half of their large campaign contributions from these sources. Seven of the top twenty committee-related contributors to committee members were commercial banks and their organizations (such as the ABA), and two of the top twenty committee-related contributors to committee members were S&L organizations (p. 102). In the House Banking Committee, most of the members (thirty-three out of fifty-two) received at least one-third of their large contributions from committee-related contributions, with eight of these members receiving at least half of their large contributions from such sources. Nine of the top twenty committee-related contributors were commercial banks; two were S&L organizations, one represented credit unions, and one represented independent bankers (p. 137).

Taken together, Makinson's descriptive statistics on the relationship between financial industry campaign contributions and the House and Senate Banking Committees suggest an organized effort by the banking industry to influence those committee members most involved with the banking industry. However, these statistics do not in and of themselves constitute evidence that these committees are targeted by industry PAC giving, or that these donations shape policy. For example, Makinson notes that more than half of the Senate Banking Committee members receive a third of their large contributions from key PACs. He does not, however, test if this apparent pattern of giving differs *significantly* from the giving of other industries, or if the contributions received by these candidates are systematically different from those received by other candidates. Moreover, what do these PAC contributions *mean*? It is safe to assume that Makinson would have us make the logical leap from "PAC contribution" to "legislation favoring contributors" but this assumption remains unstated and untested. Like the PAC studies reviewed above, Makinson has stated the "facts" and left the meaning of these facts implicit.

Finally, Makinson's statistics are a static picture of the 1990 election; they do not demonstrate changes over time relative to key pieces of legislation, such as the 1982 banking deregulation legislation or the bailout of the S&L industry in the late 1980s. To demonstrate that PAC contributions are linked to legislation, we would need to compare patterns of giving prior to and following passage of key pieces of legislation; we need to examine contributions over time.

Grenzke (1989) addressed some of the issues raised by Makinson's research. Temporally sensitive analyses of the connections between

PAC activity and legislative outcomes can be convoluted. Grenzke notes one problem created by interpreting correlations between PAC contributions and legislators' voting behavior: "[V]oting behavior may be influencing a PAC's contribution at the same time that PAC contributions may be influencing voting behavior" (p. 2). Thus, even if, for example, Makinson (1992) found a correlation between contributions and voting, these simple correlations, though suggestive, are inconclusive. To pin down the effect of PAC contributions, the researcher must show that PAC contributions and legislative outcomes are sequential.

To eliminate this problem, Grenzke suggests a dynamic research design that

> examines whether a change in the PAC's contributions between two election cycles ($t - 1$ and $t - 2$) will lead to a change in legislative voting behavior in the ensuing Congresses (t and $t - 1$) and whether a change in contributions between the next two election cycles (t and $t - 1$) simultaneously causes a change in the member's voting between the next two Congresses (t and $t - 1$), controlling for the direction in which the district and party are pushing and the member's initial voting behavior. (Grenzke 1989:13–14)

Though her dynamic model offers one solution to one part of the problem, it does not address our specific areas of concern. Grenzke selected PACs affiliated with the issue areas of education, business, construction, insurance, abortion, and private- and public-sector labor. We wish to examine different business concerns within an industry—specifically financial and nonfinancial businesses (research suggests that the issue domains of the financial and nonfinancial sectors are not necessarily the same; see, e.g., Glasberg 1989). This requires that we examine banking PACs separately, rather than aggregate all business PACs into one category.

Finally, Grenzke noted that her study found little evidence that a single PAC influences a legislator's voting behavior, but she suggested that "the combined contributions from many PACs may influence members' votes" (1989:18). We wish to explore this possibility in the cases of banking deregulation and the S&L bailout, in the context of structural bank selectivity and bank hegemony theories by comparing the PAC contributions of financial PACs to those of nonfinancial PACs.

FOLLOWING THE MONEY: HYPOTHESES, DATA, AND METHODS

If PACs are not an important source of bank power in the policy formation process, this calls into question the research of those who claim coordinated PAC activity is an indicator of corporate influence on legislation. Moreover, a lack of corporate targeting of key legislators and legislation would seem to indicate that PACs are, at best, one part of a larger structure of policy formation. Our research design allows us to explore the extent to which the financial industry brought PACs to bear on the legislative process by examining how PAC donations converge on committee members involved in key pieces of banking legislation. Although the targeting of PAC money toward certain legislators or during the time period surrounding legislation does not necessarily mean that PAC money creates votes, the absence of targeting may indicate that corporations believe increased PAC contributions have little effect on the policy formation process, that targeting has proven an ineffective means for affecting voting, that corporations have access to other, more effective mechanisms with which to influence policy, or some combination of all three. Irrespective of the exact interpretation of the absence of targeting, such a condition calls into question the methodological usefulness of PAC donations as a general measure of corporate political power.

The following hypotheses pertain to the passage of the Garn–St. Germain Act of 1982, comparing Federal Election Commission (FEC) data from the 1981–1982 period to data from the 1977–1978 and 1991–1992 periods. The 1978–1979 data set is the earliest available from the FEC. The 1991–1992 data set covers the years following the passage of the 1989 FIRREA, which bailed out the S&Ls, and represents the most recent complete data set. Each hypothesis below assumes not only that the banking industry had an interest in the Garn–St. Germain Act, but that it would express this interest through *targeted* PAC donations.

Targeting implies, in the case of hypothesis 1, that finance industry PACs give significantly more to banking committee members than to legislators not on the banking committee, and, in the case of hypothesis 2, that finance industry PACs give significantly more when key legislation is being considered than during other times. Underlying hypothesis 1 is the idea that if PAC money is used as a tool to influence policy and the finance industry is the group most interested in this legislation, then we should see industry-related PACs making significantly greater contributions to members of the banking committees than to legislators not on the banking committee. Similarly, non–committee members should garner their campaign contributions from other sources (Table 5.1a).

Table 5.1a. Bank PAC Contributions by Committee Membership

Recipient	Finance industry PACs
Banking committee members	Greater
Non–committee members	Less

Table 5.1b.   Contributions by PAC Affiliation and Committee Membership

| PAC associated with the finance industry | Banking committee member (mean; cell no.) | |
	Yes	No
Yes	Greater (cell 1)	Less (cell 2)
No	Less (cell 3)	Greater (cell 4)

Extending hypothesis 1, we should see that banking industry PAC contributions to banking committee members should be greater than contributions to non–committee members. Moreover, non–industry PACs should give less to banking committee members than to members of other committees. Using Table 5.1b, our notion of targeting predicts that cells 1 and 4 should have significantly higher PAC contribution amounts than cells 2 and 3.

The second, *dynamic* aspect of our targeting question compares the timing of bank PAC donations to the time period during which the banking committee considered the legislation. If the finance industry uses PAC contributions as a political resource, we expect that campaign contributions to banking committee members (in relation to non–committee members as specified in hypothesis 1) would increase from 1977 up until the time of the passage of the Garn–St. Germain Act and decline following passage of the FIRREA.

The usefulness of these first two analyses is, however, limited. Significance testing among multiple means will not allow us to establish the explanatory power of committee membership on PAC contributions. Thus, to explore this relationship, we place the theoretically significant variables in a general linear model in which the dependent variable is the dollar amount of campaign contributions made by bank PACs, and the independent variables are committee membership of the recipients (banking committee member or nonmember), industry sector of the contributor (financial sector or nonfinancial sectors), sector of the contributor within the finance industry (commercial banks, S&Ls, or others, including credit unions, independent banks, real estate firms, and insurance firms), and candidate's incumbency status and party affiliation. We ran regressions for the 1977–1978, 1981–1982, and 1991–1992 time periods—prior to, during, and following passage of the Garn–St. Germain Act. By hypothesis 3, if PAC contributions are a significant source of the banking industry's political power, we would expect the industry sector of the contributor to be a strong predictor of contributions to banking committee members. Moreover, the explanatory power of industry sector should increase as we move closer to the time period of the legislation.

In sum, while offering divergent interpretations of the significance of PACs, the literature we reviewed above suggests important questions for our research. Do bank PAC contributions correlate with the probank outcomes of this legislation? Did bank contributions target members of the House and Senate Banking Committees? Did they contribute more to these legislators than to legislators on other committees? Did their contributions significantly increase prior to passage of this legislation? Did their patterns of contributions differ from those of nonfinancial PACs? Finally, returning to our central theoretical question, to what extent does the analysis of PAC contributions supplant sociological analysis of the larger structural context in which legislation is created? Must research in political sociology specify the conditions under which PAC contributions are an effective political resource?

To explore these hypotheses, we coded and analyzed data from the Federal Election Commission's *Campaign Expenditures in the United States, 1977–1978 and 1979–1980, Campaign Expenditures in the United States, 1981–1982,* and *Campaign Expenditures in the United states, 1991–1992* (1986, 1984, 1995). We coded PACs according to the branch of the financial industry that they represented using *Moody's Industrial Directory* (Moody's Investor Service 1977a, 1977b, 1981a, 1981b, 1991a, 1991b) and *Ward's Business Directory* (Gale Research, Inc. 1991). Different segments of the finance industry were coded according to their business activities. The categories for the finance industry were commercial banks, S&Ls, credit unions, independent and mutual banks, securities firms, real estate firms, and other, for businesses involved in, for example, consumer credit or investment quality life insurance. Candidates were coded as members of the Senate and House Banking Committees according to listings in the 1977, 1981, and 1991 *Congressional Directory* (Joint Committee on Printing 1977, 1981, 1991). The remainder of the coding was provided by the FEC tapes. This included designations for a candidate's party and incumbency status. Because the FEC changed the way in which it codes parties other than Democrat or Republican, we split the PARTY variable to account for an increase in other-party candidates.

Using this coding, the regression equation for hypothesis 3, testing the power of committee membership to explain the amount of PAC money banking committee members received, is as follows:

$$\text{CONTRIBUTIONS} > 0 = \text{BANKCOM} + \text{INCUMBENCY} + \text{PARTY}$$
$$(\text{or DEMOCRAT} + \text{REPUBLICAN}) + \text{COMMERCIAL} + \text{S\&L}$$
$$+ \text{OTHERS,}$$

where

CONTRIBUTIONS: the dollar amount of the PAC contribution (square root transformed)

BANKCOM: a dummy variable, where 1 = on the banking
                        committee

INCUMBENCY: candidate's incumbency status, where 1 = incumbent,
                        and 0 = challenger or open seat

PARTY: the candidate's party, where 1 = Republican (1977–
                        1978 & 1981–1982)

DEMOCRAT: the candidate's party, where 1 = Democrat (1991–1992)

REPUBLICAN: the candidate's party, where 1 = Republican (1991–
                        1992)

COMMERCIAL: whether or not the PAC was associated with a commer-
                        cial bank, where 1 = commercial bank

S&L: whether or not PAC was associated with an S&L,
                        where 1 = S&L

OTHERS: credit unions, independent and mutual banks, securi-
                        ties firms, real estate firms, and financials, where 1 =
                        financial PAC not elsewhere categorized

This equation explores our targeting theme by giving primacy to committee membership. Party and incumbency are included as controls,
given that they have proven significant predictor variables in literature
exploring patterns of PAC donations. Finally, we examine the explanatory power of PAC industry identification on contributions.

BANK PACS AND THE LEGISLATIVE PROCESS:
WHAT DID THEY BUY AND WHEN DID THEY BUY IT?

As we noted above, implicit in much of the sociological literature on
PAC contributions lies the assumption that PAC contributions are a
mechanism of political influence. Based on this assumption, the following three hypotheses examine the extent to which finance industry
PACs target members of the Senate and House Banking committees.
Contrary to the assumptions of the PAC literature, we found in general
that in the case of the Garn–St. Germain Act, targeting did not occur in
the manner the PAC literature led us to predict.

Hypothesis 1 holds that banking industry PAC contributions to banking committee members should be greater than contributions to non–
committee members, and that non–industry PACs should give less to
banking committee members than to other legislators and candidates.
Given the simplicity of this hypothesis, we start our discussion with
simple, descriptive statistics. Tables 5.2–5.4 provide the mean amounts
of four types of contributions. As in Table 5.1b, cell 1 is the mean contribution from PACs associated with the finance industry to banking committee members; cell 2 is from PACs associated with the finance industry
to candidates and legislators not on the banking committees; cell 3 is

Table 5.2a.   1977–1978, Senate: Contributions by PAC Affiliation and Committee Membership

PAC associated with the finance industry	Banking committee member		
	Yes	No	Mean (N)
Yes	$1,037	$983	$990
	(110)	(762)	(872)
No	$1,170	$1,162	$1,163
	(594)	(8,547)	(9,141)
Mean	$1,149	$1,066	
	(704)	(9,309)	

Notes: Mean PAC contribution to Senate, $1,147; $R^2 = .0007$; $N = 10,013$.

from PACs not associated with the finance industry to banking committee members; and cell 4 is from PACs not associated with the finance industry to candidates and legislators not on the banking committees. Each table also includes the average PAC contribution during that donation cycle for that branch of Congress and an R^2 produced by a one-way analysis of variance, which describes how much of the variation in contributions is due to differences between the four cells.

Tables 5.2a and 5.2b, describing the 1977–1978 PAC data for the Senate and the House, respectively, indicate that contrary to hypothesis 1, contributions from PACs associated with the finance industry do not necessarily target banking committee members. In Table 5.2a we see that although the mean contributions in cell 1 are greater than those in cell 2 (not significant at alpha = .05), Senate banking committee members received, on average, *less* from finance industry PACs ($1,037) than from other PACs ($1,170). Similarly, 1977–1978 contributions in the House (Table 5.2b) show that, on average, PACs associated with the

Table 5.2b.   1977–1978, House: Contributions by PAC Affiliation and Committee Membership

PAC associated with the finance industry	Banking committee member		
	Yes	No	Mean (N)
Yes	$652	$687	$680
	(770)	(3,038)	(3,808)
No	$662	$736	$731
	(2,725)	(35,101)	(37,826)
Mean	$660	$732	
	(3,495)	(38,139)	

Notes: Mean PAC contribution to House, $726; $R^2 = .0004$; $N = 41,634$.

finance industry actually gave *less* to banking committee members ($652) than to nonmembers ($687), and, as in the Senate, PACs not associated with the finance industry gave more ($662) to banking committee members than did finance PACs ($652).

To go beyond our earlier criticism of Makinson (1992) though, we must ask if the differences between these means are significant. An analysis of the variance of the four means in the Senate shows that no mean contribution level was significantly different from any other mean at the alpha = .05 level. In the House (Table 5.2b) the mean for cell 1 ($652) was significantly different from the mean in cell 4 ($736) at the alpha = .05 level. This again leads us to reject hypothesis 1, which would be supported if the means of cells 1 and 4 were significantly different from the means of cells 2 and 3. Finally, as indicated by the extremely low R^2, little of the variation in the data is a consequence of the differences between these groups. In sum, these descriptive findings provide straightforward, prima facie evidence rejecting the notion that, at least during the 1977–1978 period, PACs associated with the finance industry target members of congressional banking committees.

Although the 1981–1982 data produce more significant differences among mean levels of contributions, like the 1977–1978 data these differences provide little support for hypothesis 1. In the Senate (Table 5.3a), we once again see that banking committee members received, on average, less from PACs associated with the finance industry ($1,353) than from other industry PACs ($1,408). In raw numbers, PACs associated with the finance industry gave more to banking committee members than to nonmembers ($1,353 vs. $1,303); this difference was not, however, significant at the alpha = .05 level. PACs not associated with the finance industry gave significantly more to non–banking committee members than did PACs associated with the finance industry at the alpha = .01 level (cell 2 vs. cell 4). Yet, because cell 1 is not significantly

Table 5.3a.   1981–1982, Senate: Contributions by PAC Affiliation and Committee
        Membership

| *PAC associated* | *Banking committee member* | | |
| *with the finance* | | | |
industry	*Yes*	*No*	*Mean (N)*
Yes	$1,353	$1,303	$1,317
	(954)	(2,471)	(3,425)
No	$1,408	$1,512	$1,496
	(4,833)	(27,307)	(32,140)
Mean	$1,399	$1,495	
	(5,787)	(29,778)	

Notes: Mean PAC contribution to Senate, $1,479; R^2 = .0009; N = 35,565.

Table 5.3b.   1981–1982, House: Contributions by PAC Affiliation and Committee
    Membership

PAC associated with the finance industry	Banking committee member		
	Yes	No	Mean (N)
Yes	$948	$915	$920
	(2,088)	(11,250)	(13,338)
No	$781	$877	$872
	(8,186)	(134,591)	(142,777)
Mean	$815	$880	
	(10,274)	(145,841)	

Notes: Mean PAC contribution to House, $875; $R^2 = .0003$; $N = 156,115$.

different from cells 2 and 3, and cell 4 is not significantly different from
cell 3, the difference between cells 2 and 4 is not relevant to hypothesis
1. Overall, it does not appear that the Senate banking committee of the
97th Congress was targeted by PACs associated with the finance industry as predicted by hypothesis 1.

The relation between committee membership and PAC contributions
becomes still more complex when we turn our attention to the 1981
House (Table 5.3b). During the 1981–1982 period, contributions from
finance industry PACs to banking committee members ($948) was signif-
icantly larger (alpha = .01) than contributions from PACs not associated
with the finance industry to banking committee members ($781). This
was, however, the only support for this hypothesis during this period.
Looking at the other relations among the means, cell 1 ($948) was signifi-
cantly larger than cell 3 ($781) and cell 4 ($877), and cell 2 ($915) were
also significantly larger than cells 3 and 4 (alpha = .01). The mean PAC
contribution to the House during the 1981–1982 period was $875. PACs
associated with the finance industry, though, had a mean contribution
of $920, while the mean donation of all other PACs was $872—a difference slightly larger than the significant difference between cells 2 and 4.

In general, cells 1 and 2 in Table 5.3b are significantly larger than cells 3
and 4. Thus, to the extent that PACs associated with the finance industry
targeted House representatives, this targeting was *dispersed* over the entire
House, as seen in the higher average contributions of finance industry
PACs than of non–finance industry PACs. Although these differences do
not support our targeting hypothesis, the significant differences between
the donations of finance industry PACs and other PACs in the House—a
difference that reappears in our discussion of hypothesis 2—lends itself to
an expanded understanding of the role of PACs in the political process, and
will therefore be discussed at greater length below.

The 1991–1992 data, from the period following the legislative resolution

Table 5.4a.   1991–1992, Senate: Contributions by PAC Affiliation and Committee
Membership

PAC associated with the finance industry	Banking committee member		
	Yes	No	Mean (N)
Yes	$1,170	$1,464	$1,382
	(1,464)	(3,789)	(5,253)
No	$1,771	$2,146	$2,093
	(5,962)	(35,947)	(41,909)
Mean	$1,653	$2,081	
	(7,426)	(39,736)	

Notes: Mean PAC contribution to Senate, $2,013; R^2 = .0003; N = 47,162.

of the S&L crisis, are consistent with the patterns we saw in the two
earlier data sets. Although none of the mean contribution levels in the
Senate (Table 5.4a) was significantly different from the other means at
the alpha = .01 level, Senate Banking Committee members received, on
average, lower contributions from PACs associated with the banking
industry ($1,170) than from other industry PACs ($1,771). Similarly, the
mean contribution from bank PACs to Senators not on the banking
committee was higher (though not significantly so) than that received by
banking committee members.

Once again, PAC contributions to representatives in the House prove
to be more interesting than those to senators (Table 5.4b). In the House,
mean bank PAC contributions to representatives who were not members of the banking committee ($900) were significantly higher (alpha =
.01) than bank PAC contributions to banking committee members
($814). At the alpha = .001 level, mean contributions to representatives
who were not banking committee members ($900, $934) were both sig-

Table 5.4b.   1991–1992, House: Contributions by PAC Affiliation and Committee
Membership

PAC associated with the finance industry	Banking committee member		
	Yes	No	Mean (N)
Yes	$814	$900	$881
	(4,038)	(14,410)	(18,448)
No	$804	$934	$925
	(11,129)	(144,437)	(155,566)
Mean	$807	$931	
	(15,167)	(158,847)	

Notes: Mean PAC contribution to House, $920; R^2 = .0005; N = 174,014.

nificantly higher than the mean donations to banking committee members. The difference between contributions from PACs associated with the banking industry to banking committee members and contributions from PACs not associated with the banking industry ($814, $804) was not significant. In sum, the 1991–1992 data do not support hypothesis 1. In both the House and the Senate, mean bank PAC donations to banking committee members were lower than mean bank PAC donations to non–committee members, in some cases, significantly so.

To close this section on hypothesis 1, we can return to the implications of Makinson's (1992) study. His description of the large donations to banking committee members certainly implied that bank committee members are targeted by bank PACs: that banks and banking committee members stand in a quid pro quo relation to one another. We found, however, that in no period, including possibly the one that Makinson studied, were mean contributions from bank PACs significantly greater to banking committee members than to nonmembers. Similarly, with the exception of 1982, contributions to banking committee members were, on average, larger from nonfinancial PACs than from PACs associated with the banking industry. Despite the presence of some large donations, on average, banking committee members have received the bulk of their PAC money from sources other than the banking industry.

Yet, when we examine hypothesis 2, we see that targeting behavior is not as straightforward as hypothesis 1 seems to assume. Hypothesis 2 examines the dynamic aspect of our targeting question by looking at changes in PAC donation patterns over time. As we outlined above, Makinson's analysis implied that PACs associated with the banking industry targeted their donations toward members of the banking committees, or conversely that banking committee members receive a disproportionate amount of their PAC money from this industry. Targeting should increase as committee members debate legislation affecting the industry with which that committee is concerned. Based on these assumptions, we predicted that if PAC contributions are a political resource, then campaign contributions to banking committee members (in relation to non–committee members as specified in hypothesis 1) should be higher in the 1981–1982 PAC data, during which time Congress was considering the 1982 Garn–St. Germain Act, than in the 1977–1978 or 1991–1992 data.

Although we find some support for hypothesis 2, this support was not in the form Makinson's (1992) statistics led us to predict. As described in Tables 5.5a and 5.5b, we saw dramatic differences between the Senate and the House in the changes of finance industry PAC contributions across time. Overall, contributions to Senate members and candidates increased 29 percent between the two periods, and changes in each of the four cells were relatively consistent with that overall increase (Table 5.5a). In particular, cells 1 and 4—which from hypothesis 1 should

Table 5.5a.   Percentage Change in PAC Donations in the
        Senate, 1977–1978 to 1981–1982

PAC associated with the finance industry	*Banking committee member*	
	Yes	*No*
Yes	31	33
No	20	30

Note: Overall change 1977–1978 to 1981–1982: 29%.

be the most heavily targeted—were the two cells that changed the least relative to overall change in contributions. However, in partial support of hypothesis 2, cell 3 (contributions to banking committee members from non–finance industry PACs) lagged behind the general increase. This may indicate that banking committee members received a larger percentage of their contributions from finance industry PACs than from others during that time period, although, as we saw in hypothesis 1, Senate Banking Committee members still received less, in actual dollars, from finance industry PACs than from other PACs (Table 5.3a).

Changes in PAC donation patterns in the House were more conspicuous than in the Senate. As we saw in Table 5.2b, the 1977–1978 data give little support to the hypothesis that banking committee members were being targeted. Indeed, whereas the mean contribution to banking committee members from the finance industry was the lowest in the table and 10 percent below the mean house donation that year, in the 1981–1982 data, on average, banking committee members received from finance industry PACs 108 percent of the mean contribution for the House—the highest mean donation in Table 5.3b. Moreover, though the House saw a 21 percent rise in overall contributions between the periods under study, finance industry PAC contributions to banking committee members increased 45 percent and to other members and candidates 33 percent (Table 5.5b). Contributions from PACs not associated with the finance industry lagged behind the overall percentage increase.

Table 5.5b.   Percentage Change in PAC Donations in the
        House, 1977–1978 to 1981–1982

PAC associated with the finance industry	*Banking committee member*	
	Yes	*No*
Yes	45	33
No	18	19

Note: Overall change 1977–1978 to 1981–1982: 21%.

Table 5.6a. Percentage Change in PAC Donations in the
Senate, 1981–1982 to 1991–1992

PAC associated with the finance industry	Banking committee member	
	Yes	No
Yes	−14	12
No	26	42

Note: Overall change 1981–1982 to 1991–1992: 36%.

Finally, when we look ten years after banking deregulation, and two years after passage of the FIRREA bailing out the S&L industry, we see in the 1991–1992 data both an absolute and percentage decline in contributions to banking committee members. The mean 1991–1992 Senate contributions to banking committee members from PACs associated with the banking industry was $1,170—a 14 percent decline from the 1981–1982 mean donation of $1,350 (Table 5.6a). Although the mean contribution to Senators increased during the decade by 36 percent, from $1,479 to $2,013, the overall increase in mean contributions from PACs associated with the finance industry was just 5 percent, from $1,317 to $1,382. Mean finance industry PAC contributions fell in the House by a like amount. As in the Senate, average finance industry PAC contributions to members of the banking committee were off 14 percent from the 1981–1982 election cycle, down from $948 to $814 (Table 5.6b). Additionally, finance industry PAC contributions to representatives not on the banking committee were off 2 percent. Overall, despite a modest average rise in House donations of 5 percent between the 1981–1982 and 1991–1992 periods, mean contributions from PACs associated with the finance industry to Representatives fell 4 percent from $920 in 1981–1982 to $881 in 1991–1992.

This indicates, as in our examination of hypothesis 1, that the targeting behavior of finance industry PACs occurred *across all candidates and members of the House*. In the 1981–1982 period, finance industry PACs

Table 5.6b. Percentage Change in PAC Donations in the
House, 1981–1982 to 1991–1992

PAC associated with the finance industry	Banking committee member	
	Yes	No
Yes	−14	−2
No	3	6

Note: Overall change 1981–1982 to 1991–1992: 5%.

disproportionately increased their donations to all House members and candidates relative to the overall increase in House donations and to the increases by PACs not associated with the banking industry. Following the 1982 Garn–St. Germain Act deregulating the banking industry, a number of smaller bailout policies and resolutions, and the culminating piece of bank legislation, the 1989 FIRREA, PAC donations from the finance industry either failed to keep pace with the overall increase in donations or actually declined.

The notion that finance industry PAC targeting was aimed less at key legislators than at the Congress as a whole is further supported by Table 5.7. Unlike the preceding tables, Table 5.7 does not examine the actual amounts of PAC contributions. Rather, it displays the extent to which being on a banking committee was associated with receiving a finance industry PAC contribution, irrespective of the amount of that contribution. First, we note the generally low correlations between committee membership and finance industry PAC contributions: banking committee members receive contributions from a variety of sources, finance industry PACs spread their contributions out within Congress, or both. Most interesting, unlike the Senate, which saw a secular increase across the years, in the 1981–1982 data for the House the relation between committee membership and finance industry PAC contributions decreased ($r = .111$). Consistent with Table 5.3b, which describes the higher than average contributions from finance industry PACs to all representatives, it appears that during that critical period when Congress debated and passed the Garn–St. Germain Act, finance industry PACs made an effort to disperse their contributions throughout the House—a pattern of spending that diminished somewhat as finance industry PAC contributions became, on average, smaller (Table 5.6b) and possibly more focused ($r = .161$).

Before turning our attention to the final hypothesis, we can make a few points in summary about these descriptive statistics. By separating PACs associated with the finance industry from other PACs, and banking committee members from other legislators and candidates, we were able to discern the extent to which PAC contributions target politicians. First, the 1977–1978 and 1991–1992 data sets contradicted hypothesis 1:

Table 5.7. Pearson Correlation Coefficients r between Banking Committee Membership and Contributions From Finance Industry PACs ($p = .0001$)

Branch of Congress	1977-1978	1981-1982	1991-1992
Senate	.067	.102	.118
House	.135	.111	.161

in both the House and the Senate, banking committee members received lower (or statistically the same) average contributions from finance industry PACs than from PACs associated with other interests. Second, to the extent that finance industry PACs targeted their donations in the 1981–1982 data, it appears these PACs targeted the entire House—not just banking committee members. As we discuss in our concluding section, this finding lends itself to an interpretation of PAC donations as a method of gaining *access* to legislators in general, rather than trying to control the behavior of a select few. Finally, the dramatic differences between the Senate and the House in changes in donation patterns were unexpected and unhypothesized. This, like the second point, is too interesting to overlook. We speculate below on the significance of this difference, arguing for the importance of specifying *the conditions under which* targeting may be expected, and, to that end, the conditions under which PAC donations are an important political resource.

The third and final hypothesis examines the ability of the variables in our tables to explain changes in contributions. We place these variables in a general linear regression model in which the dependent variable is the dollar amount of campaign contributions made by bank PACs and the independent variables are committee membership of the recipients, industry sector of the contributor, sector within the finance industry of the contributor (commercial banks, S&Ls, or others: including credit unions, independent banks, real estate firms, and insurance firms), and candidate's incumbency status and party affiliation. We ran regressions for the 1977–1978, 1981–1982, and 1991–1992 time periods—prior to, during, and following passage of the Garn–St. Germain Act. If PAC contributions are a significant source of the banking industry's political power, we expect that the industry sector of the contributor should be a strong predictor of contributions to banking committee members. Moreover, the explanatory power of industry sector should increase as we move closer to the time period of the legislation.

In general, although the regression coefficients tell an interesting story, our model explained a remarkably small amount of the variance in PAC contributions. Table 5.8 summarizes the statistics for the regression equation on a square root transformation of the dependent variable. This transformation increased the normality of the distribution and eliminated the correlation between the residuals and the model's predicted contribution values. We tried other standard transformations, which yielded similar, though somewhat less successful, results in terms of explained variance. This leads us to the obvious conclusion that the model is underspecified. In other words, as one might expect, determinants of PAC contributions are hardly limited to the independent variables we examined.

Though the model did not produce strong results, the independent

Table 5.8. General Linear Model Unstandardized Regression Coefficients for the Effects of Bank Committee Membership, Incumbency, Party, and Finance Industry Sector on the Square Root of PAC Contributions ≥ 0 in the Senate and House 1977–1978, 1981–1982, and 1991–1992

Independent variable	1977-1978 Senate b	1977-1978 Senate p	1977-1978 House b	1977-1978 House p	1981-1982 Senate b	1981-1982 Senate p	1981-1982 House b	1981-1982 House p	1991-1992 Senate b	1991-1992 Senate p	1991-1992 House b	1991-1992 House p
Bank com. member	2.24 (.784)	.004	1.30 (.272)	.0001	1.20 (.308)	.0001	.546 (.161)	.0007	-.773 (.337)	.02	-.258 (.118)	.03
Incumbency	-1.35 (.398)	.0007	-5.86 (.165)	.0001	-2.62 (.245)	.0001	-4.02 (.090)	.0001	.682 (.319)	.03	-2.54 (.094)	.0001
Party	-2.99 (.391)	.0001	-.822 (.152)	.0001	-3.60 (.221)	.0001	-1.40 (.079)	.0001				
Democrat									1.97 (12.5)	.88	1.56 (.309)	.0001
Republican									.724 (12.5)	.95	-1.57 (.311)	.0001
Commercial bank	-3.20 (1.27)	.01	-4.13 (.469)	.0001	-2.24 (.630)	.0004	-.410 (.228)	.07	-2.53 (.708)	.0003	.354 (.180)	.05
Savings & loan	-2.26 (1.65)	.17	-3.05 (.607)	.0001	-3.78 (.828)	.0001	-2.11 (.316)	.0001	-3.28 (1.66)	.05	-1.34 (.439)	.002
Others	-1.32 (1.78)	.45	-1.32 (.756)	.08	-.509 (.841)	.54	-.942 (.379)	.01	.972 (1.04)	.35	-.821 (.319)	.01
Intercept	30.33 (.353)	.0001	26.69 (.160)	.0001	36.56 (.243)	.0001	28.77 (.086)	.0001	32.80 (12.5)	.009	28.36 (.316)	.0001
Number of PAC contribs.	10,006		41,605		35,545		156,095		39,620		158,766	
R^2	.008		.032		.010		.015		.001		.017	

Note: Numbers in parentheses are the standard errors of the parameter estimates. See text for references.

variables lend themselves to three general observations about our targeting question. First, we note the consistent strength of party and incumbency (with the exception of the 1991 Senate) across the time periods. Given earlier research into ideological versus pragmatic PAC donation patterns by Clawson et al. (1992; see also Clawson et al. 1986; Clawson and Neustadtl 1989), we expected these variables to be significant, but what do they indicate about targeting? The negative relation between party and contributions (Republican = 1) indicates what Clawson et al. (1992:12) might have referred to as "pragmatic" PAC donations—contributions designed to gain access to legislators, as opposed to ideological contributions designed to modify the business climate within Congress. Moreover, it reinforces Clawson et al.'s contention that a legislator's party is less important than his or her policy positions (1992:114). Alternatively, the negative coefficients for incumbency fly in the face of our expectations. Possibly, given Democratic control of Congress during the years under study, the negative sign for incumbency might indicate support for Republican challengers—an "ideological" contribution pattern (Clawson et al. 1992:130). Our concluding analysis points to a Democratic-Republican split over this piece of legislation. Thus, the contradictory regression coefficients for party and incumbency might indicate both access and ideological giving, though they do not of themselves indicate targeting.

Second, the coefficients for banking committee membership became consistently smaller across time. However, the signs associated with these estimates are not as straightforward as they appear. As seen in the margins of Tables 5.3a and 5.3b, in the 1981–1982 period, banking committee membership is associated with lower mean PAC contributions than those received by legislators not on the banking committee. In other words, banking committee membership apparently stands in a *negative* relation to contributions. We confirmed this relationship by a correlation analysis that yielded $R = -0.017$ ($p = .001$) in the Senate and $R = -0.012$ ($p = .0001$) in the House. This implies that although contributions to banking committee members were, on average, lower than to other legislators, when committee membership is placed in an equation in which other factors affecting contribution amounts are controlled for, committee membership had a slightly positive effect—at least until the 1991–1992 period. Additionally, consistent with the notion that PACs associated with the finance industry dispersed their contributions across Congress, rather than targeting a few key senators, in the 1981–1982 period the coefficients for banking committee membership were about half as large as in the 1977–1978 period. As the finance industry increased its average donation level, banking committee members, along with the rest of Congress, received higher donations; thus, banking committee membership had a smaller coefficient. The declining coefficients might indicate a general increase in the number of legislators receiving finance industry contributions. By the time we get to the 1991–1992 period, banking committee membership becomes almost meaningless.

Finally, the coefficients for the variables tapping into the sector of the finance industry the PACs represented (commercial banks and S&Ls) are the most challenging to interpret. Although they remained negative across all three periods (all but one of the industry coefficients were negative in both branches of Congress), the coefficient for commercial bank donations in the Senate increased from 1977–1978 period (−3.20) to the 1981–1982 period (−2.2), and then decreased again to the 1991–1992 period (−2.53); S&L contributions to the Senate were the exact opposite from those of commercial banks, decreasing from −2.26 to −3.78, then increasing to −3.28. However, because the first S&L Senate coefficient is not significant ($p = .17$), we cannot be certain that there was a decrease in the first period. If it did not actually decrease, this would be consistent with the change in commercial bank contributions to the Senate and the changes in the coefficients for both S&Ls and commercial banks in the House during the 1977–1978 to 1981–1982 period.

Overall, the coefficient for contributions in the House increased across the time periods we studied. Once again, this is consistent with our examination of hypothesis 2, in which we noted an overall increase by finance industry PACs across the House of Representatives. However, with the exception of commercial bank contributions to the Senate, the commercial and S&L coefficients continued to increase following passage of the Garn–St. Germain Act. In other words, it is possible that the 1977–1978 to 1981–1982 increase was part of a more general increase in commercial bank and S&L contributions that was reflected in the increasing coefficients—not targeting of the 1981–1982 period. Moreover, that the coefficient for committee membership decreased during this period also undermines the notion that commercial banks or S&Ls singled out these representatives for special treatment.

DISCUSSION

The regression analysis did not directly support hypothesis 3 in the manner the literature would lead one to expect. It did, however, give some indication of the role PAC contributions play in the political process. Though the industry coefficients increased across time, party and incumbency—the two variables not included in our notion of targeting—proved to be equally strong predictors of contributions. Banking committee membership, with its declining coefficients, provided the least support for targeting. Our understanding of targeting specified, at the most basic level, that PACs associated with the finance industry would give more to banking committee members than others, PACs from other industries would give more to other legislators and candidates, and that donation patterns of this sort would increase in the period surrounding debate and passage of finance industry legislation. The combined findings of all three hypotheses throw this simple understanding of targeting into doubt and create a picture that suggests that rather than continuing to study PAC donation patterns based on the unexamined assumption of their importance, it is essential for the political researcher to specify the conditions under which PACs are, and may not be, an important political resource.

This study raises a number of issues about the conditions under which PACs may be used to shape legislation. First, the continued strength of party and incumbency suggest it is more sensible to interpret PAC donations as a resource designed to gain access to legislators, rather than as a targeting designed to directly influence committee members, as Makinson's research suggested. Additionally, although banks may be the most central nodes in webs of interlocking directorates, bank affiliation is not necessarily a better predictor of PAC contributions than party and incumbency. Second, we saw a *declining* relationship between banking committee membership and contributions, with the committee membership becoming possibly less significant over time. Finally, contribution patterns in the House differed dramatically from those in the Senate across all three hypotheses. We examine these observations in order.

First, the importance of party and incumbency as independent variables underscores the notion that PAC donations are less about targeting particular legislators than about supporting all legislators to whom you need access, or with whom you agree ideologically. Clawson et al. (1992) elaborated at length the nontargeting aspects of PAC contributions in their qualitative analysis of corporate PAC directors. They argued that most PAC donations are pragmatic in the sense that they are given to provide their lobbyists access to a member of Congress so that they can get their side of issues heard (p. 12). Thus, corporate PACs donate to legislators irrespective of the legislator's need or larger political vision. We saw evidence for this pragmatic style of giving in hypothesis 2, where the entire House received markedly increased donations in the 1981–1982 period from PACs associated with the finance industry, though the regression coefficients for banking committee membership actually declined. As Clawson et al. note, PAC directors do not feel that their donations buy votes:

> Virtually all [PAC officers of] access-oriented PACs went out of their way at some point in the interview to make it clear that they do not and could not buy a member's vote on any significant issue. No corporate official felt otherwise. . . . They pointed out that the maximum legal donation is

$5,000 per candidate per election. Given that in 1988 the cost of an average House seat was $388,000 and for the Senate $3,745,000, no individual corporation can make a difference. . . . Most PACs therefore feel they have little influence. (p. 90)

If you cannot directly purchase legislation, then targeting is not a useful strategy. Thus, given the importance of access over targeting, incumbency, with Democrats as the majority party, becomes a significant predictor of donation patterns.

Second, Mintz and Schwartz's (1985) interlocking directorates research and Makinson's (1992) statistics on committee membership and PAC donations provided much of the foundation of our first two targeting hypotheses. The idea that PAC donations work in a less direct—more contextual or structural—manner than the PAC literature had led us to expect gets at the question of banks as central nodes in webs of interlocking directorates and addresses our second finding regarding the decreasing relation between banking committee membership and mean contributions. In accord with the access understanding of PAC donations, the decreasing relation between contributions to banking committee membership, and the fact that in no year did banking committee members receive significantly more than non–committee members from PACs associated with the finance industry, seem to indicate that rather than targeting, finance industry PACs worked to ensure access to as many members of the entire Congress as possible; when the time to debate crucial legislation came, they spread their limited PAC money out as far as they could. This is seen most strongly in the changes in the coefficients of banking committee members in the regression equation, and in Tables 5.5b and 5.6b showing the changes in PAC donations in the House. That finance industry PACs, the most central players in the interlocking web of corporate directorates, did not target their donations leads us to a third and final question: What other resources did the finance industry, and banks in particular, bring to bear on the banking committees in particular, and political process in general?

This question can be best addressed by examining how and why Senate PAC donations were so different from those in the House for all three hypotheses. If we turn to the actual processes that created the Garn–St. Germain Act, we can better understand the split in PAC donations between the House and the Senate, and can thereby place the legislative success of the banking industry in this larger, historical-structural context.

The Garn–St. Germain Act was not Congress's first attempt to stop the decline of the S&L industry. Despite passage of the 1980 Depository Institutions Deregulation and Monetary Control Act, the S&L industry continued to falter. The administration and the two branches of Congress proffered different solutions to the (industry defined) crisis. The Reagan administration recommended that Congress let banks provide interstate banking free of the then-current intrastate restrictions. To this end, Treasury Secretary Regan outlined a deregulatory proposal that would let banks move into securities underwriting, remove many distinctions between S&Ls and thrifts, and authorize interstate banking (*New York Times* 19 September 1981:29, 26 December 1981:23). Though smaller banks and others opposed to interstate banking, including Senate Banking Committee chairman Garn, prepared for battle, Garn was not philosophically opposed to deregulation of other facets of the industry (*New York Times* 31 December 1980:1, 2 March 1981:D2). Actually, citing a "revolution" in the financial services industry that would make the different branches of the industry (i.e., commercial banks, S&Ls, securities, etc.) unnecessary, Garn offered a bill that the Treasury Department supported placing depository institutions into direct competition with the securities industry (money market mutual funds offered by securities firms were widely held as the depository institution's primary competitors for deposits and thus the cause of the S&Ls' downfall) (*New York Times* 8 October 1981:D11, 20 October 1981:D2). In other words, the administration and the Senate Banking Committee were in general agreement with the larger commercial banks that the federal government should use market-based solutions to the S&L dilemma. As we see in the current rash of bank mergers, solutions contingent upon the operation of "market forces" favor the larger competitors.

Alternatively, the House Banking Committee was more inclined to give the S&L industry direct support. The House committee worked under the S&L industry–created premise that this branch of the banking industry was a friend to the common American; S&Ls had historically provided affordable mortgages to working-class Americans when all other branches of the finance industry had turned their backs on them. Throughout the legislative process, the U.S. League (an S&L organization) and the National Association of Mutual Savings Banks lobbied House Banking Committee head St. Germain for federal aid for institutions burdened with long-term housing mortgages slowly being repaid at rates much lower than the market (*New York Times* 21 January 1982:D13; see also 28 February:C6, 1 March:D1). S&Ls favored a net-worth guarantee committing public funds to an accounting scheme that raised all institutions to a certain level of capital. While the thrift industry sought large-scale federal aid, the Reagan administration had decided to limit aid to small, informal measures (*New York Times* 27 July 1981:D1). Thus, it was over the opposition of St. Germain that the Reagan administration rejected a bank regulator's plan to deal with thrifts' short-term problems and instead offered industry deregulation (*New York*

Times 5 August 1981:D13). Treasury Secretary Regan announced that the Reagan administration opposed adopting specific thrift industry aid measures (*New York Times* 29 April 1981:D1). According to the Treasury, S&Ls were not in "serious danger." General administrative economic reforms, such as lowering the interest rates that made the market-based funds offered by securities companies so competitive, would be sufficient to rescue the thrifts. Failing that, Treasury Secretary Regan offered Treasury and Federal Reserve funds as support for the FSLIC and FDIC (*New York Times* 3 May 1981:D2, 6 March:D1, 24 March:D6).

Following intensive lobbying from the thrift industry and fearing having to bear the blame for the failure of the thrift industry, Congress authorized banks and S&Ls to offer one-year, tax-exempt savings certificates (*New York Times* 23 June 1981:D1, 24 June 1981:D1, 25 June 1981:D14, 29 June 1981:D1). This program proved so popular and profitable that the S&L industry mounted another drive, this time unsuccessful, to receive congressional permission to continue the program past the end of 1982 (*New York Times* 14 September 1982:D1, 27 September:D2). That the S&Ls successfully lobbied at one point for one measure, and shortly after lobbied unsuccessfully for the same measure points to the *varying effectiveness of corporate political resources*.

The House approved a bill setting temporary guidelines for mergers to aid ailing thrifts, *which St. Germain threatened to kill if the Senate altered it* (*New York Times* 29 October 1981:D13). Early in 1982, S&Ls began to see full-fledged bailout proposals coming from Congress and other sources (*New York Times* 24 February 1982:D2). St. Germain offered a bill to provide $7.5 billion to ailing thrifts (*New York Times* 23 February 1982:D6). The House Banking Committee, split on party lines, approved the St. Germain bill to create an $8.5 billion Treasury-backed fund guaranteeing the net worth of failing depository institutions (*New York Times* 12 May 1982:D1). This proposal became the Garn–St. Germain Act of 1982; its cash outlay was in the form of promissory notes designed to bolster the net worth of the depository institution holding them (a "networth guarantee") (*New York Times* 15 May 1982:44, 21 May 1982:D1).

To explain the different PAC donation patterns in the House and the Senate, we needed to explore the actual positions of the House and Senate. What we saw, in partial explanation of the increased S&L PAC coefficients in the House (from -3.05 to -2.11), was strong support in the House for the S&L's position, and much weaker support in the Senate and the administration. Was House support a consequence of increased finance industry PAC donations, or did House support create increased donations? We cannot tell—though we may note that the coefficient continued to increase up until the most current period (-1.34). Given that we have argued that PAC donations are a resource through which corporate donors gain access to legislators, it would seem in this case that PACs may have made it possible for S&Ls to get their side heard outside the public debates that are part of the legislative record. But this is certainly only a small part of the entire, structurally embedded policy process.

We argue that the debate among the administration, branches of Congress, regulators, and the industry occurred within a particular structural context formed by policy precedents established both through processes of bank hegemony and within an ongoing federal deregulatory movement. First, though some observers in both the state and the industry viewed the Garn–St. Germain Act as a bailout for the industry (and thus a departure from the state's preferred laissez-faire role), most legislators, wishing to distance themselves from previous policies that amounted to corporate welfare, characterized the legislation as simply a continuation of the role the state has always played in the S&L industry (and thus not a bailout). Some congresspersons took great pains to make tortured and largely unconvincing assertions that the net-worth provision in the Garn–St. Germain Act was not a bailout (see, for example, U.S. Congress: House 1982:928–29).

Second, in addition to the strong bailout precedent, Congress also labored under the historic relation between the state and the S&L industry. As illustrated above, S&Ls' federally mandated role as providers of low-cost mortgage money meant S&Ls had historically received the benefit of pro-S&L federal intervention. This relationship between the state and the S&Ls included federal controls on deposit interest rates, and a rate differential enabling S&Ls to attract more deposits than other branches of the finance industry. Finally, deregulation was the "obvious" solution for Congress to choose given the ongoing federal deregulatory movement. Deregulation was, and in some cases remains, the prevailing solution to the underlying weakness of the U.S. economy. Before 1982, Congress had deregulated the airline, natural gas, over-the-road trucking, and telecommunication industries. It is within the context created by these three structural factors that the 1982 act was enacted. In other words, rather than the Garn–St. Germain Act being a dramatic step that created a new structure of relations between the state and the industry, this bailout, along with prior bank-negotiated bailouts of other finance industry investments, the historic relation between the state and S&Ls, and a larger federal deregulatory movement, was built upon an ongoing structure of relations. Given these structural filters, alternatives to deregulation and bailout were not considered.

What does all this mean then about the role PACs play in the legislative process? We interpret these findings as consistent with the theoretical perspective we developed earlier in our analysis. That is, Clawson et al. are correct in their analysis that PACs are not about "buying" legislation; they are about buying access to congresspersons to influence their perspectives for policymaking. Bank PACs do not target members of the House and Senate Banking Committees because they already have access to those members: those committees routinely seek out testimony from banking community representatives for analysis of issues and problems and for input into legislative creation. Therefore, banks do not need to use PAC donations to purchase access to the members of these committees. Additionally, banks fully understand that important bills affecting the banking community must eventually be presented to and passed by the entire Congress, not just by the banking committees. It is therefore necessary to buy access to non–committee members, since they will not necessarily hear the banks' testimony given before the banking committees.

In sum, business dominance theorists are correct to point to PACs as important resources for corporations to influence legislation in general. But the assumption underlying their research—that corporate PAC donations are somehow converted into desired legislation—does not stand. Rather, PACs operate as one of many resources that shaped bank deregulation and the S&L bailout. Notably, too, while business dominance theorists may analyze PACs in an investigation of policy creation, they do not typically examine policy implementation. Our analysis traces both policy creation and implementation; the implementation phase of state policy is one place where PACs would appear to have limited influence. In the case of the legislation examined here, the dialectics of finance capital in the process of the state project of economic intervention played a more compelling role in the development of policy.

6

Too Big to Fail?
A Tale of Two Banks

Although Congress bailed out the S&L industry, thrifts were not alone in their crises touched off by deregulation and overheated real estate speculation and leveraged buyout investments. Commercial banks, the banking sector that more commonly participated in real estate and stock and bond speculation and investment, found itself beset by crises similar to those plaguing the thrifts. The commercial banks' crises differed from those of the S&L institutions in that commercial banks did not suffer the contradictions of high-interest-rate payouts on deposits and low-interest-rate receipts on old mortgages. But deregulation fostered a banking environment of little or no oversight, encouraging speculative investments that were highly risky even for commercial banks. And in the absence of regulatory oversight, the ravages of the bottom falling out of real estate markets in the late 1980s and the collapse of the junk bond market seriously hurt many commercial banks as they did the thrifts.

Yet Congress did not bail out the entire commercial bank industry as it did the S&Ls. Instead, some banks received federal bailout assistance, others were allowed to quietly fail, and still others were forced to involuntarily shut down operations quickly. What distinguishes these bank crises such that they receive differential application of the bailout process?

Some analysts acknowledge that *size* of corporation may differentiate capitalist interests (see, for example, Weinstein 1968; Glasberg 1989), and others recognize that *type* of corporation may differentiate these (see, for example, Glasberg 1989). However, in the case of bank closings, type of corporation is a less important variable: while there are certainly different kinds of banks, all corporations involved are financial institutions. Does the type of financial institution make a difference here? Did S&L institutions receive preferential treatment over commercial banks because of the bailout legislation? Is size of bank still a differentiating factor here? Officials in the Treasury Department, the Federal Reserve Board, and the FDIC publicly insisted that they applied a "too big to fail" rule of thumb to determine which banks to bail out and which ones to let die, or force to die. Or did they?

Might there be other factors (besides size) explaining why some banks are forced to shut down and others are bailed out? A comparative analysis of two commercial banks which differed in size as well as the characteristics of their constituents enables us to begin to unpackage the processes that affect the implementation of the bailout as a state project, and to explore the factors, beyond simple economics, that might contour state projects.

BANK OF NEW ENGLAND

The Bank of New England was worth $23 billion, and provided corporate loans and home mortgages for middle-income and wealthy suburban families. It participated in the huge lending consortia providing loans to developing countries. And it was an acquisitive conglomerate, enjoying the freedoms accorded such financial institutions by the Garn–St. Germain Act of 1982, which deregulated the industry. Scores of large banks, corporations, wealthy New England families, and municipalities deposited their money in BNE. Between 1987 and 1991 BNE tripled in size and began to speculate heavily in real estate: by the time of its closing in 1991, 38 percent of its assets were in real estate loans (U.S. Congress: House 1991b:5). By early December 1990, deposits at BNE declined 21 percent and its assets had shrunk from $32 billion to $22 billion (U.S. Congress: House 1991b:61). The bank reported losses of $1 billion for 1989, a loss of approximately 4.3 percent of its net worth (U.S. Congress: House 1991b:5, 85). The posted loss at Bank of New England prompted rumors among nervous New Englanders about a bank failure. The Treasury Department responded by depositing $1.8 billion in tax receipts and operating cash for the Treasury's account at BNE. That deposit meant that the Treasury account alone comprised over 10 percent of BNE's total of $18 billion in deposits. Such large deposits were uninsured by strict application of the FDIC's limit of insurance to $100,000 (U.S. Congress: House 1991b:86–87).

Amid criticisms of favoritism, the Treasury maintained that such deposits were not unusual: nearly three thousand banks throughout the United States hold Treasury deposits of payroll tax receipts from employers' withholdings and corporate tax payments (U.S. Congress: House 1991b:85). However, a spokeswoman for the comptroller of the currency offered that "a valid question should be whether these funds should go into a bank with potentially significant problems" (*Hartford Courant* 1991a). Senator Donald W. Riegle, Jr., chairman of the Senate Banking Committee, was more pointed in his criticism of using Treasury tax receipts to shore up an ailing bank: "[T]his is putting taxpayers at risk," because it creates the false image of a healthy bank and because any subsequent failure of the bank would prompt an even bigger federal bailout (ibid.).

Indeed, a House financial institution subcommittee report noted that BNE was insolvent as early as June 30, 1990, an assessment vehemently denied by BNE officials (U.S. Congress: House 1991b:105). The House report, however, insisted that federal regulators had been too liberal in valuating BNE's assets, particularly in their inclusion of the market value of the bank's insurance. When the insurance was excluded, the House report discovered that as of June 30, 1990, BNE had $21.105 billion in assets and $21.164 billion in liabilities, making the bank insolvent with a negative net worth. According to an earlier agreement with federal regulators following a $1.1 billion loss in 1989, BNE was required to maintain a 3 percent net worth (U.S. Congress: House 1991b:60–61, 74–77, 86, 136–41).

There were other disturbing indicators of BNE's serious condition. The ratio of its nonperforming assets to total loans was 13 percent, which was nearly ten times the value of shareholders' equity. Its ratio of capital to assets was less than 2 percent; federal regulations require a ratio of at least 3 percent (U.S. Congress: House 1991a:86). Its stock price steadily fell from $25 per share in early 1989 to $0.50 per share by the time of its federal takeover in January 1991. It also had almost $6 billion in delinquent loans, much of it in commercial real estate (U.S. Congress: House 1991c:42, 138).

BNE officials apparently knew of the bank's deepening crisis early in 1989, but according to a Securities and Exchange Commission complaint, had "'knowingly and recklessly' understated its allowance for loan- and lease-loss provisions in the third quarter of 1989" (*Hartford Courant* 1990d). As a result, its stockholders were taken by complete surprise when BNE announced the $1.1 billion loss for the year. Those same stockholders, however, still received a dividend payout from BNE after that announcement (U.S. Congress: House 1991b:5).

By all accounting standards, BNE was a failed bank. Yet most observers remained unconcerned, because BNE was considered "too big to fail," but that insouciance was ill-placed, because BNE was considered by many to be the leading edge of future bank troubles: its failure was presumed to be the first domino in bank runs by nervous customers at other banks throughout the region, prompting a "devastating economic impact" on the region (U.S. Congress: House 1991b:27–28).

In an effort to rescue the bank, BNE entered into negotiations (which later collapsed) with bondholders in late December 1990 to exchange $705 million in debt for 92 percent equity in BNE's common stock. In addition, the bondholders wanted two new senior secured debt issues totalling $100 million. While these issues would not pay interest, they

could be redeemed in five years for cash or more stock. Such an arrangement would raise BNE's capital-assets ratio to the required level of 3
percent (U.S. Congress: House 1991a:79). Despite the promise for recovery such an agreement posed, observers agreed that it would simply be
a temporary bandaid, since the bank's primary problem was its proportion of nonperforming loans, which had climbed to $2.84 billion by
September 30 (U.S. Congress: House 1991a:79). BNE clearly shared the
critical problem of precarious real estate loans in bad times suffered by
many banks, including Freedom National Bank.

In an effort to reduce some of its liabilities, BNE sold twenty-two
branches of its Rhode Island subsidiary to Citizens Bank of Providence
for $75 million (U.S. Congress: House 1991a:79). Ironically, the next day
Governor Bruce G. Sundlun of Rhode Island ordered the closing of
forty-five financial institutions insured by Rhode Island Share and Deposit Indemnity Corp. (RISDIC), a private insurer that was nearly broke
itself (U.S. Congress: House 1991b:45). Nevertheless, BNE continued its
slide, posting a $450 million fourth-quarter 1990 loss (p. 13). The an-
nouncement caused the bank's bondholders to withdraw their proposed
debt-to-equity swap with the bank. Rumors and predictions for a federal
bailout of BNE began to circulate. Said one analyst, "This may be the
knockout punch for the Bank of New England. . . . In my opinion, the
company won't be resuscitated without government action" (*Hartford
Courant* 1991i).

The bank's imminent collapse provoked renewed debate over the
FDIC's concept that a bank could be too big to fail. According to this
concept, implemented in 1984 when Continental Illinois National Bank
failed, the regulators determined that certain banks are too vital to the
economy to be allowed to go bankrupt, whether they were insured or
not. The larger banks typically did business with major corporations and
wealthier families, invested in commercial real estate, and had large
investors. More importantly, larger commercial banks typically deposited substantial amounts of money in other large commercial banks. In
fact, at BNE, large interbank depositors constituted "the largest single
group" of depositors with accounts exceeding the $100,000 insured limit
(U.S. Congress: House 1991b:13). Smaller banks, which have never benefited from the concept of too big to fail typically provided small business loans and residential mortgages, and drew their deposits from
moderate-income families and small investors. And they were not the
recipients of large interbank deposits. FDIC chairman L. William Seidman admitted that regulators were treating cases differentially at a congressional hearing in December when he testified that "it's unfair that
we are treating small banks badly and differently than big banks" (ibid.).
Yet regulators continued to do just that.

On January 6, 1991, the FDIC seized BNE, providing $750 million to bolster the bank's financial health, and guaranteeing all deposits, including those valued at over $100,000. Seidman estimated the bank's uninsured accounts to total more than $2 billion. Many of these larger accounts were business and interbank deposits. Moreover, the FDIC decided to protect $55 million in deposits in BNE's offshore branches, despite the fact that BNE had not paid to insure those deposits, and such protection is not legally authorized. Only $7.4 million of that total came from individual European customers; the remainder came primarily from American commercial banks, corporations, and institutions (pp. 11, 33).

Federal regulators worried that failure to protect these accounts would hurt the region's economy (pp. 13, 28). Therefore, the FDIC applied the too large to fail concept once again. Apparently, too large to fail meant that a bank's customers were large banks and corporate customers; banks servicing small business, local community, and moderate-income families were not large enough, even if they were the only bank serving a particular community, and even if their loss would have a severe impact on that community. Seidman argued that the FDIC chose to take over BNE and protect even its very large deposits, many of which were corporations, other banks, charities, and municipalities. Failure to cover these deposits, in Seidman's view, would have rippled throughout the economy and caused more bank failures around the country (pp. 13, 28, 44). Seidman also defended the takeover as the solution with the lowest cost to the FDIC and as the most supportive of stability to the New England and national banking systems. The price of this "lowest-cost" solution was expected to be $2.3 billion, making it one of the most expensive bank bailouts in the United States (pp. 52, 82).

The federal takeover of BNE meant that the bank would be restructured into a new "bridge bank," which, as mandated in 1987 by law, could function for up to three years while a buyer was sought. The bridge bank is run by a five-person board of directors appointed by the FDIC. BNE's restructuring bailout was the eighth time the FDIC created a bridge bank (*Hartford Courant* 7 January 1991:A6; *New York Times* 7 January 1991:D8). The federal protection accorded all depositors, including the uninsured, large commercial banks, municipalities, the state of Connecticut treasury, and many major corporations (including Ames Dept. Stores, Inc., Cigna Corp., Heublein Inc., and United Technologies Corp.) caused these depositors to decide to keep their deposits at BNE's Connecticut subsidiary, Connecticut Bank and Trust (*Hartford Courant* 1991f).

Interestingly enough, the FDIC even retained the bank's management, the same management that oversaw BNE's continued slide. When asked why the bank was allowed to continue doing business, and why management was retained, Seidman said, "We thought . . . management was in there doing an effective job" (*Hartford Courant* 7 January 1991:A6). Yet Robert L. Clarke, comptroller of the currency, conceded that his examiners noticed problems with how BNE was lending money as early as 1987, and his office notified the bank's managers (U.S. Congress: House 1991b:24). Said Clarke, "[M]ost of the banks that we have those kinds of conversations with respond to what we tell them to do. This bank did not respond as well as we would have liked as early as we would have liked." The bank continued to do business as usual until the takeover and bailout, at which time Clarke admitted, "In retrospect, I think it would have been appropriate to get more aggressive in eliciting that response" (p. 48). Such an admission makes the retention of the bank's management all the more curious.

The protection given depositors and management was not extended to BNE's shareholders. They lost their entire investment in the bank. Bondholders, on the other hand, would share the profits of the bank's sale, estimated to be $40 million, with the FDIC (*Hartford Courant* 7 January 1991:A1). Shareholders are a group all three theories of the state identify as a favored group in such bailouts, yet even they suffered a significant loss in the sale of the bank.

The FDIC's announcement that all deposits, large and small, would be protected and guaranteed and its encouragement to nervous municipalities, corporate customers, and individuals alike to maintain their deposits with the bank prevented a run on the bank and allowed BNE to continue operating and serving its largely white, middle-class, corporate, and municipal customers. Noted Rep. Henry B. Gonzalez, chairman of the House Committee on Banking, Finance and Urban Affairs, "At the Bank of New England, the wealthy depositors with more than $100,000 were warmly received by the FDIC and assured they would get every dime plus interest, courtesy of the Federal insurance funds" should the bank fail (U.S. Congress; House 1991a:4).

Meanwhile, the FDIC began to accept bids from other banks to purchase the newly restructured BNE. Eventually, BankAmerica Corp. of San Francisco, Bank One Corp. of Columbus, Ohio, and Fleet/Norstar Financial Group of Providence offered bids for the bank (*Hartford Courant* 1991b). BankAmerica, parent company of Bank of America, had 1,296 branches in seven western states (ibid.). Bank One, which had previously purchased the troubled MCorp in Texas in 1989, did business in six midwestern and southwestern states. Fleet was the only bidder with existing branches in Connecticut, but its headquarters was in Rhode Island (*Hartford Courant* 1991h). The FDIC takeover made BNE an attractive purchase since any buyer "would be purchasing institutions with virtually clean portfolios because the FDIC would absorb most or all of the bad loans" (*Hartford Courant* 1991b). This should make it easier to sell the bank, thereby enabling BNE to emerge restructured into a healthier institution.

The big winner in the bidding war was Fleet/Norstar. Fleet acquired BNE in April 1991 for $625 million. The cost to the FDIC (and taxpayers) was $2.5 billion. What did Fleet get for their money? They got 320 branches of BNE banks in three states, 12,000 employees (many of whom would have to be laid off as Fleet closed down BNE branches that were located too close to existing Fleet branches), and $16 billion in deposits. What they did not get was $5 billion in bad loans from BNE (*Wall Street Journal* 1991).

However, the differential treatment accorded banks by the FDIC in addressing their crises continued to anger legislators. Some congresspersons expressed concern with the fact that the bidders for BNE were out-of-state banks. They detested the idea of "the steady erosion of banking powers away from our community toward the city [or toward another state], which further removes any sort of local sensitivity, any sense of local priorities, any sense of what is good for the local economy, steadily taking away local authority" (U.S. Congress: House 1991b:38). They speculated that the banks likely to take over BNE were perhaps the same big, nonlocal banks supported by the FDIC because they were too big to fail. Rep. Carroll Hubbard, Jr., of rural Kentucky continued to take issue with the principle of too big to fail: "Do you know of any banks in my district that are too big to fail?" (p. 19). Seidman agreed that he doubted there were. House Banking Committee Chairman Henry B. Gonzalez complained about the consequences of the concept in which major corporations and institutions are protected at the expense of small depositors at small banks: "Deposit insurance should be operated solely for its real purpose: the protection of ordinary depositors . . . regardless of size and regardless of the intent of the law" (*Hartford Courant* 1991g). 0Many congresspersons groused about how "the big boys in Boston got their money while [the] lawmakers' constituents often did not" (*Hartford Courant* 1991c). Certainly, the constituents in Harlem, Bedford-Stuyvesant, and Fort Green in New York City, communities serviced by Freedom National Bank, did not get theirs. The federal regulators' response to Freedom National's financial troubles contrasts sharply with its reaction to the Bank of New England just one month later.

FREEDOM NATIONAL BANK

Freedom National Bank in Harlem, New York, was closed by federal regulators on November 9, 1990, as a result of mounting losses on outstanding loans. Freedom National was the fourth largest U.S. bank owned by African-Americans, and New York City's sole minority-owned commercial bank, worth an estimated $121 million at the time of its demise (*Time* 1990). It was founded in the political consciousness of the civil rights movement in 1964 by a group of African-American and Jewish investors organized by Jackie Robinson, the first African-American professional baseball player to break that sport's color barrier (U.S. Congress: House 1990e:1–2).

Freedom National's mission was to provide investment capital for poor and minority communities' projects and for mortgages and development. These are the very communities and customers that white commercial banks have traditionally shunned as bad risks, despite Community Reinvestment Act stipulations mandating such investments (pp. 5, 17–19, 24). After decades of bank redlining and disinvestment in the city's largest African-American community, Harlem finally had a bank whose activities were devoted to providing small business loans to minority-owned enterprises, low-cost mortgages to low- and moderate-income families, and loans for community-based redevelopment projects in Harlem and elsewhere in the city. For example, Freedom National provided the financing to renovate the historic Apollo Theater, a symbol of Harlem's African-American cultural energy and sophistication (p. 31). Freedom National was also cited as "the only bank in [New York] City that would provide a construction loan to the minority developer involved in Tomkins Avenue," a housing project built by minority construction companies in Bedford Stuyvesant, a largely African-American neighborhood in Brooklyn (pp. 11, 18). And at least six church organizations throughout the city were able to build their churches because of construction loans provided by Freedom National (pp. 24–25). New York City Mayor David Dinkins referred to Freedom National as "the financial backbone of the Harlem community at a time when few other institutions showed much interest in doing business there" (*New York Times* 10 November 1990:B2; see also U.S. Congress: House 1990e:16–17).

Indeed, when asked whether the big commercial banks were complying with their agreements to reinvest in the communities (as stipulated by the Community Reinvestment Act), Chief Charles Joshua of Central Brooklyn Coordinating Council, noted,

> We are urban planners, we help to plan for communities with other agencies and we found that we have been targeting our efforts towards our minority contractors and minority builders so they get a fair share of the action. We found that it is difficult for them to approach these other banks, Manufacturers Hanover and others, Chase and Chemical, in order to get loans in order to build the house. We have a problem, we have a very serious problem. (U.S. Congress: House 1990:24)

And Percy Sutton, a former congressman and now chairman of Inner City Broadcasting, told Congress,

[T]here is something about the color of my skin that limits my ability to have access to capital. If I could tell you what it took me before I was able to buy my first radio station, a visit to 63 lending institutions . . . , rejected over and over again. I had all of the abilities. I had been in the State Assembly . . . , I had been a Borough President, I understood budgets. . . . yet, when I sought a loan, $2 million, they turned me down over and over again. (pp. 33–34)

Thus, while Freedom National's available capital to provide minority communities and projects was certainly relatively small, it did offer access to investment capital that the major commercial banks were unwilling to provide.

Scores of nonprofit organizations and charities addressing the needs of minority, poor, and working-class constituents deposited their money with Freedom National "as an expression of community solidarity" (*Nation* 1991:1). They believed their deposits would greatly contribute to the African-American community's economic independence and empowerment. Turner/Santa Fe Construction Corporation testified that it became a depositor at Freedom National as part of its commitment to affirmative action and equal opportunity: "We felt that by depositing funds here, we were helping the same minority and women owned businesses whom we regularly include in both our companies' projects" (U.S. Congress: House 1990e:14). Together, these charities and community service organizations provided day care, foster care, housing, crime victim assistance, and programs addressing the needs of the elderly (pp. 7–15, 72–73). Freedom National thus became an institutional symbol of local empowerment.

However, Freedom National often tottered on the edge of insolvency. In 1974, for example, the pressures of the national recession forced Freedom National to write off more than 10.5 percent of its $19 million loan portfolio as losses. This prompted a rescue effort by a consortium of eleven major banks who invested almost $4 million in the bank (pp. 73). By the early 1980s, Freedom National was once again recording modest profits, having grown from assets of $35 million to $125 million. Freedom National even opened a branch in Brooklyn's Bedford Stuyvesant (p. 74).

The recovery was short-lived, however. A hostile takeover attempt, coupled with yet another national recession (the effects of which were particularly pronounced in the African-American community) and internal mismanagement, sent Freedom National reeling again. The bank had made several investments that the regulators termed "unsound," costing it nearly $1 million. Moreover, the bank lost money in its high-quality stock investments because it "did not adjust to swings in the stock market after the Wall Street collapse of 1987" (*New York Times* 3

December 1990:B4). Compounding these problems were poor and "unorthodox" record-keeping practices. For example, regulators found that the bank sometimes approved checking account overdrafts to help financially strapped customers avoid defaulting on loans.

These bookkeeping and management problems grew more complicated during a hostile takeover attempt by Travers J. Bell, Jr., who ran the city's only African-American-owned brokerage firm on the New York Stock Exchange. Some members of Freedom National's board considered his attempt an "assault" on the bank, largely because he wanted to divert Freedom National's missions toward more aggressive loans and investments and quicker growth by acquiring smaller banks. Disagreement among Freedom National's board members as to the prudence of Bell's strategy created difficulties for the bank (U.S. Congress: House 1990e:25).

Bell's takeover attempt ultimately failed, but the damage of the internal struggles generated by his threat continued. His holding company had managed to secure three seats on Freedom National's board, giving influence over the bank to people outside the community for the first time in the bank's history. Bell's representatives began to aggressively promote their strategies for the bank's growth. This conflicted with the vision of slow growth, community-based loans, and loans to major U.S. corporations with clear track records supporting affirmative action and nondiscrimination favored by Freedom National's president and its local board members (pp. 21–22). Said one former board member, "in trying to sort out the allegiances, we got distracted from running the bank" (*New York Times* 3 December 1990:B4).

The implication in this analysis of incompetency among Freedom National's managers was challenged in hearings before the House Committee on Banking, Finance, and Urban Affairs. Several witnesses at that hearing argued that Freedom National was no different than the hundreds of other banks and S&L institutions that had become insolvent or were in danger of becoming so in the late 1980s and early 1990s. Isaiah Robinson, Freedom National's last chairman, termed the bank

> an accurate and reliable barometer of the economic conditions of the country. In periods of economic growth and easy credit, Freedom blossomed with a rapid asset growth, increased deposits, high loan production and solid earnings. Conversely, in periods of economic weakness and tight money, Freedom suffered a more accelerated depreciation of assets, deposits, loan defaults and limited earnings. (U.S. Congress: House 1990e:72)

Percy Sutton noted that his own shares in Citibank and Manufacturers Hanover Trust had plunged, but he doubted (and no one in government or the media doubted) that this was caused by the incompetency of the bank's managers. Rather, he attributed it to the recession in the national economy (U.S. Congress: House 1990e:34–35). He questioned why similar declines at Freedom National should be interpreted as incompetency instead of the product of the same national economic dynamics (U.S. Congress: House 1990e:35). William Tatum, the publisher of Amsterdam News in Harlem answered that question noting that such a suggestion of incompetency at Freedom National Bank was cruelly racist:

> [I[t puts doubt in some minds about the abilities of African American people. In all of the controversy around cities and low institutions around the country, I haven't heard one report that suggested that incompetence was a factor. Billions of dollars of debt has been created for the American taxpayer, but no one has said that any of these white bankers were incompetent. They were reckless and they were greedy, but they were never incompetent. (p. 27)

Moreover, the bank's special mission placed it in a unique economic and political tension, which set it apart from large commercial banks serving the needs of white, middle-class, and wealthy customers. Freedom National's constituents and borrowers were precisely the most vulnerable to economic crises of chronic unemployment and underemployment, and therefore frequently unable to maintain mortgage and loan payments. Such a tenuous business base meant that any downturns in the general economy that would irritate or somewhat depress larger, wealthier communities could spell disaster for a bank like Freedom National.

The combined effect of both management and political economic problems sent Freedom National into a tailspin: between 1988 and 1990, the bank recorded $7 million in losses, a loss of approximately 5.4 percent of its net worth (*New York Times* 12 November 1990:B5, 13 November 1990:B3). The situation was aggravated in mid-March 1990, when the Treasury and the Federal Reserve Bank of New York cut their tax and loan receipts deposit accounts at the bank from $15 million to $8 million, a move that observers argued "hastened" the bank's insolvency (*New York Times* 29 January 1991:A1; U.S. Congress: House 1990e:75). Where the Treasury Department had deposited almost $2 billion in tax receipts to help save the Bank of New England, it chose here not only *not* to deposit any more tax receipts but to withdraw significant deposits. The move deepened Freedom National's crisis.

The threatened loss of the city's only African-American-owned bank galvanized a coalition of politicians and African-American religious and business leaders to try to breathe new life into the institution. They struggled over the course of several days to raise the $6 million needed to ward off the bank's imminent federal liquidation, scheduled for 9:00 A.M., November 13, 1990 (U.S. Congress: House 1990e:41–55). By the evening prior to the deadline, the coalition had verbal pledges from investors all around the world for more than $12 million, but they had not yet received formal letters of credit to confirm and document the pledges. The FDIC was not satisfied with the uncertified pledges, and held fast to its 9:00 A.M. deadline.

Testimony given at the House hearings revealed that the struggle to raise the money needed to keep Freedom National alive occurred in an impossible context created by the FDIC and the OCC. The OCC had declared Freedom National insolvent on Friday, November 9, 1990, the Friday before a long holiday weekend for Veterans' Day. Since it was a holiday, all banks would be closed until Tuesday morning, the morning the FDIC and the OCC had agreed was Freedom National's deadline. All efforts by Freedom National's managers and friends to contact potential investors and banks for verification that money was indeed on deposit for Freedom National and ready to be drawn were thus futile. On Tuesday morning, despite impassioned pleading by Freedom National and by Congressman Charles Rangel for an extension of at least a few hours, the FDIC began to settle the bank's accounts and reimburse small depositors' money (p. 42). Harlem Congressman Rangel was furious over the move, and characterized it as, "mean spirited. . . . We needed more time" (*Time* 1990). Congressman Charles Schumer was equally angered over the callous way both the FDIC and the Office of Comptroller of the Currency (OCC) had placed Freedom National in an impossible position. When David A0. Bomgaars of the OCC defended the move to close Freedom National because he felt it could not raise the required capital "in a reasonable amount of time," Schumer fumed:

> What would you define as a reasonable amount of time? This is a group that assembled on Friday evening during a holiday weekend and by all reports, did a damn good job of—considering it was a weekend and everything else—of making real progress. . . . And to say that at 9 that morning everything had to be in place . . . seems unfair, seems unreasonable to any banking institution. . . . [W]hy 3 hours, . . . or even 2 days or 3 days, to say, hey, OK, put up or shut up, wouldn't have been reasonable, wouldn't have been fair, wouldn't have been the least that could have been done? (U.S. Congress: House 1990e:44)

Indeed, other banks have been given greater amounts of time to raise the necessary capital or to find a suitable merger partner. Several banks in the Southwest were granted anywhere from six months to two years to continue operations before being closed. And Freedom National's Robinson pointed to "a bank in downtown Manhattan . . . also found to be insolvent, but . . . is still open and doing business under a conservatorship" (p. 72). In the final analysis, the federal government set an impossible deadline for Freedom National to meet in order to line up potential investors, ensuring the bank's forced closing (p. 93).

The quick move by federal regulators to close Freedom National Bank was inconsistent with their more typical response to failing or insolvent financial institutions. More typically, federal regulators place failing banks into conservatorship for up to a year before liquidating the bank. During this period of conservatorship, depositors with accounts totaling more than $100,000 are given the opportunity to move their money to safer, more solvent institutions to protect their investments. This is because the federal deposit insurance that covers customers' money will only guarantee deposits up to a total of $100,000. Any deposits exceeding that amount run the danger of losing all or a substantial part over that amount. Sometimes, as was the case with the $4.5 billion bailout of Continental Illinois National Bank and Trust Company in 1984, the FDIC will insure all deposits, including those totaling more than $100,000. Such protection was not extended to the large depositors at the African-American-owned Harlem bank.

In the case of Freedom National, many of the charities and nonprofit organizations with such large deposits at the bank discovered that the federal regulators' decision to liquidate the bank meant that they would lose millions of dollars of their deposits. Ironically, these charities assumed their deposits would be safe, since each of them maintained several accounts, none of which exceeded the $100,000 limit. This was because such nonprofit organizations are required by their governmental and private funding agencies to maintain separate accounts for their carefully monitored charitable activities, and to protect their accounts for insurance coverage. Such a strategy turned out to be no protection at all.

For example, Brooklyn's Fort Greene Senior Citizens Council maintained twenty-four separate checking accounts at Freedom National totaling $350,000. However, the FDIC insisted on a strict interpretation of the meaning of the insurance limit, defining it as the total of multiple deposits per single customer and treating each organization as a single customer. The FDIC therefore initially reimbursed the Senior Citizens Council only $100,000. As a result of the losses, the Council was unable to fund its vital community programs, including the daily provision of meals for eight thousand elderly people and the maintenance of day care centers servicing more than two hundred low-income children. In the absence of a full refund of its deposits, the council could not pay its teachers, social workers, and food suppliers, and had to shut down operations by Thanksgiving (U.S. Congress: House 1990e:8).

Some observers question why Freedom National's depositors did not realize that such a strategy was useless; that is, they should have known better. Testimony given to Congress suggests that the nonprofit organizations believed their accounts were different from the types of accounts more commonly found in large commercial banks such as the Bank of New England. In large commercial banks the deposits are typically personal, organizational, or corporate assets, and as such are clearly restricted de jure to $100,000 of insurance coverage (regardless of the number of accounts into which the assets are distributed). In contrast, the deposits of the nonprofit organizations at Freedom National were not organizational assets, but rather accounts of government funds for various projects and services. Grace Harewood, Executive Director of Fort Greene Senior Citizens Council, noted to Congress, "In the case of government funded programs, the Council understood that it served as a principal agent and trustee for the Government funds. At no point did the Council consider these funds to be our assets. We are required to give strict line accounting for the funds" (ibid.). Several other agencies also indicated to Congress their understanding that the accounts were "not our monies, this is public monies that we are entrusted" (p. 11).

Moreover, in contrast to the assurances extended by the FDIC to the large depositors at the Bank of New England, Freedom National's depositors were never notified that their funds were in jeopardy because of the bank's impending closing. Reverend Dr. Philius Nicolos of the Evangelical Crusade of Fishers of Men told Congress that not only had "no one ever told us. I [even] made a deposit personally for the church on Thursday at the bank, about 2 [P.M.], and Friday I hear over the news that the bank is closed" (p. 9, see also pp. 19–20).

Despite the daunting scenario of hardship for the communities and organizations served by the bank, the FDIC shut down Freedom National Bank, citing as its basis for the decision the concept of too big to fail: the Bank of New England is too big and therefore bailed out, but Freedom National is not large enough and therefore must be liquidated. Unfortunately, the concept of too big to fail is not clearly defined. First, hearings before the House Committee on Banking, Finance and Urban Affairs revealed that the FDIC has no written policy or regulation defining a policy of too big to fail, nor are there any memoranda or legislation enunciating such a policy (pp. 61). When asked who makes such determinations, Steven A. Seelig from the FDIC replied that the FDIC's board of directors and William Seidman as its chairman did. It is worth noting that these positions are all political appointments. That such a decision could be made by political appointees on the basis of an ad hoc informal rule of thumb creates a strong potential for personal prejudice and arbitrariness in decision-making at the very least, and political manipulation and racism at worst. Both the Reagan and Bush administrations' hostility to affirmative action efforts were no secret, thus setting a favorable stage for such decision-making to run against Freedom National's favor.

There is evidence that several small banks, some of which were in far worse shape than Freedom National, were saved, suggesting that their

size or importance to the economy could not be construed as the definition of too big to fail. For example, the National Bank of Washington,
which had an offshore branch, was bailed out. Congressman Schumer
castigated the FDIC, arguing that "National Bank of Washington was
hardly an essential institution. . . . [E]ven though it was larger [than
Freedom National], it was a far less important institution to America as a
whole as Freedom National Bank" (pp. 5–7).

Other, smaller minority banks have been bailed out in the past, including the First Woman's Bank. First Woman's Bank "had less capital
than the value of their furniture and fixtures account" (p. 88). Yet the
Superintendent of the FDIC, Muriel Siebert, resisted the FDIC's pressure to close it, saying, "the first woman Superintendent [herself] is not
going to close the First Women's Bank" (ibid). She refused to close it,
and instead got an agreement from clearinghouse banks to send some of
their personnel to help operate the bank and raise the money it needed
to stay solvent. That the same was not done for Freedom National
smacked to many of racism. The fact that the superintendent charged
with closing First Woman's Bank was a woman saved that bank from
being closed. Had that superintendent been a man, it is questionable
whether the bank would have survived.

Such idiosyncracies point to the roots of Freedom National's treatment: the superintendent in charge of overseeing their shutdown was
not a member of a racial minority. Given the historical and racial bias in
these higher circles of American institutions (Dye 1990), the chances of
that happening are remote. An analysis of the social characteristics of
professional employees at key banking regulatory agencies shows that
as recently as 1992, racial minorities represented only 10 percent of such
employees at the Federal Reserve Board, and only 15 percent of such
employees at the FDIC in 1990 (Ullmann 1994:42). Although the category "professional employees" covers a wide range of occupations relative
to authority to make important decisions, these figures are telling in
light of evidence suggesting that the higher one looks in corporate and
governmental hierarchies of authority, the less likely one is to find racial
minorities (U.S. Department of Labor 1991).

Moreover, a 1990 House of Representatives staff report showed that
the Federal Reserve Bank boards of directors lacked diversity: there was
not a single racial minority among more than sixty top positions on the
board, including the Board of Governors and the twelve Federal Reserve
Bank presidents. These are positions that empowered their holders to
greatly affect monetary policy. The staff report pointedly concluded that
"this complete lack of . . . diversity . . . raises the . . . question of how
sensitive the Federal Reserve Board is or can be to the needs of the many
diverse segments of our population" (U.S. Congress: House 1990k:V).

Given Siebert's testimony concerning her motivations in preserving the First Woman's Bank, it would appear that the lack of racial diversity in the Federal Reserve Board introduced institutional bias in Freedom National's closing, shaped by the manner in which banks are defined as worthy of saving or deserving of destruction. That there was no one to share Siebert's perspective relative to minority banks' importance to the communities they serve increases the likelihood that administrators would fail to appreciate its unique role in the community and in the banking industry.

FDIC decisions concerning which banks are too big to fail and which ones are not also has little to do with the cost to the agency of bailing out the bank. The bailout of Continental Illinois Bank in 1984 cost the FDIC $4 billion, of which only $2 billion has been recovered to date. The FDIC negotiated that bailout with Continental Illinois for four to five months while it continued to operate (yet refused to give Freedom National even so much as one day's extension after a holiday weekend to arrange for investors to raise enough money to head off insolvency). Had the FDIC forced Continental Illinois into bankruptcy it would have cost the agency "just under $2 billion" (U.S. Congress: House 1990e:62). In contrast, the closing of Freedom National cost the FDIC $30 million; bailing it out would have cost just $10 million (pp. 62–63). Thus, the notion of too big to fail is not governed by comparative costs to the FDIC of bailing out or closing a given bank.

Even if the notion of too big to fail were consistently governed by size or cost alone, provisions for both the FDIC and the OCC stipulate that minority-owned institutions should be given special consideration in determining their fate, because of the special constituency they serve and the crucial role they play in underserved or redlined communities (p. 60). The failure of both the FDIC and the OCC to extend the deadline they insisted Freedom National had to meet in order to remain open suggests that they did not adhere to this stipulation.

To its credit, the FDIC did try to locate another large bank to acquire Freedom National, but to no avail. Here, large commercial banks appear to have played at least an indirect role hastening Freedom National's demise. The FDIC invited sixty large banks to bid on Freedom National to acquire it. In cases such as this, the FDIC takes the bad assets and only sells the good assets to the acquiring bank, as they had done with the Bank of New England. This means that the acquiring bank buys only the clean assets, thereby enriching its own assets with no risk. Yet all sixty large banks the FDIC talked to declined to bid on Freedom National (p. 42). The FDIC then sought a bank to act as a paying agent while a prospective buyer of Freedom National could be located. A paying agent in effect honors and clears checks written by Freedom National checking account customers, thereby allowing them to continue to write checks.

For Freedom National's nonprofit and charity organizations, this would have meant being able to pay personnel and suppliers, and continue operations such as day care and elder care. For its poor and working-class customers this would have meant being able to pay their bills on time. The FDIC asked five of the largest commercial banks in New York City to act as Freedom National's paying agent, and all five refused (p. 55). Why would the large commercial banks refuse to help Freedom National and its customers continue to do business?

Two years prior to Freedom National's collapse, during its own struggles on its board, its charter had been amended. The testimony given to Congress suggests that the amendment was implemented by the board's new management to attract support from the big commercial banks (p. 25). The amendment, which the big banks forced on Freedom National as the condition for their support, stipulated that should the bank become insolvent, first payment would go to holders of preferred stock, who would be paid the value of their stock as well as any accrued interest. It just so happens that the holders of Freedom National's preferred stock were none other than Chase Manhattan Bank, Citicorp, Manufacturers Hanover Trust, Equitable Life Insurance, and Morgan Community Development Corporation (p. 22). Since, as Percy Sutton had pointed out, the stocks of even the big commercial banks had fallen because of the recession, they stood to benefit more from Freedom National's insolvency than from its bailout. This is because the big banks were positioned to recover their investment plus interest in an insolvency. A bailout would potentially place even the preferred stock at greater risk of declining value due to the stubborn national recession. It was clear that within the financial community, not all financial institutions were equal. The greater power of the big banks enabled them to position themselves more advantageously than Freedom National or its constituents, and to greatly influence the outcome of decisions at a critical point for the minority bank.

Financial institutions, particularly the large commercial banks in New York City, stood to gain a great deal from Freedom National's insolvency. These banks were not interested in obtaining Freedom National's clean assets, because Freedom National's customers were neighborhoods, organizations, and individuals whom the banks had long viewed as undeserving and hence had ignored. The business the banks would have acquired was not of the sort with which the large banks had previously bothered to concern themselves. Thus, one could not argue that the big banks sought to eliminate Freedom National Banks as competition, since they were not competitors. However, the big banks would gain all of the value of their preferred stock plus accrued interest, in effect draining resources from these redlined and "undeserving" neighborhoods, at the same time enriching their own assets. The large financial institutions that held Freedom National's preferred stock were in a position to determine that bank's fate, and chose to refuse to help.

Congressman Schumer noted the implicit racism in the behavior of the larger banks, the FDIC, and the OCC:

> [A]s regulators, we as government officials have sort of an obligation to do a little more for the Freedoms, to go beyond the bureaucratic rules because there are other forces pushing in the other direction. (p. 61)

Congressman Hon. Major R. Ownes was blunter: "What Mr. Schumer is talking about in gentile and polite language is discrimination and racism. . . . Some banks are too big to fail, small banks can go to hell" (ibid.).

Yet despite the protestations of many, including Representative Rangel and New York State Attorney General Robert Abrams, Seidman refused to accept any suggestion that Freedom National was too important to Harlem and New York City's other minority communities to be allowed to fail, or that its loss would have a severe impact on the social and economic systems of those communities. The FDIC insisted it was being quite generous in its ultimate reimbursement of $0.50 on the dollar for large depositors (*New York Times* 30 November 1990:B3).

In essence, the only source of even limited investment capital for minority enterprises and support for poor and working-class community needs had been eliminated in a city known as the world's financial hub. At the very least, the federal government demonstrated insensitivity to the unique and critical role of Freedom National in the community (U.S. Congress: House 1990e:88). Community members saw the bank's demise as "a death in the family" (p. 1). Many were struck by Freedom National's position as a tremendous resource of community empowerment. Earl Dicks, a building manager who had owned shares in the bank since its establishment in 1964, noted, "Freedom's failure was the passing of a neighborhood dream of economic independence" (*New York Times* 3 December 1990:B4). Poet Abiodun was more blunt when he argued that the bank's closing was "a step backward for the empowerment of black people. . . . Freedom Bank is now an enslaved bank" (*New York Times* 12 November 1990:B1).

Was closing Freedom National the only viable option available to the FDIC? The answer, according to testimony given to Congress, was no:

> They could have merged it with a stronger bank; they could have sought out other banks in the community; they could have come in and said we have to put this bank in receivership and protected the deposits of this bank. . . . [F]ormer chairman of the Federal Reserve Andy Brimmer has indicated that 360 banks failed in 1989 and 1990, that the FDIC took the

unusual action of paying off the depositors in only fifteen cases, and three of them are black-owned banks which include our own Freedom Bank. In the other cases they found purchasers. (U.S. Congress: House 1990e:4)

The racial element of differential application of bank bailouts was forcefully articulated by Dr. Wyatt Lee Walker, a pastor at Canaan Baptist Church of Christ and a former chairman of the bank's board: "Had this been a white bank of comparable size and circumstance, the decision to shut its doors would not have been made so precipitously" (*New York Times* 12 November 1990:B1). Isaiah E. Robinson, Freedom National's chairman at the time of its closing, argued, "We had problems, but we're not the only bank with problems . . . , and it seemed discriminatory to us that the regulators moved so fast to close us down" (*New York Times* 3 December 1990:B4). The feelings of many among Freedom National's customers as well as congresspersons were perhaps best summed up by William Tatum, the publisher of the *Amsterdam News*: "Freedom should not have failed. Freedom was pushed" (U.S. Congress: House 1990e:29).

DISCUSSION

The comparative analysis of regulators' differential response to crises in the Bank of New England and Freedom National Bank highlights the factors that can contour the implementation of state projects. Here, race and class issues that are ingrained in the fabric of the American political economy altered the balance of class forces that affected decisions concerning the differential application of the bailout.

Existing theories of the state share a common tendency to treat capitalists themselves as the dominant force in capitalist society, either because of the power of capitalists as agents or the constraining power of the structure of capital. While none of these theories explicitly states that all finance capitalists are the same, none of them specifically identify what factors (other than perhaps size) might cause some finance capitalists or their organizations to benefit more from their influence than others. The differential power of finance capitalists to benefit from corporate welfare policies introduces one element that affects the balance of class forces. Moreover, the size of the bank in question was not the only or even the most important factor influencing whether it would be bailed out or foreclosed. The social characteristics of each bank's constituents appear to have played critical roles in the decision-making processes affecting how bailout legislation was implemented in each case.

The business dominance perspective provides few keys to understanding the differential treatment of these two banks. While large financial interests do dominate state decision-making on many levels, there is no evidence in the analysis here that such interests filled either the important positions in the state or the crucial informational or advisory bodies of the state. In the case of Freedom National, the bank's executives appealed strenuously to the FDIC not to close it down, and later to insure the accounts totaling more than $100,000, to no avail (ultimately, accounts over $100,000 at Freedom National were given $0.50 on the dollar, while those at the Bank of New England were protected in full).

A structuralist explanation suggests at least two expectations concerning the treatment of the two banks.

(1)   The FDIC's bailout process in these cases should have been constrained by previous precedents (Skocpol and Amenta 1986:149). While it is true that the 1984 bailout of Continental Illinois Bank set a precedent for bailing out BNE, that precedent did not constrain the FDIC in its treatment of Freedom National.

(2)   The bailout process should have been a state response to finance capital accumulation problems, a response that advantaged the banks relative to other interests. It is true that BNE's crisis occurred in part because of the collapse of New England's real estate market, a market (particularly the commercial real estate market) in which that bank had heavily speculated. Freedom National also suffered finance capital accumulation crises, in part because of the depressed labor market for racial minorities in the city. Since Freedom National's customers were vulnerable to such economic exigencies, they were unable to maintain their loans. However, the FDIC moved to support the finance capital accumulation crisis at BNE, but not at Freedom National.

The structuralist perspective, then, fails to explain fully the two banks' differential treatment by the FDIC. This is because in neither of the outcomes implied by the structuralist explanation did the FDIC relate consistently to the two banks in the predicted fashion.

A class dialectic analysis suggests that the FDIC mediated the power struggles between the banks on one hand, and labor, consumers, and community interests on the other. In these cases, we should have witnessed labor, community, and consumer interests managing to mobilize their resources to incorporate their interests into the FDIC's policy. In the case of BNE, it is clear that bailing out the bank protected consumers' deposits, supported community and regional economic stability, and preserved jobs and pension funds' security. However, in the case of Freedom National, community and consumer interests, as well as the bank's own interest in survival, were not incorporated into the FDIC decision-making, despite the mobilization of resources. What differentiated the two banks here was the characteristics of their respective depositors. While BNE's major depositors were corporations and governments, Freedom National's were community charities, nonprofit organizations, and working-class families. Freedom National's constituents were unable to mobilize enough resources to constrain or influence the FDIC's discretion in closing down the bank. BNE's corporate, governmental and middle-class constituents did not need to engage in such arduous struggles to elicit protection from the FDIC. Thus, a class dialectic analysis partially explains the differential application of bailout policy here. However, the class dialectic explanation is limited in its inability to explain the racial element in this comparative analysis, unless that variable is subordinated to the variable of class. It is unclear here whether that was in fact the case. Therefore, the class dialectic perspective is only partially useful in explaining these cases.

A contingency perspective provides us with the most useful framework for understanding the different experiences of these two banks. That the financial interests themselves did not equally dominate or benefit from the process of decision-making speaks to the question of the balance of class forces that affect state policies. Here, the financial institutions became the institutional representatives of their respective constituents whose interests and perceived value to the economy apparently took precedence over the finance capital accumulation interests of the banks themselves.

Furthermore, a contingency perspective alerts us to the difference between de jure formal policy and de facto informal implementation. The policy of too big to fail is in fact not a formal policy or statute that has simply been differentially applied; it is an ad hoc informal policy or rule of thumb that is arbitrarily and inconsistently applied. Issues of capital accumulation by the larger financial institutions did not seem to motivate the behavior of the large commercial banks, or of the FDIC or the OCC. Instead, such decision-making and application of an ad hoc rule of thumb appear, at least in the comparative analysis here, to have been influenced by politics as well as class and racial bias.

The differential treatment accorded the two banks also revealed the importance of race and class in the politics of finance affecting the bailout as part of a state project. Freedom National Bank infused limited but much-needed investment capital into New York's African-American community in Harlem, a community that had suffered redlining and disinvestment by banks for decades. Its presence in the community represented local empowerment and solidarity at a time when such empowerment was constantly threatened by federal cutbacks in badly needed programs and municipal cutbacks in services. While the total amount of dollars supplied to the community was indeed small compared to the investment potential of the large commercial banks, the loss of the city's only black-owned financial institution meant that the community was once again dependent on white financial institutions that had a long history of disregard for it and an intransigent refusal to invest there.

In contrast, BNE serviced the needs of mostly white, middle-class New England suburbs, relatively large corporations in the region's cities, and municipal governments (which largely ignored the needs of their poor and minority constituents). Moreover, BNE held large interbank deposits from major commercial banks, and these deposits constituted the majority of its deposit accounts exceeding the $100,000 insured limit. The Treasury Department's willingness to put massive amounts of taxpayers' money at risk to shore up the bank's losses represents BNE's "most favored bank" status, and indicates the Fed's assumption that BNE was too big to fail.

Although Freedom National was quite small compared to BNE in dollar value, it rivaled BNE in community social and political value. To say that BNE was simply too big to fail ignores the historical and structural processes that facilitated the growth of such banks at the same time that they hindered similar growth of banks like Freedom National. Bank deregulation in 1982 enhanced the barrier to entry posed by large banks like BNE to local community-based minority and working-class banks like Freedom National, because it allowed the larger banks to acquire smaller banks and other financial institutions, thereby making it nearly impossible for the small minority banks to compete. Here, the state's policy initiative of bank deregulation in 1982 favored previously advantaged large commercial banks over smaller (and in this case minority-owned) banks. Differential bailout decisions reinforce this.

The decision to bail out BNE but not Freedom National also indicates the role of bank hegemony in altering the balance of class forces created by interbank deposits. The bailout of BNE reinforced the structural hegemony of large commercial banks by providing state subsidies of those banks' risks as customers and as lenders, and by facilitating bank mergers. The contrast between the federal response to BNE and Freedom National suggested that corporate welfare is not uniformly applied to all corporations, even within the same industry. A federal program such as the FDIC, which was originally designed to protect the small depositor, had become a form of corporate welfare advancing large finance capital accumulation interests and, ironically, a weapon against the interests of small depositors. What began as a program to prevent the working class from being victimized by the vagaries of the economy became a patron of the reproduction of past inequalities.

What dimensions, then, differentiated these two cases? Although the evidence does not clearly demonstrate that the race and class of each bank's constituents were the decisive factors motivating the FDIC's decision-making, those factors do stand out as dimensions that distinguish these two cases. Comparative analyses of future bank bailout processes should look for evidence of these dimensions and for patterns that are either consistent or inconsistent with those found here. This will contribute to our ability to determine whether these are, in fact, the influential factors affecting differential application of bank bailout processes.

One question nags in light of the manifest unfairness of the differential treatment of these two banks: How was it possible for such inequity to occur largely unchallenged? Part of the answer has to do with the balance of class forces affected by a national atmosphere of racial politics in the Bush administration. Racial divisions within the working class intensified throughout the 1980s, reducing the possibility of a more widespread and effective organized resistance to the capital accumulation interests that were influencing the bailout process. The infamous Willy Horton ads that Bush's campaign ran set the tone in which thinly veiled racism reemerged as acceptable, setting back decades of progress obtained through struggles by the civil rights movement. That campaign had thrown down a gauntlet to the Democratic party to defend itself against charges that it was the party of racial minorities who were overtaking white Americans. In earlier decades, the Democratic party might have been counted on to attempt to make a major issue out of the iniquitous treatment of Freedom National Bank; but the now racially charged atmosphere of national politics made the Democratic party fearful of being cast as the party of racial minorities (and therefore vulnerable to losing a large proportion of the white electorate). That fear operated as a powerful deterrent to Democratic challenges to the racial dimensions of the politics of finance here.

According to economists' predictions, we can reasonably expect to see more bank crises in the near future. What do these two cases suggest we should look for in future cases in order to develop an explanatory model to consistently explain them all? First, when we attempt to define the meaning of "too big to fail," we should look not only at the characteristics of the banks themselves (large vs. small, commercial bank vs. S&L, regionally important, ownership characteristics), but also at the characteristics of their customers: Are they corporate or governmental depositors and borrowers? Are they big commercial banks making interbank deposits? Are they charities and nonprofit organizations? Are they suburban or urban wealthy, middle-class, working-class, or poor? What is the racial composition of the banks' customers? What are the emerging patterns of criteria the FDIC uses in future cases in defining too big to fail? These questions suggest an examination of the balance of class forces in examining not only de jure policymaking leading to corporate welfare, but also de facto implementation of policy.

CHAPTER

7

Reconceptualizing the Welfare State

Far from being dismantled, the welfare state is very much alive and well in the United States. It is only when we redefine the welfare state as a combination of both social and corporate welfare that we can see the expansion of the welfare state in recent decades. The thrust of the new federalism of the 1980s and 1990s was not to dismantle the welfare state, but simply to shift the emphasis of the welfare state from social to corporate welfare. In essence, particularly in light of the unprecedentedly enormous growth of the federal deficits in the past decade, the new federalism expanded the welfare state, with a heavy emphasis on corporate welfare. This can be seen in the dramatic growth of Department of Defense expenditures over the 1980s, which occurred alongside huge slashes in entitlement and social welfare expenditures (Phillips 1990; Ackerman 1982). Nowhere is the rise of the corporate welfare component of the welfare state more apparent than in the bailout of the S&L industry, wherein the state socialized and subsidized the risks and costs of finance capital investments.

Observers might wonder why Congress took the unprecedented step of bailing out an entire industry (as opposed to a single corporation), when other industries, such as the family farm and the steel industry, while also in crisis were not similarly accorded the help of Congress. Congressional documents suggest that the S&L industry was bailed out because it is part of an industry that controls a unique resource: finance capital. There are no alternatives to access to finance capital. In comparison, there are many alternatives to other industries. If the family farm disappears altogether, the United States can still produce sufficient food: major food producers have been buying up the land of bankrupt small family farms and mass producing processed food products. The steel industry has been consolidated, at times through acquisitions and mergers, and at times through worker buyouts, thereby keeping the plants operating. In other instances, alternative materials can be used, such as aluminum in place of steel. Such is not the case with finance capital. One either accesses finance capital or one goes without it. And without it, not much can happen. Congress fully recognizes this, and therefore agrees to violate the principle of laissez-faire to develop state projects for economic intervention that preserves the banking system. As banking goes, so goes the United States.

Although it is true that larger, commercial banks have certainly been buying up the assets of failed S&L institutions, Congress recognized the danger of allowing too much consolidated control of such a unique and crucial resource. Moreover, Congress remained cognizant of the special market niche served by the S&L institutions: affordable mortgages, a market largely abandoned by the larger commercial banks. And, unlike other industries, the banking industry had previously established a precedent of congressional bailouts of their investments in Chrysler Corporation in the late 1970s and Mexico in the early 1980s. More importantly, the Chrysler bailout produced a quid pro quo wherein Congress agreed to pass bank deregulation legislation if banks agreed to convert substantial amounts of Chrysler's debt to equity. No other industry has ever displayed such ability to set the agenda or to bargain so advantageously with Congress to formulate policy. The Chrysler and Mexico bailouts, and the quid pro quo, were accomplished by the power bank hegemony processes, produced by the banks' collective control of finance capital.

These past precedents set the stage for the bailout of the S&L industry. Other industries did not have this precedent or quid pro quo agreements working on their behalf. Indeed, when individual corporations have been bailed out, such as Chrysler and Lockheed (and over four hundred others since World War II), it has been because of the collective power of the banking community in pressing for the necessary legislation.

Thus, a sociological reconceptualization of the welfare state enables us to appreciate an analysis that, contrary to many analyses in the existing literature as well as in the popular press, the Reagan and Bush administrations did not, in fact, dismantle the welfare state. They did, however, redefine the focus of the welfare state in the United States, from an emphasis on social welfare to an emphasis on corporate welfare.

CORPORATE WELFARE VS. SOCIAL WELFARE PROCESSES

Our findings suggest that we cannot simply assume that processes of social and corporate welfare policy formation are the same. Corporate welfare policy formation is more likely to be attended by participation by powerful corporations, whereas social welfare policy formation is not. The likely exception to this would be the formulation of universal health care policies, which directly affect pharmaceutical and insurance corporations. Indeed, hearings on health care reform in 1995 elicited heated responses from both of these industries. However, processes of social welfare policy formation are generally less likely than corporate welfare policy formation processes to attract such active participation by corporations.

Unlike the hearings attending other bailouts and social welfare policy legislation, bank deregulation and S&L bailout legislation were marked by an imbalance of voices and perspectives. The deregulation and bailout hearings were strongly dominated by representatives of the banking community (including all of its various, often competing elements, such as large commercial banks, S&L institutions, credit unions, small regional banks, and independent banks). Other competing or critical perspectives and voices were rarely included. Indeed, the views of consumer and community groups were marginalized out of these hearings, to be heard before hearings concerning other bills entirely. As a result, the committee responsible for gathering information and formulating the bills heard only a narrow range of perspectives, the vast majority of which reinforced the interests and perspectives of the banking community in general, and the larger commercial banks in particular.

We found that, as anticipated, corporations participated in the development and implementation of corporate welfare policies. Specifically, financial institutions played a major role in the hearings leading to the creation of bank deregulation legislation and, later, legislation bailing out the S&L industry. This is a clear departure from processes and relationships attending the development and implementation of social welfare policies, wherein corporations do not play such pivotal roles. We speculated that it may be that corporations do not generally have much directly at stake in social welfare policies, whereas they certainly do have vested interests in the development of corporate welfare policies. Financial corporations had clear interests in both bank deregulation and S&L bailout legislation.

Our analysis of the S&L bailout highlighted an important difference between corporate and social welfare, a difference that affects not only our sociological conceptualization of the welfare state but also public debate concerning the federal budget and the future of the welfare state. Many of the most expensive corporate welfare programs are defined as off-budget, including the bailout. Thus, when debates occur in Congress concerning which programs to cut, these are not part of the discussion. On the other hand, social welfare expenditures are on-budget, thereby implying that they alone are responsible for budget deficits and thus focusing any debate on deficit reductions on which social welfare programs to cut. Moreover, since they are defined as off-budget, corporate welfare expenditures are not threatened by automatic, across-the-board budget cuts imposed by the Gramm-Rudman Act should Congress fail to meet specified deficit reduction goals. By defining corporate welfare expenditures such as the bailout as off-budget, the new federalism of the 1980s de facto protected that part of the welfare state while appearing to be attempting to reduce the welfare state. That sleight of hand, which continues into the 1990s, obscures the expansion of the welfare state.

It is true that some items that can be construed as at least indirect corporate welfare are on-budget, such as payments on the national debt. But note that these remain politically untouchable and are not included in debates to balance the budget and reduce the deficit. That they could be on-budget but as untouchable as if they were off-budget attests to the power of finance capital to contour the process of the welfare state. More notably, none of the social welfare expenditures are treated as so sacred. Even Social Security, widely considered a social contract, is not immune from debates about cutting expenditures, redefining entitlement, and shifting greater burdens to recipients.

Our analysis illustrates the dynamics of the welfare state. It extends the concept of the welfare state beyond the narrow definition of social welfare. While many scholars acknowledge the benefits to private corporations of social welfare policies and expenditures, none have explicitly investigated the process of corporate welfare or included the concept of corporate welfare in their implicit definitions of the welfare state. Our analysis identifies the dynamics that produced the S&L bailout and suggests those which may operate to generate welfare policies designed directly for corporations.

Moreover, this research reconceptualizes the notion of the welfare state as a process of power involving shifting relative emphases on corporate and social welfare policies and expenditures. This reconceptualization enables us to decipher some of the dynamics that influence that shift. Viewing the welfare state as a power process involving state projects and struggles to shift the line between corporate and social welfare components as part of those state projects offers an opportunity to understand the significance of politics and policies of the past decades. We have seen and continue to witness not so much dismantling the welfare state as a shift in its emphasis from social to corporate welfare.

THEORIES OF THE STATE

Framing the reconceptualization of the welfare state in a contingency theory of the state reveals the welfare state as a dynamic process rather than as a static structure. That process involves historical precedents of state projects and processes of class struggles affecting the mixture between corporate and social welfare over time. Our findings thus reinforce attempts to synthesize theories of the state.

No single case study can support a new grand theory of the state. This is not our intention. Rather, in keeping with the spirit of accommodationism, we have specified at length the conditions under and the extent to which the capitalist state has performed as a capitalist state—in this case by implementing corporate rather than social welfare policies. The "conditions" specified by accommodationism and analyzed below include the structure of the state and its political processes, the institutional inertia of historical trends and settings, and the reciprocally modifying relation between the state and class forces outside the state. The preceding case study examined how political processes and historical context (state project), intra- and interclass activities (balance of class forces), and the structure of the state-industry relation (structural selectivity) created the FIRREA and the FIRREA-AHP, shaped their implementation, and excluded other policy options.

State policy is shaped by a number of conditions. The deregulation and bailout of the S&L industry began within the S&L crisis. In the context of this crisis, and under the province of an ongoing deregulatory state project, the sometimes contentious factions of the banking industry unified to shape the state's imminent response to the crisis. As a consequence of this unity, the banking industry created and defined the powers of the congressional Depository Institution Deregulation Committee (DIDC). However, the DIDC created a new context within which this tenuous intraclass unity dissolved. Given the authority to create their own regulations, representatives of the commercial banks sought to disrupt the structural relation between S&Ls and the state. Once out from under the protection of the state, the S&Ls would fall prey to market forces and the flagging S&L segment of the industry would be absorbed by the commercial banks. [1]

This scenario did not, however, come to pass. The historic, structural relation between the state and the industry shaped both the S&L crisis and, as an expression of the larger deregulatory project, banking deregulation. [2] Beginning with the depression-era Glass-Steagall Act and going through regulation-Q, the state-industry relation was structured to preserve the S&L industry's health through regulatory subsidization of its activities in the housing market. As the state sought solutions to the crisis, the structure of the state-industry relation, in conjunction with the larger deregulatory state project, created policy that contradictorily amplified both the level of investment risk in the banking industry and the level of corporate welfare—the amount of risk the state took on to support the S&L industry. The state had a "public service" relationship with private industry, particularly with those corporations that are too large to fail, which included a de facto bailout policy. The structure created by these forms of corporate welfare precluded either letting the S&L industry fail, or opening it up to the forces of the market. [3]

Contradictorily, this structure did not preclude the inclusion of the Affordable Housing Program on the legislative agenda. As with the creation of the DIDC, discussion surrounding the creation of the FIR-REA and the administration's desire to keep this bailout off-budget spurred intraclass unity—this time among the "noncapitalist" community, labor, and consumer groups. In opposition to the administration and Treasury Department, community groups mobilized or, in the case of the Campaign for Financial Democracy (CFD), were formed to extend the rights of noncapitalist groups using the legislative opportunity the bailout process provided. However, this de jure legislative success met with a later bureaucratic veto. This veto occurred in the context of the same structural relation between the state and the industry that both created the bailout and selected against legislative alternatives that would remove the S&L's regulatory subsidy. Under these conditions, the RTC upheld the state's historic role in supporting the private, for-profit housing market, rather than subvert this market by providing housing to those who could not afford it.

By unpacking the preceding analysis, we return to the four themes we derived from the accommodationist theory. First, the processes of state policy formation and implementation are characterized by sporadic fragmentation and antagonisms within class groupings. The conditions under which intraclass unity and political activity occur should be a part of one's research agenda—not assumed a priori (see Akard 1992; Brents 1992; Prechel 1990). Although the objective interests of the different segments of the banking industry intersect, these common interests do not mean we can presuppose the industry is always unified.

Rather, as posited by the second accommodationist theme, class unity and political organization is affected by the presence of a perceived threat from the state and by that class's organizational resources (Prechel 1990). In this case, class unity (and disunity) responded to not only a perceived threat, as in the case of finance capital organizing to control the solution to the S&L crisis, but also to a perceived political opportunity. The commercial banks broke away from the industry coalition (DIDC) in an attempt to eliminate the S&L segment of the industry; community, consumer, and labor groups organized when, in the process of creating the FIRREA, Congress was faced with the task of disposing of the worthless property held by failed savings institutions. We argue, therefore, that it is less important to say that there is a single specific causal agent creating class unity, than to say that class-based state theory research needs to specify the conditions that promoted or thwarted class unity in the case under study.

The third theme underscores the reciprocally modifying relation between state and societal policy determinants; policy emerges, and the state is modified in a dialectic fashion out of contradiction and conflict (Quadagno 1992). As Quadagno argued, neither the state nor social groups ultimately determine or shape one another. Rather, the state shapes the political activity (mass turmoil) of social groups, and mass turmoil shapes the structure of the state. Her "state transformation" theory was dramatically supported by the formation of the FIRREA-AHP, the protests surrounding its implementation, and its subsequent alteration. Within the political context described above, noncapitalist groups organized and helped shape the state's response to the crisis represented by the state's de jure commitment to the AHP. Within the new context created by this state policy, the de facto bureaucratic veto led to mass turmoil—the AHP created the setting for ACORN's break-ins of RTC-owned property, and its suing of the RTC to prevent the sale of affordable property to an investor. In response, the state modified the same initial piece of legislation. That this institutional response was derivative of the original legislation supports Quadagno's understanding of mass turmoil theory, and the more general accommodationist position that the relation between state and societal forces is both dynamic and reciprocally modifying.

The fourth theme draws together and historicizes the preceding three. One must specify the historical conditions under which both class unity and the passage of policy favorable to a particular class may occur. For example, perceived threats and opportunities are contingent upon the conjunction, in a given historical context, of some state project and the larger structure of relations between state and social forces. As Jenkins and Brents (1989) and Gilbert and Howe (1991) argued, the effectiveness of a group or protest strategy depends upon the larger political-economic context: noncapitalist groups are more successful when their capitalist opponents are divided; some state structures are more vulnerable to external protest or control than others. The historic relation between the state and the industry made deregulation the policy of choice; corporate welfare, in the form of the bailout, was a continuation of the de facto state policy of rescuing firms that are too big to fail; the bureaucratic veto of the AHP maintained the state's historic role in the subsidization of the private accumulation of capital.

This analysis incorporates and qualifies elements of the grand state theories. It accepts the business dominance position that the capitalist class gains strength through coordinated political activity, the state-centered focus on bureaucratic, political precedent, and the structuralist's attention to state's structural position in the larger political economy. Yet, this contingency-sensitive understanding of the state-society relation moves beyond the stagnant grand-theory debates of the past. This systematic understanding of contingency incorporates the historicity found in the accommodationist position, and presents a set of middle-range concepts around which the disparate facts produced by state theory research can be organized.

In sum, our analysis of the deregulation and bailout of the banking industry gave evidence of all four themes found in the new accommodationist research. The banking industry argued for and received deregulatory and bailout legislation. Noncapitalist group demands were made part of the bailout but were vetoed in implementation. The conditions under which this occurred included (1) an industry crisis requiring some form of state intervention, (2) an ongoing deregulatory state project, (3) context-specific intraclass unity, and (4) a historic, structural relation between the state and industry that, as explained above, precluded alternatives to state intervention. No one of these conditions is, a priori, a necessary part of the of the state-society relation, but all were a part of the historical context in which this legislation was created.

The notion of state projects, then, facilitates the identification of the conditions under which the elements specified by various theories of the state are likely to become more or less significant in the production of policy. In the analysis presented here, we found that the FIRREA legislation bailing out the S&L industry resulted from historical precedents in the state project of economic intervention, the balance of class forces, and structural selectivity filters that together created the conditions affecting the significance of the elements identified by various state theories. That is, the finance capital accumulation interests were able to "win" the advantageous legislation in the FIRREA because the state confronted an imminent economic crisis in the collapse of the S&L industry. Moreover, the consequent loss of moderate-income Americans' access to affordable mortgages threatened to prompt a legitimacy crisis for state managers. And prior legislation bailing out hundreds of other firms and municipalities over the previous several decades reinforced the selectivity filter through which these interests pressed their case.

The ability of these interests to control the content of the legislation, however, was modified significantly by the balance of class forces at the time. The competing segments of the financial community overrode some of their differences concerning the details of the bailout's implementation to coalesce around the need for the bailout legislation; but this level of organization among capital accumulation interests was modified by the organization of a variety of nonaccumulation interests into a larger, unified group (the CFD) to press for the linkage of the bailout to affordable housing issues.

Both sets of coalitions in the balance of class forces (i.e., capital accumulation coalitions and nonaccumulation coalitions) were prompted by imminent threats and opportunities to organize. For example, finance capital accumulation interests were ironically threatened by bank deregulation legislation that was originally designed precisely to address accumulation problems in the industry. The various segments of the banking community enjoyed a long history of experience and opportunity to transcend their differences and organize into a formidable force in previous struggles with the state for advantageous policies in the state project of economic intervention. And the various segments of the banking community maintain ongoing organizations and associations to press their perspectives in the formation of the selectivity filters through which state managers define problems and legislative solutions. These ongoing organizations were easily mobilized in this case. On the other hand, nonaccumulation interests faced the imminent threat of the loss of access to affordable mortgages should the S&L industry collapse, and confronted the real threat of diminished access to affordable housing of any kind. Moreover, they faced imminent threats to the solubility of their deposit accounts at the thousands of S&L institutions that were in serious danger. The opportunity for nonaccumulation interests to organize into a larger, national coalition was facilitated by the existing organizations of labor unions, consumer organizations, and community organizations, which enabled these to pool their organizational resources and mobilize their networks quickly.

The balance of class forces then, defined by the organizations of capital accumulation and nonaccumulation interests, which were in turn shaped by imminent threats or perceived threats and opportunities to organize, contributed to the passage of the FIRREA with the inclusion of the AHP.

State managers' ability to press their own agenda became apparent in the decision to keep the FIRREA largely off-budget. That is, while both capital accumulation and nonaccumulation interests were well-organized, neither was particularly active in the debate concerning whether to keep the legislation on-budget or off-budget. That aspect of the legislation was debated solely by state managers in Congress, whose own agendas concerned the preservation of their legitimacy; the avoidance of obvious and public exacerbation of the federal deficit; and the avoidance of politically dangerous public debates over whether or not to cut corporate welfare programs like the FIRREA or social welfare entitlement programs to balance the budget. The absence of organized opposition from capital accumulation interests or nonaccumulation interests, and the imminent threats perceived by state managers, became the conditions under which the legislation was passed as off-budget.

However, passage of the legislation is but one aspect of the levels of power apparent here. It would seem clear that the state managers in Congress ultimately governed in the passage of the legislation. That governing, however, was strongly influenced by the selectivity filters of prior legislative precedent, the structural importance of finance capital to the larger economy, and the organization of accumulation interests to dominate the hearings leading up to the passage of the bailout legislation. These filters biased the managers' collective definition of a finance capital accumulation crisis and their assumptions of appropriate legislative solutions that favored the broad accumulation interests of the banking community.

The final legislation appears to indicate that all parties involved in this policy "won": finance capital accumulation interests won a federal bailout of the S&L industry, nonaccumulation interests won an inclusion of an affordable housing provision in the bailout, and state managers in Congress won the placement of the bailout off-budget. What is most telling in this case, however, is the answer to the question, Who benefits? Although nonaccumulation interests won the inclusion of the affordable housing provision in the legislation, the implementation of the policy resulted in advantages accruing to wealthy speculators rather than to moderate-income and working-class families. Caught between the contradictory requirements of recovering the best prices for the defaulted property the federal government now held on one hand, and of providing the right of first refusal to moderate-income families on the other hand, the state managers in the RTC exercised their legislative veto over the provision and sold the properties to the highest bidders. In the end, state managers benefited from the treatment of the legislation off-budget, so that the issue no longer has the potential to taint congresspersons up for reelection or the national elections of 1996. S&L institutions benefited from the federal assumption of the industry's liabilities and from the opportunity to reorganize to remain a force in the financial community. Large commercial banks benefited from the bailout legislation, which allowed them to acquire the solvent properties of the failed thrifts while the federal government absorbed the liabilities. Working-class and moderate-income families whose access to affordable mortgages was threatened by the collapse of the thrift industry benefited from the preservation of that industry; but they did not benefit from the de facto implementation of the bailout, because of the bureaucratic veto of the affordable housing provision by the state managers in the RTC.

This discussion underscores the importance of identifying not only the conditions under which various elements of theories of the state are more or less likely to become significant in policymaking, but also the levels of power at work in these policymaking processes. Who governs, who wins, and who benefits are likely to be different, depending upon the dialectics of the state project and the balance of class forces at a given historical juncture.

Our contingency-sensitive analysis points to three theoretical conclusions:

1. Contingency is not synonymous with pluralism. It does not imply that anything goes, but that state policy is embedded within historical structures that *systematically bias the state* toward some policies at the exclusion of others. Is the state a capitalist state? The state is a capitalist state to the extent that state power supports the private accumulation of capital. The corporate welfare policies described above indicate the state's capitalist bias.
2. Yet it was possible for these events not to occur. We assume, and feel it is necessary to assert the nearly tautological position that, had the structure of the state–banking industry relation been different, different policies might have been created. This points once again to the importance of specifying the conditions under which the state functions in a certain manner.
3. The concepts we used above helped us specify "the conditions under which . . . "

We believe the recent accommodationist turn in state theory research holds promise. The concepts we present here do not represent a new grand theory melded together from the remains of older theoretical systems. A single case study cannot support a new grand theory and, as the notion of state projects highlights, we suspect no single reductionist theory can encapsulate the sundry processes underlying the entire range of state policies. We have proposed a set of middle-range concepts designed to guide future research agendas. These concepts sensitize the researcher to biases within the nonneutral structure of the state and to the historic relation between the state and the economy, in this case, in the still growing analysis of state welfare policy.

In keeping with our understanding of corporate welfare, Representative Kennedy argued, comparing the difficulty the RTC was having implementing the AHP and the ease with which it helped other investors buying the assets of failed S&Ls:

> You've got three of the top free-market advocates in the country sitting at the table [, but e]ssentially you are sitting on an organization that is really socialism for the rich. (U.S. Congress: House 1991a:50)

In sum, this state theory includes the contingencies inherent in recent accommodationist literature, yet provides a framework that could guide future research agendas. It accepts the business dominance position that the capitalist class gains strength through coordinated political activity, the state-centered focus on bureaucratic self-interests and political precedent, and the structuralist's attention to the strategic control of key economic resources, the state's position in the larger political economy, and the contradictory class powers embedded within state structures themselves. As with the accommodationist literature, the contingency-sensitive understanding of the state-society relation moves beyond the stagnant grand-theory debates of the past. This systematic understanding of contingency incorporates the historicity found in the accommodationist position, and moves toward the development of a theoretical system around which the disparate facts produced by state theory research can be organized.

At the risk of sounding redundant, we reiterate: A case study of a single set of related policy decisions is not sufficient to establish a fully developed state theory, but it does suggest ways to systematize the theoretical elements of one. Case studies of other policies, including deregulation of other industries and corporate welfare policy initiatives, need to be done. Taken together, these may help to develop a database upon which to compare and test more fully our findings here. Future research thus needs to further systematize the notions of state projects and balance of class forces.

THE FUTURE OF THE WELFARE STATE

A careful analysis of the S&L crisis and the subsequent bailout of the industry, framed in a reconceptualization of the welfare state, may inform policy. The Republican's Contract with America has opened a strong debate concerning the future of the welfare state. A serious discussion of the differences between social and corporate welfare, and an analysis of the real costs of each, whether on-budget or off-budget, must occur. It is not particularly helpful or accurate to focus on the caricature of the single-mother "welfare queen" as the reason for the tremendous budget deficits we have amassed since 1980. To do so will result in continued attacks against social welfare programs with little resultant reductions in the federal deficit. To make a dent in the deficit, we must recognize that corporate welfare programs are much more costly, but also more invisible given their off-budget status.

We also stand poised for a national debate concerning the future of the banking industry in general and the S&L industry in particular. Questions are increasingly being raised throughout Congress and among business analysts addressing the future of the FDIC and the FSLIC. Questions are being raised in Congress concerning whether to alter both of these institutions in order to prevent another crisis such as that of the banking industry. Some observers and congresspersons are beginning to question the wisdom of deregulating the banking industry. An analysis of the S&L crisis that links it to theories of the state in general and theories of the welfare state in particular may frame these questions in a theoretical context that can contribute to how these questions are answered.

Thus, if we view the S&L crisis as the result of greedy, unscrupulous, or criminal individuals, then we need only convict these individuals and hire more industry examiners to resolve the problem. However, if we understand the crisis and its resolution as the result of patterned structural relationships and class struggles between the state, financial institutions, labor, and community and consumer groups over shifting the line between social and corporate welfare, then we are pointed toward policies that alter those structures that facilitated the crisis as an institutional problem. We may begin to examine how resolution proposals may transfer wealth from the poor, the working class, women, and children to corporations and the wealthiest families in the United States. And we may place debates about social welfare programs in this larger context, examining the relationship between corporate and social welfare and thereby engaging in a more thorough discussion of national priorities and how we pay for them.

NOTES

1.   This would seem to imply that class unity is contingent not only upon the perceived *threat* of government intervention, but also upon perceived *opportunities*.

2.   The deregulatory state project involved a unified set of state policies across a number of industries and state apparatuses geared toward, in the case of the S&L industry, greater market-based risk taking and increased public subsidization of the risks associated with the private accumulation of capital.

3.   This is the sort of process suggested by the concept "structural selectivity."

References

Ackerman, Frank. 1982. *Reagonomics: Rhetoric vs. Reality*. Boston: South End Press.

Akard, Patrick J. 1992. "Corporate Mobilization and Political Power: The Transformation of U.S. Economic Policy in the 1970s." *American Sociological Review* 57:597–615.

Alexander, Herbert E. 1984. *Financing Politics: Money, Elections, and Political Reform*, 3rd edition. Washington, DC: Congressional Quarterly Press.

Allen, Michael Patrick. 1991. "Capitalist Response to State Intervention: Theories of the State and Political Finance in the New Deal." *American Sociological Review* 56:679–89.

Allen, Michael Patrick and Phillip Broyles. 1989. "Class Hegemony and Political Finance: Presidential Campaign Contributions of Wealthy Capitalist Families." *American Sociological Review* 54:275–87.

Altman, Edward I. and S. A. Nammacher. 1985. *The Anatomy of the High-Yield Debt Market*. New York: Morgan Stanley.

Amenta, Edwin and Sunita Parikh. 1991. "Comment: Capitalists Did Not Want the Social Security Act: A Critique of the 'Capitalist Dominance' Thesis." *American Sociological Review* 56:124–29.

Amenta, Edwin and Theda Skocpol. 1988. "Redefining the New Deal: World War II and the Development of Social Provision in the U.S." Pp. 81–122 in *The Politics of Social Policy in the United States*, edited by Margaret Weir, Ann Shola Orloff, and Theda Skocpol. Princeton, NJ: Princeton University Press.

Bane, Mary Jo and David T. Ellwood. 1994. *Welfare Realities: From Rhetoric to Reform*. Cambridge, MA: Harvard University Press.

Barth, James R. 1991. *The Great Savings and Loan Debacle*. Washington, DC: American Enterprise Institute.

Barth, James R., Philip F. Bartholomew, and Carol J. Labich. 1989. "Moral Hazard and the Thrift Crisis: An Analysis of 1988 Resolutions." Research paper no. 160, Office of Policy and Economic Research, Federal Home Loan Bank Board, Washington, D.C.

Bater, Jeff. 1994. "Greenspan: Banking System Recovers." United Press International, September 22.

Bearden, James. 1982. *The Board of Directors in Large U.S. Corporations.* Ph.D. dissertation, SUNY-Stony Brook.

Benda, Charles G. 1979. "State Organization and Policy Formation: The 1970 Reorganization of the Post Office." *Politics and Society* 9(2): 123–51.

Berkowitz, Edward and Kim McQuaid. 1980. *Creating the Welfare State: The Political Economy of Twentieth Century Reform.* New York: Praeger.

Block, Fred. 1977. "The Ruling Class Does Not Rule: Notes on the Marxist Theory of the State." *Socialist Review* 33:6–28.

———. 1981. "The Fiscal Crisis of the Capitalist State." *Annual Review of Sociology* 7:1–27.

Block, Fred, Richard Cloward, Barbara Ehrenreich, and Frances Fox Piven. 1987. *The Mean Season: The Attack on the Welfare State.* New York: Pantheon.

Bluestone, Harry and Bennett Harrison. 1982. *The Deindustrialization of America: Plant Closings, Community Abandonment, and the Dismantling of Basic Industry.* New York: Basic Books.

Bowles, Samuel and Herbert Gintis. 1982. "The Crisis of Liberal Democratic Capitalism: The Case of the United States." *Politics and Society* 11(1):51–93.

Bradsher, Keith. 1994. "S&Ls See New Threat, This Time from Banks." *New York Times,* October 20:D6.

Brandes, Stuart D. 1976. *American Welfare Capitalism, 1880–1940.* Chicago: University of Chicago Press.

Brents, Barbara G. 1992. "Class Political Organizing and Welfare Capitalism." *Critical Sociology* 19:69–101.

Burnett, Michael A. and Frank Philippi. 1990. "New Developments in Regulation of the High-Yield Bond Market and Junk Bond Investments." Pp. 145–53 in *The High-Yield Debt Market: Investment Performance and Economic Impact,* edited by Edward I. Altman. Homewood, IL: Dow Jones-Irwin.

Burris, Val. 1992. "Elite Policy-Planning Networks in the United States." *Research in Politics and Society* 4:111–34.

Buser, Stephen A., Andrew W. Chen, and Edward J. Kane. 1981. "Federal Deposit Insurance, Regulatory Policy, and Optimal Bank Capital." *Journal of Finance* 36(March):51–60.

Calavita, Kitty and Henry N. Pontell. 1990. "'Heads I Win, Tails You Lose': Deregulation, Crime, and Crisis in the Savings and Loan Industry." *Crime and Delinquency* 36(3):309–41.

———. 1991. "'Other People's Money' Revisited: Embezzlement in the Savings and Loan Insurance Industries." *Social Problems* 38(1):94–112.

Chappell, Henry. 1982. "Campaign Contributions and Congressional

Voting: A Simultaneous Probit-Tobit Model." *Review of Economics and Statistics* 64:77–83.

Clawson, Dan and Alan Neustadtl. 1989. "Interlocks, PACs, and Corporate Conservatism." *American Journal of Sociology* 94:749–73.

Clawson, Dan, Alan Neustadtl, and James Bearden. 1986. "The Logic of Business Unity: Corporate Contributions to the 1980 Congressional Elections." *American Sociological Review*. 51: 797–811.

Clawson, Dan, Alan Neustadtl, and Denise Scott. 1992. *Money Talks: Corporate PACs and Political Influence*. New York: Basic.

Clawson, Marion. 1981. *New Deal Planning: The National Resources Planning Board*. Baltimore: Johns Hopkins University Press.

Cloward, Richard and Frances Fox Piven. 1983. "Toward a Class-Based Realignment of American Politics: A Movement Strategy." *Social Policy* 13(3):3–14.

Cobb, Stephen. 1976. "Defense Spending and Defense Voting in the House: An Empirical Study of an Aspect of the Military-Industrial Complex Thesis." *American Journal of Sociology* 82(1):163–82.

Congressional Quarterly, Inc. 1990. "Sweeping Thrift Bailout Bill Cleared." *Congressional Quarterly Almanac* 46:118–30.

Cypher, James N. 1975. "An Institutional Economic Theory of the Military-Industrial Complex." *Kapitalistate* 3(Spring):47–53.

Devine, Joel. 1983. "Fiscal Policy and Class Income Inequality: The Distributional Consequences of Governmental Revenues and Expenditures in the United States, 1949–1976." *American Sociological Review* 48(5):606–22.

Dobbin, Frank R. 1992. "The Origins of Private Social Insurance: Public Policy and Fringe Benefits in America, 1920–1950." *American Journal of Sociology* 97:1416–50.

Domhoff, G. William. 1978. *The Powers That Be: Processes of Ruling Class Domination in America*. New York: Vintage/Random House.

———. 1987. "Corporate Liberal Theory and the Social Security Act: A Chapter in the Sociology of Knowledge." *Politics and Society* 15:297–330.

———. 1990. *The Power Elite and the State: How Policy is Made in America*. Hawthorne, NY: Aldine de Gruyter.

———. 1991a. "American State Autonomy via the Military? Another Counterattack on a Theoretical Delusion." *Critical Sociology* 18:9–56.

———. 1991b. "Class, Power, and Parties during the New Deal: A Critique of Skocpol's Theory of State Autonomy." *Berkeley Journal of Sociology* 36:1–49.

Dye, Thomas. 1990. *Who's Running America? The Bush Era*. Englewood Cliffs, NJ: Prentice-Hall.

———. 1995. *Who's Running America? The Clinton Years*. Englewood Cliffs, NJ: Prentice-Hall.

Eichenwald, Kurt. 1990. "S&L Sues Executives of Drexel." *New York Times*, December 13:D5.

Ely, Bert. 1990. "Crime Accounts for Only 3% of the Cost of the S&L Mess." Mimeo, July 19.,

Esping-Andersen, Gosta. 1990. *The Three Worlds of Welfare Capitalism.* Princeton, NJ: Princeton University Press.

Esping-Anderson, Gosta, Roger Friedland, and Erik Olin Wright. 1976. "Modes of Class Struggle and the Capitalist State." *Kapitalistate* 4–5:184–220.

Evans, Peter B., Dietrich Rueschemeyer, and Theda Skocpol. 1985. *Bringing the State Back In.* Cambridge: Cambridge University Press.

Federal Election Commission. 1984. *Campaign Expenditures in the United States, 1981–1982.* Ann Arbor, MI: Inter-university Consortium for Political and Social Research.

———. 1986. *Campaign Expenditures in the United States, 1977–1978 and 1979–1980*, Vol. 1. Ann Arbor, MI: Inter-university Consortium for Political and Social Research.

———. 1995. *Campaign Expenditures in the United States, 1991–1992.* Ann Arbor, MI: Inter-university Consortium for Political and Social Research.

Finegold, Kenneth. 1981. "From Agrarianism to Adjustment: The Political Origins of New Deal Agricultural Policy." *Politics and Society* 11:1–27.

Frendreis, John and Richard Waterman. 1985. "PAC Contributions and Legislative Behavior: Senate Voting on Trucking Deregulation." *Social Science Quarterly* 66:401–12.

Galbraith, John Kenneth. 1985. *The New Industrial State*, 4th ed. Boston: Houghton-Mifflin.

Gale Research, Inc. 1991. *Ward's Business Directory*. Foster City, CA: Information Access.

Gilbert, Jess and Caroline Howe. 1991. "Beyond 'State vs. Society': Theories of the State and New Deal Agricultural Policies." *American Sociological Review* 56:204–20.

Ginsberg, Benjamin and John Green. 1986. "The Best Congress Money Can Buy: Campaign Contributions and Congressional Behavior." Pp. 75–89 in *Do Elections Matter?* edited by Benjamin Ginsberg and Alan Stone. Armonk, NY: Sharpe.

Glasberg, Davita Silfen. 1987a. "Chrysler Corporation's Struggle for Bailout: The Role of the State in Finance Capitalist Society." *Research in Political Sociology* 3:87–110.

———. 1987b. "International Finance Capital and the Relative Autonomy of the State: Mexico's Foreign Debt Crisis." *Research in Political Economy* 10:83–108.

———. 1988. "The Political Economic Power of Finance Capital and

Urban Fiscal Crisis: Cleveland's Default, 1978." *Journal of Urban Affairs* 10(3):219–39.

———. 1989. *The Power of Collective Purse Strings.* Berkeley: University of California Press.

Glasberg, Davita Silfen and Dan Skidmore. 1992. "State Policy Formation and Unintended Consequences: Bank Deregulation and the Savings and Loan Crisis." Paper presented at the annual meetings of the American Sociological Association, Pittsburgh.

———. 1996. "Bank Hegemony Processes and Corporate Welfare: Bailing Out the Savings and Loan Industry." Pp. 183–205 in *Corporate Control, Capital Formation, and Organizational Networks: Intercorporate Relations in Japan and the United States*, edited by Takuyoshi Takada, Beth Mintz, and Michael Schwartz. Tokyo: Chou University Press.

Gleiber, Dennis, James King, and H. R. Mahood. 1987. "PAC Contributions, Constituency Interest and Legislative Voting: Gun Control Legislation in the U.S. Senate." Paper presented at the annual meeting of the Midwest Political Science Association. Chicago.

Gopian, David J. 1984. "What Makes PACs Tick? An Analysis of the Allocation Patterns of Economic Interest Groups." *American Journal of Political Science* 28:259–81.

Gordon, Linda. 1994. *Pitied But Not Entitled: Single Mothers and the History of Welfare.* New York: Free Press.

Gough, Ian and Anne Steinberg. 1981. "The Welfare State, Capitalism, and Crisis." *Political Power and Social Theory* 2:141–71.

Grenzke, Janet M. 1989. "PACs and the Congressional Supermarket: The Currency Is Complex." *American Journal of Political Science* 33:1–24.

Griffin, Larry G., Joel A. Devine, and Michael Wallace. 1983. "On the Economic and Political Determinants of Welfare Spending in the Post-World War II Era." *Politics and Society* 12:331–72.

Habermas, Jurgen. 1973. *Legitimation Crisis.* Boston: Beacon.

Harrington, Michael. 1984. *The New American Poverty.* New York: Penguin.

Hartford Courant. 1990a. "Deposits at BNE under Close Watch by Senate Panel, GAO." December 15:C1–C2.

———. 1990b. "BNE, SEC Resolve Complaint Involving Financial Disclosure." December 22:B1.

———. 1990c. "CBT's Parent Gets Plan to Reduce Debts." December 22: A1, A4.

———. 1991a. "U.S. Bailout Forecast for BNE Corp." January 5:D1, D4.

———. 1991b. "Regulators Still Examining Bank of New England Finances." January 6:A1, A9.

———. 1991c. "Ease of Bailout Masked Tense Decisions." January 8:A1, A11.

————. 1991d. "BankAmerica Bidding for Former BNE Banks." January 8:B1–B2.

————. 1991e. "Two More Large Banks Interested in BNE Assets." January 9: B1–B2.

————. 1991f. "BNE Case Spurs Call for Limit on FDIC Coverage." January 13:E1–E2.

Hays, Gorey and Richard Hornik. 1990. "No End in Sight: Politicians Hurl Blame as the $500 Billion S&L Crisis Races out of Control." *Time* (August 13):50–52.

Heins, John. 1988. "Tom Speigel's (Dubious) Claim to Fame." *Forbes* (November 14):153–56.

Hershey, Robert D., Jr. 1990. "Thrift Office Will Open Its Cases; Also Tells Ex-Chief of Columbia Savings to Repay $19 Million." *New York Times*, July 6:D1.

Hilder, D. B. 1988. "Bank Board Staff Expects to Offer Rules Curbing Thrifts' 'Junk Bond' Investments." *Wall Street Journal*, September 28:B4.

Hooks, Gregory. 1990. "The Rise of the Pentagon and U.S. State Building: The Defense Program as Industrial Policy." *American Journal of Sociology* 96:358–404.

————. 1993. "The Weakness of Strong Theories: The U.S. States' Dominance of the World War II Investment Process." *American Sociological Review* 58:37–53.

Hymer, Stephen. 1981. "The Multinational Corporation and the Law of Uneven Development." Pp. 283–302 in *Complex Organizations: Critical Perspectives*, edited by Mary Zey-Ferrell and Michael Aiken. Glenview, IL: Scott, Foresman.

Jenkins, J. Craig and Barbara G. Brents. 1989. "Social Protest, Hegemonic Competition, and Social Reforms." *American Sociological Review* 54:891–909.

Jessop, Bob. 1982. *The Capitalist State: Theories and Methods.* New York: New York University Press.

————. 1990. *State Theory: Putting the Capitalist State in Its Place.* University Park: Pennsylvania State University Press.

Joe, Tom and Cheryl Rogers. 1985. *By the Few for the Few: The Reagan Welfare Legacy.* Lexington, MA: Lexington.

Joint Committee on Printing. 1977. *Congressional Directory.* Washington, DC: U.S. Government Printing Office.

————. 1981. *Congressional Directory.* Washington, DC: U.S. Government Printing Office.

Joint Committee on Printing. 1991. *Congressional Directory.* Washington, DC: U.S. Government Printing Office.

Kane, Edward J. 1986. "Appearance and Reality in Deposit Insurance: The Case for Reform." *Journal of Banking and Finance* 10(June):175–88.

———. 1989. *The S&L Mess: How Did It Happen?* Washington, DC: Urban Institute Press.

Karpik, Lucien. 1977. "Technological Capitalism." Pp. 41–71 in *Critical Issues in Organizations,* edited by Stewart Clegg and David Dunkerly. London: Routledge and Kegan Paul.

Kau, James B. and Paul Rubin. 1982. *Congressmen, Constituents, and Contributors.* Boston: Martinus Nijihoff.

Keim, Gerald and Asghar Zardkoohi. 1988. "Looking for Leverage in PAC Markets: Corporate and Labor Contributions Considered." *Public Choice* 58:21–34.

Kerwin, Kathleen. 1990. "Can Ed Harshfield 'Make the Taxpayer Whole'?" *Business Week* (September 10):78.

Labaton, Stephen. 1990a. "U.S. Blocks Columbia 'Junk' Sale." *New York Times,* September 11:D1.

———. 1990b. "U.S. Files $6.8 Billion Claim against Drexel." *New York Times,* November 15:D1, D6.

———. 1990c. "In Court, U.S. Blames Drexel for Much of the S&L Crisis." *New York Times,* November 16:A1, D4.

Langbein, Laura I. 1986. "Money and Access: Some Empirical Evidence." *Journal of Politics* 48:1052–62.

Lev, Michael. 1990. "Columbia 'Junk Bond' Sale Set." *New York Times,* July 26:D1.

———. 1991a. "U.S. Seizes Columbia Savings." *New York Times,* January 26:31, 43.

———. 1991b. "U.S. Closes Columbia Savings." *New York Times,* September 14:37.

Levine, Rhonda. 1988. *Class Struggle and the New Deal: Industrial Labor, Industrial Capital and the State.* Lawrence: University of Kansas Press.

Lipset, Seymour Martin. 1981. *Political Man: The Social Bases of Politics,* 3rd edition. Baltimore: Johns Hopkins University Press.

Lukes, Steven. 1974. *Power: A Radical View.* London: Mac Millan.

Makinson, Larry. 1992. *The Cash Constituents of Congress.* Washington, DC: Congressional Quarterly.

Mandel, Ernest. 1975. *Late Capitalism.* London: New Left.

Maney, Ardith L. 1989. *Still Hungry after All These Years: Food Assistance Policy from Kennedy to Reagan.* New York: Greenwood.

McCammon, Holly. 1994. "Disorganizing and Reorganizing Conflict: Outcomes of the State's Legal Regulation of the Strike since the Wagner Act." *Social Forces* 72(4):1011–49.

Middlemas, Keith. 1983. "Corporate Bias." Pp. 330–37 in *States and Societies,* edited by David Held et al. New York: New York University Press.

Miliband, Ralph. 1969. *The State in Capitalist Society.* New York: Basic.

———. 1983. *Class Power and State Power.* London: Verso.

Miller, S. M. 1978. "The Recapitalization of Capitalism." *Social Policy* 9(3):5–13.

Mills, C. Wright. 1956. *The Power Elite.* New York: Oxford University Press.

Mintz, Beth and Michael Schwartz. 1985. *The Power Structure of American Business.* Chicago: University of Chicago Press.

Mizruchi, Mark S. 1989. "Similarity of Political Behavior among Large American Corporations." *American Journal of Sociology* 95:402–24.

Mizruchi, Mark S. and Thomas Koenig. 1986. "Economic Sources of Corporate Political Consensus: An Examination of Interindustry Relations." *American Sociological Review* 51:482–91.

Moody's Investor Service. 1977a. *Moody's Bank & Finance Manual.* New York: Moody's Investor Service.

———. 1977b. *Moody's Industrial Manual.* New York: Moody's Investor Service.

———. 1981a. *Moody's Bank & Finance Manual.* New York: Moody's Investor Service.

———. 1981b. *Moody's Industrial Manual.* New York: Moody's Investor Service.

———. 1991a. *Moody's Bank & Finance Manual.* New York: Moody's Investor Service.

———. 1991b. *Moody's Industrial Manual.* New York: Moody's Investor Service.

Nation. 1991. "Redlining a Black Bank." January 7–14, 1.

National Commission on Financial Institution Reform, Recovery, and Enforcement. 1993. *Origins and Causes of the S&L Debacle: A Blueprint for Reform.* Washington, DC: Government Printing Office.

Neustadtl, Alan. 1990. "Interest-Group PACmanship: An Analysis of Campaign Contributions, Issue Visibility, and Legislative Impact." *Social Forces* 69(2):549–64.

Neustadtl, Alan and Dan Clawson. 1988. "Corporate Political Groupings: PAC Contributions to the 1980 Congressional Elections." *American Sociological Review* 51:781–96.

New York Times. 1989. "Saving Units' 'Junk Bonds.'" July 19:D17.

———. 1990a. "'Junk Bond' Deal Joined by Investor." July 28:30.

———. 1990b. "Bank in Harlem Fails and U.S. Takes Control." November 10:B2.

———. 1990c. "Coalition Struggles to Raise Funds to Save Freedom Bank." November 13: B3.

———. 1990d. "Columbia Expects Loss on 'Junk' Sale." August 17:D3.

———. 1990e. "Ex-Savings Chief Curbed." July 7:30.

———. 1990f. "FDIC to Pay 50c on $1 for Large Deposits at Freedom Bank." November 30: B3.

———. 1990g. "Freedom Bank Is Paying Off Its Depositors." November 14, 1990: B1–2.

————. 1990h. "Freedom Bank's Demise: A Trail of Risky Loans and Fast Growth." December 3:A1, B4.

————. 1990i. "Freedom Bank's Failure Hits Harlem like a Death in the Family." November 12:B1, B5.

————. 1990j. "New Charge in S&L Case." September 7:D2.

————. 1991a. "Big Cut in U.S. Bank Deposits Hastened Fall of Freedom Bank in Harlem." January 29:A1, D18.

————. 1991b. "U.S. Is Taking Over Northeast Bank to Head Off a Run." January 7:A1, D8.

————. 1991c. "Few of the Working Poor Get Houses in S&L Rescue Plan." June 26:A1, D6.

O'Connor, James. 1973. *The Fiscal Crisis of the State.* New York: St. Martin's.

————. 1981. "The Fiscal Crisis of the State Revisited . . . ." *Kapitalistate* 9:41–61.

————. 1987. *The Meaning of Crisis: A Theoretical Introduction.* New York: Basil Blackwell.

Offe, Claus. 1972a. "Political Authority and Class Structure." *International Journal of Sociology* 2:73–108.

————. 1972b. "Advanced Capital and the Welfare State." *Politics and Society* 2:479–88.

————. 1974. "Structural Problems of the Capitalist State: Class Rule and the Political System. On the Selectiveness of Political Institutions." Pp. 31–58 in *German Political Studies,* Volume 1, edited by Klaus Von Beyme. Beverly Hills, CA: Sage.

————. 1984. *Contradictions of the Welfare State.* Cambridge, MA: MIT Press.

Phillips, Kevin. 1990. *The Politics of Rich and Poor: Wealth and the American Electorate in the Reagan Aftermath.* New York: Random House.

Piven, Frances Fox and Richard A. Cloward. 1978. *Poor People's Movements: How They Succeed and Why They Fail.* New York: Pantheon.

————. 1982. *The New Class War: Reagan's Attack on the Welfare State and its Consequences.* New York: Pantheon.

Polsby, Nelson. 1980. *Community Power and Political Theory,* 2nd edition. New Haven, CT: Yale University Press.

Poulantzas, Nicos. 1969. "The Problem of the Capitalist State." *New Left Review* 58(November/December):67–78.

————. 1976. "The Capitalist State: A Reply to Miliband and Laclau." *New Left Review* 58 (November/December):67–78.

————. 1978. *State, Power, and Socialism.* London: Verso.

Prechel, Harland. 1990. "Steel and the State." *American Sociological Review* 55:634–47.

Purdy, Penelope. 1990. "A Bank They Called 'Desparado.'" *New York Times,* July 17:A21.

Quadagno, Jill. 1984. "Welfare Capitalism and the Social Security Act of 1935." *American Sociological Review* 49:632–47.

———. 1989. "Organized Labor, State Structures and Social Policy Development: A Case Study of Old Age Assistance in Ohio, 1916–1940." *Social Problems* 36(2):181–96.

———. 1992. "Social Movements and State Transformation: Labor Unions and Racial Conflict in the War on Poverty." *American Sociological Review* 57:616–34.

———. 1994. *The Color of Welfare: How Racism Undermined the War on Poverty.* New York: Oxford University Press.

Quadagno, Jill and Madonna Harrington Meyer. 1989. "Organized Labor, State Structures, and Social Policy Development: A Case Study of Old Age Assistance in Ohio, 1916–1940." *Social Problems* 36:181–96.

Roose, Diana. 1975. "Top Dogs and Top Brass: An Inside Look at a Government Advisory Committee." *Insurgent Sociologist* 5(3):53–63.

Sabato, Larry J. 1984. *PAC Power: Inside the World of Political Action Committees.* New York: Norton.

Schmitter, Phillipe C. 1974. "Still the Century of Corporatism?" *Review of Politics* 36(1):85–127.

Sheak, Robert. 1990. "Corporate and State Attacks on the Material Conditions of the Working Class." *Humanity and Society* 14(2):105–27.

Sidel, Ruth. 1986. *Women and Children Last: The Plight of Poor Women in Affluent America.* New York: Penguin.

———. 1990. *On Her Own: Growing Up in the Shadow of the American Dream.* New York: Viking Penguin.

Skidmore, Dan and Davita Silfen Glasberg. 1996. "State Theory and Corporate Welfare: The Crisis and Bailout of the Savings and Loan Industry from a Contingency Perspective." *Political Power and Social Theory* 10:149–91.

Skocpol, Theda. 1980. "Political Response to Capitalist Crisis: Neo-Marxist Theories of the State and the Case of the New Deal." *Politics and Society* 10:155–201.

———. 1985. "Bringing the State Back in: Strategies of Analysis in Current Research." Pp. 3–37 in *Bringing the State Back In*, edited by Peter B. Evans, Dietrich Rueschemeyer, and Theda Skocpol. Cambridge: Cambridge University Press.

———. 1988. "The Limits of the New Deal System and the Roots of the Contemporary Welfare Dilemmas." Pp. 293–311 in *The Politics of Social Policy in the United States*, edited by Margaret Weir, Ann Shola Orloff, and Theda Skocpol. Princeton, NJ: Princeton University Press.

———. 1992. *Protecting Soldiers and Mothers: The Political Origins of Social Policy in the United States.* Cambridge, MA: Harvard University Press.

Skocpol, Theda and Edwin Amenta. 1986. "States and Social Policies." *Annual Review of Sociology* 12:131–57.

Skocpol, Theda and John Ikenberry. 1983. "The Political Formation of the American Welfare State in Historical and Comparative Perspective." *Comparative Social Research* 6:87–148.

Stein, Benjamin J. 1989. "Watch Dog, Awake! Fervent Plea to the New Chairman of the SEC." *Barron's* (November 13):6–7, 32–36.

Stevenson, Richard W. 1990a. "$3.5 Billion 'Junk Bond' Sale Sought." *New York Times*, March 15:D1, D21.

———. 1990b. "Columbia Savings Reports Large Losses." *New York Times*, April 2:D1, D12.

———. 1990c. "S&L Tries Recasting Itself as Victim." *New York Times*, November 19:D1, D5.

Taggart, Robert A. 1988. "The Growth of the 'Junk' Bond Market and Its Role in Financing Takeovers." Pp. 5–24 in *Mergers and Acquisitions*, edited by Alan J. Auerbach. Chicago: University of Chicago Press.

Thomas, Paulette. 1991. "RTC Is Selling Part of Columbia S&L to Investors and Liquidating the Rest." *Wall Street Journal*, September 16:A6.

Time. 1990. "Freedom: Not Just Another Bank." November 26:71.

Tolchin, Martin. 1991. "Mildest Possible Penalty Is Imposed on Neil Bush." *New York Times*, April 19:D2.

U.S. Congress: House. 1979. *The Chrysler Corporation Financial Situation*. Committee on Banking, Finance, and Urban Affairs, Subcommittee on Economic Stabilization. 96th Congress, 1st session. Washington, DC: Government Printing Office.

———. 1980. *Oversight Hearings on Depository Institutions Deregulation Committee*. Committee on Banking, Finance, and Urban Affairs, Subcommittee on Financial Institutions, Supervision, Regulation, and Insurance. 96th Congress, 2d session. Washington, DC: U.S. Government Publications Office.

———. 1981a. *Conduct of Monetary Policy*. Committee on Banking, Finance, and Urban Affairs. 96th Congress, 2d session. Washington, DC: U.S. Government Publications Office.

———. 1981b. *The Deposit Insurance Flexibility Act*. Committee on Banking, Finance, and Urban Affairs, Subcommittee on Financial Institutions, Supervision, Regulation, and Insurance. 97th Congress, 1st session. Washington, DC: U.S. Government Publications Office.

———. 1981c. *Oversight Hearings on Depository Institutions Deregulation Committee*. Committee on Banking, Finance, and Urban Affairs, Subcommittee on General Oversight and Renegotiation. 97th Congress, 1st session. Washington, DC: Government Printing Office.

———. 1982a. *Housing and Urban-Rural Recovery Act of 1982, pts. 1–4*. Committee on Banking, Finance, and Urban Affairs, Subcommittee on Housing and Community Development, 97th Congress, 2d session. Washington, DC: U.S. Government Publications Office.

———. 1982b. *The Depository Institutions Amendments of 1982*. Committee on Banking, Finance, and Urban Affairs, Subcommittee on Financial Institutions, Supervision, Regulation, and Insurance. 97th Congress, 2d session. Washington, DC: U.S. Government Publications Office.

U.S. Congress: House. 1984. *Inquiry into Continental Illinois Corporation and Continental Illinois National Bank*. Committee on Banking, Finance, and Urban Affairs, Subcommittee on Financial Institutions Supervision, Regulation and Insurance. 98th Congress, 2d session. Washington, DC: Government Printing Office.

———. 1988. *Junk Bonds: 1988 Status Report*. Committee on Banking, Finance, and Urban Affairs, Subcommittee on General Oversight and Investigations. 100th Congress, 2nd session. Washington, DC: Government Printing Office.

———. 1989a. *The Other Side of the Savings and Loan Industry*. Committee on Banking, Finance and Urban Affairs, Subcommittee on Financial Institutions Supervision, Regulation and Insurance. 101st Congress, 1st session. Washington, DC: Government Printing Office.

———. 1989b. *Financial Institutions Reform, Recovery, and Enforcement Act of 1989, pts. 1 and 2*. Committee on Banking, Finance and Urban Affairs, Subcommittee on Financial Institutions Supervision, Regulation and Insurance. 101st Congress, 1st session. Washington, DC: Government Printing Office.

———. 1989c. *Administration Plan to Resolve the Savings and Loan Crisis*. Committee on Banking, Finance, and Urban Affairs. 101st Congress, 1st session. Washington, DC: U.S. Government Publications Office

———. 1989d. *Domestic Economic Issues, Financial Providers, and Safety and Soundness of the U.S. Financial System*. Committee on Banking, Finance and Urban Affairs, 101st Congress, 1st session. Washington, DC: Government Printing Office.

———. 1989e. *Failure of Independent CPAs to Identify Fraud, Waste, and Mismanagement and Assure Accurate Financial Position of Troubled S&Ls*. Committee on Banking, Finance and Urban Affairs. 101st Congress, 1st session. Washington, DC: Government Printing Office.

———. 1989f. *Financial Condition of the Federal Savings and Loan Insurance Corporation and Federal Deposit Insurance Corporation at Year End, 1988*. Committee on Banking, Finance and Urban Affairs. 101st Congress, 1st session. Washington, DC: Government Printing Office.

———. 1989g. *FSLIC Assistance Programs*. Committee on Banking, Finance, and Urban Affairs, 101st Congress, 1st session. Washington, DC: Government Printing Office.

———. 1989h. *Status and Activities of the RTC and the Oversight Board*. Committee on Banking, Finance, and Urban Affairs, Subcommittee on Financial Institutions Supervision, Regulation and Insurance. 101st Congress, 1st session. Washington, DC: Government Printing Office.

———. 1989i. Conference Report, *Financial Institutions Reform, Recovery and Enforcement act of 1989.* 101st Congress, 1st session. Washington, DC: Government Printing Office.

———. 1989j. *Oversight Hearing to Examine the Impact of FIRREA on the Federal Home Loan Bank System.* Committee on Banking, Finance, and Urban Affairs. Subcommittee on General Oversight and Investigations. 101st Congress, 1st session. Washington, DC: U.S. Government Printing Office.

———. 1989k. *Junk Bonds: 1988 Status Report.* Committee on Banking, Finance and Urban Affairs. Subcommittee on General Oversight and Investigations. 100th Congress, 2nd Session. Washington, DC: U.S. Government Printing Office.

———. 1989l. *Issues Concerning Investing in High-Yield Bonds by FSLIC Insured Depository Institutions.* Committee on Banking, Finance and Urban Affairs. Subcommittee on General Oversight and Investigations. 101st Congress, 1st Session. Washington, DC: U.S. Government Printing Office.

———. 1990a. *Oversight Hearings on the Resolution Trust Corporation.* Committee on Banking, Finance, and Urban Affairs. 101st Congress, 2nd session. Washington, DC: U.S. Government Printing Office.

———. 1990b. *Semiannual Report and Appearance by the Oversight Board of the Resolution Trust Corporation.* Committee on Banking, Finance, and Urban Affairs. 101st Congress, 2nd session. Washington, DC: U.S. Government Printing Office.

———. 1990c. *Disposition of Residential Properties, Single Family and Multi-Family, with Emphasis on Affordable Housing.* Committee on Banking, Finance, and Urban Affairs. Subcommittee on Financial Institutions Supervision, Regulation and Insurance. Resolution Trust Corporation Task Force. 101st Congress, 2nd session. Washington, DC: U.S. Government Printing Office.

———. 1990d. *Financial Inst Reform, Recovery and Enforcement Act of 1989, FIRREA, and its Impact on the Federal Home Loan Bank System.* Committee on Banking, Finance, and Urban Affairs. Subcommittee on General Oversight and Investigations. 101st Congress, 2nd session. Washington, DC: U.S. Government Printing Office.

———. 1990e. *Closing of Freedom National Bank.* Committee on Banking, Finance, and Urban Affairs, Subcommittee on Financial Institutions, Supervision, Regulation, and Insurance. 101st Congress, 2d session. Washington, DC: U.S. Government Publications Office.

———. 1990f. *Oversight Hearings on the Financial Institutions Reform, Recovery, and Enforcement Act of 1989.* Committee on Banking, Finance, and Urban Affairs, Subcommittee on Financial Institutions, Supervision, Regulation, and Insurance. 101st Congress, 2d session. Washington, DC: U.S. Government Publications Office.

U.S. Congress: House. 1990g. *Oversight of the Resolution Trust Corporation.* Committee on Banking, Finance, and Urban Affairs. 101st Congress, 2nd session. Washington, DC: U.S. Government Printing Office.

―――. 1990h. *Year End Asset Sales, Institutions Resolution, Management, and the Strategic Plan.* Committee on Banking, Finance, and Urban Affairs. Subcommittee on Financial Institutions Supervision, Regulation and Insurance. Resolution Trust Corporation Task Force. 101st Congress, 2nd session. Washington, DC: U.S. Government Printing Office.

―――. 1990i. *Silverado Banking, Savings and Loan Association, Part 1.* Committee on Banking, Finance, and Urban Affairs. 101st Congress, 2nd session. Washington, DC: U.S. Government Printing Office.

―――. 1990j. *Silverado Banking, Savings and Loan Association, Part 2.* Committee on Banking, Finance, and Urban Affairs. 101st Congress, 2nd session. Washington, DC: U.S. Government Printing Office.

―――. 1990k. *A Racial, Gender, and Background Profile of the Directors of the Federal Reserve Banks and Branches.* Committee on Banking, Finance, and Urban Affairs. 101st Congress, 2nd session. Washington, DC: U.S. Government Printing Office.

―――. 1991a. *RTC Semiannual Report for Period Ending April 30, 1991.* Committee on Banking, Finance, and Urban Affairs. 102nd Congress, 1st session. Washington, DC: Government Printing Office.

―――. 1991b. *Failure of the Bank of New England.* Committee on Banking, Finance and Urban Affairs. 102d Congress, 1st session. Washington, DC: Government Printing Office.

―――. 1991c. *The Failure of the Bank of New England Corporation and its Affiliate Banks.* Committee on Banking, Finance and Urban Affairs. 102d Congress, 1st session. Washington, DC: Government Printing Office.

―――. 1991d. *Asset Disposition by the RTC including the Present Status of the SAMDA Program.* Committee on Banking, Finance, and Urban Affairs. Subcommittee on Financial Institutions Supervision, Regulation and Insurance. Resolution Trust Corporation Task Force. 102st Congress, 1st session. Washington, DC: U.S. Government Printing Office.

―――. 1991e. *Resolution Trust Corporation's Asset Disposition Policies.* Committee on Banking, Finance, and Urban Affairs. Subcommittee on General Oversight and Investigations. 102nd Congress, 1st session. Washington, DC: U.S. Government Printing Office.

―――. 1992a. *HR 4241; Resolution Trust Corporation Funding Act of 1992.*

Committee on Banking, Finance, and Urban Affairs, Subcommittee on Financial Institutions Supervision, Regulation and Insurance. 102d Congress, 2d session. Washington, DC: Government Printing Office.

————. 1992b. *Semiannual Appearance by the Thrift Depositor Protection Oversight Board.* Committee on Banking, Finance, and Urban Affairs. Subcommittee on Financial Institutions Supervision, Regulation and Insurance. Joint Hearing. 102nd Congress, 2nd session. Washington, DC: U.S. Government Printing Office.

————. 1993a. *Status report of the Resolution Trust Corporation.* Committee on Banking, Finance, and Urban Affairs. Subcommittee on General Oversight, Investigations, and the resolution of failed financial institutions. 103rd Congress, 1st session. Washington, DC: U.S. Government Printing Office.

————. 1993b. *Resolution Trust Corporation's Affordable Housing Program.* Committee on Banking, Finance, and Urban Affairs. Subcommittee on Housing and Community Development. 103rd Congress, 1st session. Washington, DC: U.S. Government Printing Office.

————. 1993c. *Semiannual Appearance of the Thrift Depositor Protection Oversight Board.* Committee on Banking, Finance, and Urban Affairs. 103rd Congress, 1st session. Washington, DC: U.S. Government Printing Office.

U.S. Congress: Senate. 1980a. *Depository Institutions Deregulation Committee.* Committee on Banking, Housing, and Urban Affairs. 96th Congress, 2d session. Washington, DC: Government Printing Office.

————. 1980b. *Fourth Meeting on the Condition of the Financial System.* Committee on Banking, Housing, and Urban Affairs. 96th Congress, 2d session. Washington, DC: Government Printing Office.

————. 1981a. *Competition and Conditions in the Financial System.* Committee on Banking, Housing, and Urban Affairs. 97th Congress, 1st session. Washington, DC: Government Printing Office.

————. 1981b. *Financial Institutions Restructuring and Services Act of 1981, pts. 1–3.* Committee on Banking, Housing, and Urban Affairs. 97th Congress, 1st session. Washington, DC: Government Printing Office.

————. 1981c. *Federal Role in Conventional Home Financing.* Committee on Banking, Housing, and Urban Affairs, Subcommittee on Housing and Urban Affairs. 97th Congress, 2d session. Washington, DC: Government Printing Office.

————. 1982a. *Securities Activities of Depository Institutions.* Committee on Banking, Housing, and Urban Affairs, Subcommittee on Securities. 97th Congress, 2d session. Washington, DC: Government Printing Office.

————. 1982b. *Capital Assistance Act and Deposit Insurance Flexibility Act.* Committee on Banking, Housing, and Urban Affairs. 97th Congress, 2d session. Washington, DC: Government Printing Office.

U.S. Congress: Senate. 1989. *Problems of the Federal Savings and Loan Insurance Corporation (FSLIC), pts. 1–4.* Committee on Banking, Housing, and Urban Affairs. 101st Congress, 1st session. Washington, DC: Government Printing Office.

———. 1990a. *Hearing on the Semiannual Report of the Resolution Trust Corporation—1990.* Committee on Banking, Housing, and Urban Affairs. 101st Congress, 2d session. Washington, DC: Government Printing Office.

———. 1990b. *The Resolution Trust Corporation Asset Disposition.* Committee on Banking, Housing, and Urban Affairs. 101st Congress, 2d session. Washington, DC: Government Printing Office.

———. 1990c. *Second Oversight Hearing on the Resolution Trust Corporation.* Committee on Banking, Housing, and Urban Affairs. 101st Congress, 2d session. Washington, DC: Government Printing Office.

———. 1991a. *Refunding the RTC.* Committee on Banking, Housing, and Urban Affairs. 102d Congress, 1st session. Washington, DC: Government Printing Office.

———. 1991b. *Real Estate Disposition Activities of the Resolution Trust Corporation.* Committee on Banking, Housing, and Urban Affairs, Subcommittee on Consumer and Regulatory Affairs. 102d Congress, 1st session. Washington, DC: Government Printing Office.

———. 1991c. *Strengthening the Supervision and Regulation of the Depository Institutions.* Committee on Banking, Housing, and Urban Affairs. 102st Congress, 1st session. Washington, DC: U.S. Government Printing Office.

———. 1992a. *Hearing on the Semiannual Report of the Resolution Trust Corporation—1992.* Committee on Banking, Housing, and Urban Affairs. 102nd Congress, 2nd session. Washington, DC: U.S. Government Printing Office.

———. 1992b. *RTC's Operations and the Affordable Housing Program.* Committee on Banking, Housing, and Urban Affairs. 102d Congress, 2d session. Washington, DC: Government Printing Office.

———. 1992c. *Second Hearing on the Semiannual Report of the Resolution Trust Corporation—1992.* Committee on Banking, Housing, and Urban Affairs. 102nd Congress, 2nd session. Washington, DC: U.S. Government Printing Office.

U.S. Department of Labor. 1991. "A Report on the Glass Ceiling Initiative." Washington, DC: Government Printing Office.

Ullmann, Owen. 1994. "Is the Fed Facing a Political Correction?" *Business Week* (January 10):42.

Useem, Michael. 1984. *The Inner Circle.* New York: Oxford University Press.

Vallochi, Steven. 1989. "The Relative Autonomy of the State and the Origins of British Welfare Policy." *Sociological Forum* 4:349–65.

Wall Street Journal. 1991. "Fleet/Norstar, Aided by KKR, Wins Bidding Battle for Bank of New England." April 23:3, 16.

Wallace, Anise C. 1990. "Savings Units Trim 'Junk' Holdings." *New York Times,* April 2:D7.

Weinstein, James. 1968. *The Corporate Ideal in the Liberal State, 1900–1918.* Boston: Beacon.

Weir, Margaret, Ann Shola Orloff, and Theda Skocpol (eds.). 1988. *The Politics of Social Policy in the United States.* Princeton, NJ: Princeton University Press.

Wertheimer, Fred. 1980. "The PAC Phenomenon in American Politics." *Arizona Law Review* 22(2):603–26.

Whitt, J. Allen. 1979. "Toward a Class Dialectic Model of Power: An Empirical Assessment of Three Competing Models of Political Power." *American Sociological Review* 44:81–100.

———. 1980. "Can Capitalists Organize Themselves?" Pp. 97–114 in *Power Structure Research,* edited by G. William Domhoff. Beverly Hills, CA: Sage.

———. 1982. *The Dialectics of Power: Urban Elites and Mass Transportation.* Princeton, NJ: Princeton University Press.

Wilhite, Allen and John Theilmann. 1982. *The Dialectics of Power: Urban Elites and Mass Transportation.* Princeton, NJ: Princeton University Press.

———. 1987. "Labor PAC Contributions and Labor Legislation: A Simultaneous Logit Approach." *Public Choice* 53:267–76.

Witte, Edwin E. 1972. "Organized Labor and Social Security." Pp. 241–74 in *Labor and the New Deal,* edited by Milton Derber and Edwin Young. New York: DeCapo.

Wright, Erik Olin. 1978. *Class, Crisis, and the State.* London: Verso.

Zeitlin, Maurice, Lynda Ann Ewen, and Richard E. Ratcliff. 1974. "New Princes for Old? The Large Corporation and the Capitalist Class in Chile." *American Journal of Sociology* 80:87–123.

Zeitlin, Maurice and Richard E. Ratcliff. 1975. "Research Methods for the Analysis of the Internal Structure of Dominant Classes: The Case of Landlords and Capitalists in Chile." *Latin American Research Review* 10(3):5–61.

Zey, Mary. 1993. *Banking on Fraud: Drexel, Junk Bonds, and Buyouts.* Hawthorne, NY: Aldine de Gruyter.

Zey, Mary and Brande Camp. 1996. "The Transformation from Multidivisional Form to Corporate Groups of Subsidiaries in the 1980s: Capital Crisis Theory." *Sociological Quarterly* 37(2):327–51.

Index